FURNITURE MAKING

Making and Restoring Furniture

Furniture is the mass noun for the movable objects intended to support various human activities, such as seating, storing, working and sleeping. Most often, at least in the present day - furniture is the product of a lengthy design process and considered a form of decorative art. In addition to furniture's functional role, it can also serve a symbolic or religious purpose, for instance in churches, temples or shrines. It can be made from many materials, including metal, plastic, and wood, using a variety of techniques, joins and decoration, reflecting the local culture from which it originated. Furniture construction can be extremely technical, or very simple, dependent on the desired end product and skills of the maker.

Numerous courses are available to provide a grounding in furniture making, generally designed to broaden practical (as opposed to art historical) knowledge of materials, tools and design. For the amateur maker, such options can be an extremely useful route into building and restoring their own furniture. Typically, restoring furniture has been seen as a job solely for the trained craftsman, however with the advent of readily available courses, books and online tutorials, it has never been easier to start yourself. Furniture construction and restoration does take a good deal of preparation and persistence, not to mention a keen eye for detail, but can be successfully achieved by any enthusiastic individual.

One of the first things to assess, is what to look out for when purchasing (or evaluating your own) old furniture. As a general rule, if you are restoring furniture yourself, look for older mass-produced items, produced after the mid-nineteenth century. These (with some exceptions) will not have very high values, but are incredibly well made - able to last a long time in the family home. If in doubt, do ask an expert however! One should also be aware, that there are certain more recent styles and designers of furniture which are incredibly rare, for example Art Deco, Arts and Crafts, De Stijl and Bauhaus. Another key thing to look out for are 'dovetail joints'; they are strong and require skill to assemble, and are thereby generally a good sign of a well-constructed piece of furniture. Solid wood or plywood backing, for instance on the back or inside of drawers, are also good indicators of age, as solid wood will generally tell you that it is pre-twentieth century, whereas plywood was only utilised after this date. Perhaps more obviously, inscriptions and manufacturer's stamps can tell the owner a lot about their piece of furniture.

Painting and stencilling wood furniture is probably the most common, and easiest starting activity for the amateur furniture restorer. When finishing wood, it is imperative to first make sure that it has been adequately cleaned, removing any dust, shavings or residue. Subsequently, if there are any obvious damages or dents in the furniture, wood putty or filler should be used to fill the gaps. Imperfections or nail holes on the surface may be filled using wood putty (also called plastic wood;

a substance commonly used to fill nail holes in wood prior to finishing. It is often composed of wood dust combined with a binder that dries and a diluent (thinner), and sometimes, pigment). Filler is normally used for an all over smooth-textured finish, by filling pores in the wood grain. It is used particularly on open grained woods such as oak, mahogany and walnut where building up multiple layers of standard wood finish is ineffective or impractical.

After the furniture is thus smartened, it should then be sanded (without entirely removing the finish) and primed before a base coat of paint is applied. Aerosols will provide a smoother finish than paintbrushes. If stencilling afterwards, make sure that the base colour is completely dry before the final step is embarked upon.

Recovering dining room chairs is another popular activity, involving skills with fabric as well as woodwork - also fashionable is metal furniture restoration. Metal work provides slightly different problems to those of traditional wood and chair restoring; one of the main questions is - do you actually want to make the piece 'as good as new?' Rust and signs of wear can be removed to varying degrees, with many choosing to leave their pieces of furniture worn and torn; achieving 'the industrial look', popular in design circles. This is especially the case for small-scale furniture like lighting, various ornaments such as candlesticks and even larger pieces such as cast-iron beds. If a metal piece is going to be painted, it is imperative to first remove the rust however. This is a time consuming, but ultimately rewarding task to complete, and can be done by a professional for larger objects. Once the metal is rust free, all that remains is to prime and paint! Antiquing effects can also be used, i.e. sanding off layers of paint (of differing colours if the maker prefers) - finished off with a clear protective finish.

Today, British professional furniture makers have self organised into a strong and vibrant community, largely under the organisation 'The Worshipful Company of Furniture Makers', commonly referred to as the Furniture Makers or the Furniture Makers Company. Its motto is 'Straight and Strong'! Members of the Company come from many professions and disciplines, but the common link is that all members on joining must be engaged in or with the UK furnishing industry. Thus the work of the Company is delivered by members with wide ranging professional knowledge and skills in manufacturing, retailing, education, journalism; in fact any aspect of the industry. There are many similar organisations across the globe, as well as in the UK, all seeking to integrate and promote the valuable art that is furniture making. Education is a key factor in such endeavours, and maintaining strong links between professional practitioners, didactic colleges and the amateur maker/restorer is crucial. We hope the reader enjoys this book.

A History of Furniture

Furniture is the mass noun for the movable objects intended to support various human activities, such as seating, storing, working and sleeping. Most often, at least in the present day - furniture is the product of a lengthy design process and considered a form of decorative art. In addition to furniture's functional role, it can also serve a symbolic or religious purpose, for instance in churches, temples or shrines. It can be made from many materials, including metal, plastic, and wood - using a variety of techniques, joins and decoration, reflecting the local culture from which it originated.

Furniture has been a part of the human experience since the development of non-nomadic cultures, and even before this in its crudest form. Evidence of furniture survives from the Neolithic Period and later in antiquity in the form of paintings, such as the wall Murals discovered at Pompeii; sculpture, and examples have been excavated in Egypt and found in tombs in Ghiordes, in modern-day Turkey. Perhaps one of the most interesting archaeological sites is Skara Brae, a Neolithic village located in Orkney (an archipelago in northern Scotland). The site dates from 3100–2500 BC and due to a shortage of wood in Orkney, the people of Skara Brae were forced to build with stone, a readily available material that could be worked easily and turned into household items. Each house shows a high degree of sophistication and was equipped with an extensive assortment of stone furniture, ranging from cupboards, dressers and beds to shelves, stone seats, and limpet tanks. The stone dresser was regarded as the most important item, as it symbolically faced the entrance in each house and was therefore the first item seen when entering.

The furniture of the Middle Ages was usually heavy, oak, and ornamented with carved designs. Along with the other arts, the Italian Renaissance of the fourteenth and fifteenth century marked a rebirth in design, often inspired by the Greco-Roman tradition. A similar explosion of design, and renaissance of culture in general, occurred in Northern Europe, starting in the fifteenth century. The seventeenth century, in both Southern and Northern Europe, was characterized by opulent, often gilded Baroque designs that frequently incorporated a profusion of vegetal and scrolling ornament. Starting in the eighteenth century, furniture designs began to develop more rapidly. Although there were some styles that belonged primarily to one nation, such as 'Palladianism' in Great Britain (derived from and inspired by the designs of the Venetian architect Andrea Palladio) or 'Louis Quinze' in French furniture (characterised by supreme craftsmanship and the integration of the arts of cabinet-making, painting, and sculpture), others, such as 'Rococo' and 'Neoclassicism' were perpetuated throughout Western Europe.

The nineteenth century is usually defined by concurrent revival styles, including Gothic, Neoclassicism, and Roccoco. The design reforms of the late century introduced the 'Aesthetic movement' (essentially promoting the beauty of objects above any other social or political themes) and the 'Arts and Crafts movement' (An international design movement that flourished between 1860-1910, led by William Morris. It stood for traditional craftsmanship using simple form, often applying medieval, romantic or folk styles of decoration). Art Nouveau, in turn was influenced by both of these movements. This latter development was perhaps the most influential of all, inspired by natural forms and structures; evident primarily in architecture, but also the beautiful objects crafted to fill such spaces. Noted furniture designers in this style included William H. Bradley; the 'Dean of American Designers', Goerges de Feure, the Parisian designer who famously produced the theatre designs for *Le Chat Noir* cabaret, and Hermann Obrist, a German sculptor of the Jugendstil (the German branch of Art Nouveaux) movement.

The first three-quarters of the twentieth century are often seen as the march towards Modernism in furniture design. Modernism, in general, includes the activities and creations of those who felt traditional forms of art, architecture, literature, religious faith and social activities were becoming outdated in the new economic, social, and political environment of an emergent industrialized world. Art Deco, De Stijl, Bauhaus, Wiener Werkstätte, and Vienna Secession designers all worked to some degree within the Modernist idiom. Born from the Bauhaus and Art Deco/Streamline styles came the post WWII 'Mid-Century Modern' style using materials developed during the war including laminated plywood, plastics and fibreglass. Prime examples include furniture designed by George Nelson Associates, Charles and Ray Eames, Paul McCobb and Danish modern designers including Finn Juhl and Arne Jacobsen. Post-modern design, intersecting the Pop art movement, gained steam in the 1960s and 70s, promoted in the 1980s by groups such as the Italy-based Memphis movement. The latter group worked with ephemeral designs, featuring colourful decoration and asymmetrical shapes.

As is evident from this short history, the history of artistic developments is inextricably linked with the progression of furniture design. This is hardly surprising, as after all, many artists, thinkers and designers would stringently resist any artificial separation between traditional fine art and functional design. Both respond to their wider context and environment, both, perhaps in differing ways, seeking to impact on reality and society.

Today, British professional furniture makers have self organised into a strong and vibrant community, largely under the organisation 'The Worshipful Company of Furniture Makers', commonly referred to as the Furniture Makers or the Furniture Makers Company. Its motto is 'Straight and Strong'! Members of the Company come from many professions and disciplines, but the common link is that all members on joining must be engaged in or with the UK furnishing industry. Thus the work of the Company is delivered by members with wide ranging professional knowledge and skills in manufacturing, retailing, education, journalism; in fact any aspect of the industry. There are many similar organisations across the globe, as well as in the UK, all seeking to integrate and promote the valuable art that is furniture making. Education is a key factor in such endeavours, and maintaining strong links between professional practitioners, didactic colleges and the amateur maker/restorer is crucial. We hope the reader enjoys this book.

FURNITURE MAKING

Designs, Working Drawings, and Complete
Details of 170 Pieces of Furniture,
with Practical Information
on Their Construction

By
R. S. BOWERS, JOHN BOVINGDON
and other Designer-Craftsmen

With 1,082 Illustrations

EDITOR'S PREFACE

This book presents a variety of designs for articles of domestic furniture, accompanied by information on the execution of the work. The method is to give a general view of the piece, the working drawings, and enough detail drawings to allow of the craftsman thoroughly understanding the construction. The object being to give as many designs as possible, it has not been thought desirable to occupy space with elementary information on the woodworking and other processes involved in the production of cabinet work. A companion volume, " The Complete Woodworker " (1,000 illustrations), more than supplies the craftsman's needs in this direction.

The one hundred and seventy examples of furniture suitable for cultured homes which this book contains have been contributed by possibly a score of different designers and practical craftsmen, among whom especial mention must be made of Messrs. R. S. Bowers, John Bovingdon, and J. D. Bates, who have contributed the major part of the book, and of Messrs. P. R. Green, George Eldridge, and C. S. Taylor.

Many of the present designs were originally contributed to " Work " by men whose particular forte is practical craftsmanship, and in all such cases the information on construction has been carefully retained in a revised form, but trouble has been taken to re-design the examples, a very heavy task cheerfully undertaken and, I think, skilfully carried out by my friend Mr. R. S. Bowers.

The reader should remember always that full-size working drawings are absolutely essential for successful and economical work; although he may be tempted to consider their preparation a waste of time, he will soon discover that in their absence mistakes are very easily made —and mistakes affecting the cutting up of expensive wood are likely to be costly. The well-known method of enlarging by means of squares may frequently be adopted, there being many diagrams throughout the book that will give the key to the correct procedure.

Nearly every example in the book is capable of almost infinite modification and variation, suggestions as to which have been given in many cases. Before starting to make any one of the articles of furniture here depicted the reader should assure himself that it will answer his requirements as regards dimensions, general design, and details and method of construction; and any necessary alteration to adapt the article to his individual needs should be decided on before setting out the work, and, of course, incorporated in the full-size drawing. Before attempting any piece of furniture, the reader is advised to study the construction of other examples, as from them fresh ideas and much useful information may often be gleaned. With regard to the ornamentation and the finish of the work there is still greater scope for individuality; and it will be understood that in the case of nearly every example shown in these pages there are many alternatives that can be adopted with success. But let ornament be used with restraint!

Space is not wasted in this book by illustrating and describing small fittings the nature of which in most cases may be taken for granted and with regard to which a cabinet-maker's ironmongery catalogue may be consulted with advantage. Neither is there tedious repetition of information as to the various woods in which the articles of furniture may be constructed; but it may be of interest to note that a list containing the names and chief particulars of some hundreds of different woods is given in "The Complete Woodworker," a companion volume in this library.

Should the reader fail to understand a detail of construction he should state his difficulty as concisely as possible to "Work," the Weekly Journal of Handicrafts, edited by the Editor of the present library, and information will then be freely forthcoming in its pages; but he will note that answers are not sent by post.

B. E. J.

La Belle Sauvage,
    London, E.C.

CONTENTS

CHAPTER	PAGE
1. Book-stands, Racks and Troughs	1
2. Bookshelves	12
3. Bookcases and China or Curio Cabinets	19
4. Writing Cabinets and Bureaux	35
5. Overmantels and Mirrors	48
6. Enclosures to Unsightly Mantels	61
7. Clock Cases	65
8. Veneering and Inlaying as a Decorative Medium	84
9. Hall Furniture	92
10. An Eighteenth-century Hall Seat	114
11. Two Old Chests	122
12. Music Stools	129
13. Music Cabinets	135
14. Draught-screens, Fire-screens and Easels	148
15. Hanging Cabinets or Cupboards	157
16. Corner Cupboards	168
17. Stools	175
18. Dining-room and Drawing-room Chairs	182
19. Settees, Armchairs, and Window Seats	196
20. Cosy-corner Fittings	205
21. Urn and Plant Stands and Pedestals	213
22. Small Tables	223
23. Showcase or Curio Tables	239

Contents

CHAPTER	PAGE
24. Writing-tables and Desks	245
25. Large Tables	255
26. Sideboards	269
27. A Bedroom Suite	289
28. Another Bedroom Suite	312
29. Miscellaneous Bedroom Furniture	331
30. Bedside Tables and Reading-stands	346
31. Stuffover Chair and Settee	353
32. A French Side Table	356
33. Recess Fitments	361
34. Kitchen and Scullery Furniture	369
35. Miscellaneous Furniture	387
Index	405

FURNITURE MAKING

CHAPTER I

BOOKSTANDS, RACKS AND TROUGHS

Double-shelf Bookcase Table, Figs. 1 to 8.—The double-shelf bookcase table which constitutes the first example given in this book is of simple construction, but effective

Fig. 1.—Double-shelf bookcase table

when neatly made. Oak, walnut, or mahogany would be the most suitable material to use, but any cheaper kind of hard wood, stained and polished, would do. It is 2 ft. 9 in.

square by 2 ft. 6 in. high, but these dimensions may be varied if desired. The legs, which are got out first, are 2 ft. 5¼ in. long by 2 in. square; they are shown plain and tapered at the bottom, but they can be turned or otherwise shaped if so preferred. The top rails are 3 in. by ¾ in., and are mortised into the legs, finishing ⅜ in. back from the outer faces of the legs (see Fig. 6). The rails supporting the bottom shelf A (Fig. 2) are 1¾ in. by ¾ in., and are also mortised into the legs (see Fig. 7), but in this case they finish flush with them. The bottom rails are 6¼ in. from the floor, and the

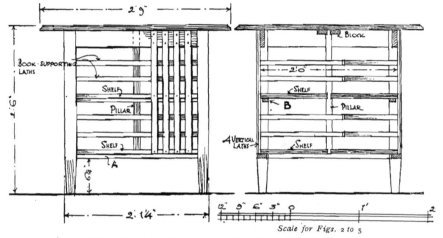

Figs. 2 and 3.—Elevation and section of bookcase table

rails above are midway between the bottom rails and the lower edge of the top rails. The last mentioned (see B, Fig. 3) are 1¼ in. by ¾ in. mortised as before, but flush with the inside faces of the legs as shown.

Each shelf is made up of two boards, 2 ft. by 1 ft. by ⅝ in., glued together, with a rectangular piece, 1⅝ in. square, cut from each corner to admit the table legs. A ½-in. hole is bored in the exact centre for the extremities of the pillars that support the laths against which the books rest.

One side of the bookcase table should now be built up permanently, and the remaining rails glued to the other

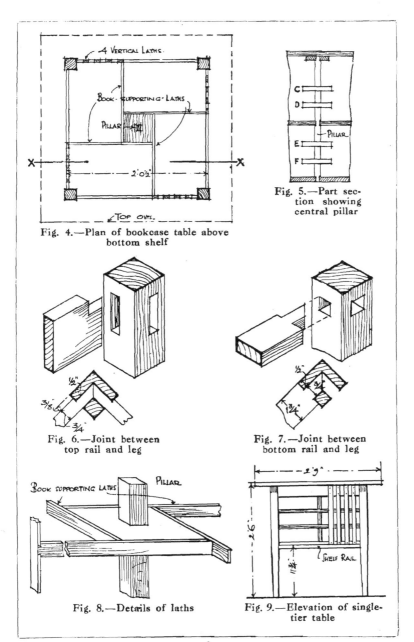

Fig. 4.—Plan of bookcase table above bottom shelf

Fig. 5.—Part section showing central pillar

Fig. 6.—Joint between top rail and leg

Fig. 7.—Joint between bottom rail and leg

Fig. 8.—Details of laths

Fig. 9.—Elevation of single-tier table

legs. Then place the shelves in position, glue the two portions together, and secure the lower or single shelf, noting that its edges are ⅜ in. back on each face from those of the rail A (Fig. 2).

Two pillars, 1 in. square are required, all four ends being fashioned into pins to fit the holes in the two shelves, a block being secured to the under surface of the table top (*see* Fig. 3). Pass each pillar through the centre of a couple of 5-in. squares of 1-in. stuff (C D E, and F, Fig. 5) and glue the latter to the pillars at equal distances from the extremities and each

Fig. 10.—Single-trough bookstand with fretted ends

other. The horizontal book-supporting laths are to be attached to the edges of these squares, which obviate the necessity for making the pillars 5 in. thick. Glue the lower pillar to the two shelves and secure the upper shelf with glue, and with screws passing through the rails from the under surface.

The table top is 2 ft. 9 in. square by ¾ in. thick, and is made by gluing two or three lengths of material together, planing up, and working a suitable moulding on the edge. It *is* secured to the rails with screws driven into it obliquely through the rails, a cavity being first made for each screw-

Bookstands, Racks and Troughs

head; or buttons may be employed at two or three points on each side. The buttons have a tongue to fit a slot in the rail inner face, and are screwed to the under surface of the table top as described on page 116. Another method is to glue triangular blocks in the angle of the top and rail.

Before the top is secured, the upper pillar must be glued to the shelf and block, the latter being first glued and screwed to the top.

The vertical laths to the sides are 1 in. wide by ¼ in. thick, and long enough to reach from the top to the upper edge of the bottom shelf rail, against which they butt neatly; sixteen are required, and they should finish ⅛ in. behind the legs and bottom rail. Sixteen similar laths, 1 ft. 2¾ in. long, but horizontal, are needed to form book

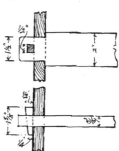

Figs. 13 and 14.—Wedged tenon joint at end of bookstand rails

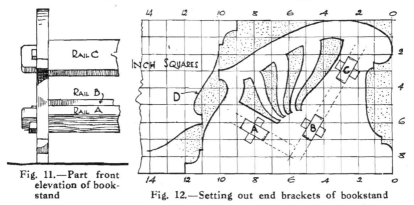

Fig. 11.—Part front elevation of bookstand

Fig. 12.—Setting out end brackets of bookstand

supports, one running outwards from each side of the pillar squares to the innermost vertical lath, to which they are united with a lap dovetail (*see* Fig. 8). These laths should be spaced out as equally as possible. Glue and screw the vertical laths in place, using either round- or flat-headed brass screws. Let the nicks of the screw-heads be perpendicular, and make no attempt to conceal the flat-

6 Furniture Making

headed ones, which should be flush with the surface of the wood.

Single-shelf Bookcase Table, Fig. 9.—A single-tier table may be constructed on precisely the same principle as that already described, and can easily be adjusted to suit any special series of volumes. The legs, rails, and bottom shelf are exactly as previously described, the sixteen vertical laths are altered only in length, and only eight of the horizontal internal laths (Fig. 8) will be required. This table is more graceful in appearance than the double-shelf one, the first being essentially suggestive of a library.

Fig. 15.—Double-trough bookstand

Single-trough Stand, Figs. 10 to 14.—In selecting timber for this bookstand, stuff that would harmonise with the table on which the stand is to be set should be considered. The stand consists of two main parts, the brackets and the rails. The former are both cut out of a piece of wood 1 ft. 9 in. long, 9 in. wide, and $\frac{5}{8}$ in. thick, to the outline given, material being economised by reversing the second bracket and keeping it close to the first as at D (Fig. 12). This would be best done with a bow saw, the edge being finished with a spokeshave. To take out the fret pattern, a number of holes should be bored, the pattern then being carefully pared out with a chisel and gouge.

Bookstands, Racks and Troughs

This method of cutting out the fret is adopted because of the comparative thickness of the brackets.

The position of the rails should now be set off, the angle of the one marked A being 30° and of the other two 60°. In cutting the mortises for the tenon joints, the holes should be bored and then carefully pared to shape.

Three rails are required, one for the shelf, 3 ft. 3 in. long (or as may be required to suit the table), 2 in. wide, and ⅝ in. thick,

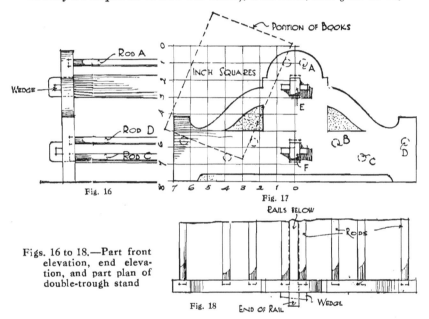

Figs. 16 to 18.—Part front elevation, end elevation, and part plan of double-trough stand

and two exactly similar for the back. The tenons should be cut out, and the mortise (Figs. 13 and 14) in each formed to allow the wedge, which fixes the joint, to be put in position.

If in whitewood the stand can be stained, care being taken that the work is carried out so as to leave no brush marks, and polished with beeswax and turpentine.

Double-trough Stand, Figs. 15 to 18.—A selection of standard reprints, such as Messrs. Cassell & Co.'s " People's Library," are to be found in most homes, and are worthy of, and very suitable for, a handy table rack of their own.

The rack illustrated by Figs. 15 to 18, consists of two ends and a few rods, and, as the latter are to be obtained readily at any time, the rack may be said to be extensible. Therefore, it can be made initially with short rods and extended subsequently when further books have to be accommodated. The ends of the rack can be got out of any stuff, from pine to inlaid ebony, the form and finish being as plain or as elaborate as taste dictates.

In Figs. 16 and 17 are given end and part front elevations of the rack, which, as will be seen, is of double form. The outline of the ends is merely a suggestion, which may be modified as desired.

First of all decide the form to be adopted, and get out the two ends from stuff about $\frac{5}{8}$ in. thick. The edges can be finished sharp and square, or they may be chamfered slightly. The various holes required in each piece are pitched as shown in Fig. 17. Only two are cut right through the wood, those for the main rails at E and F. The rest are simply recessed $\frac{1}{4}$ in. deep by $\frac{7}{16}$ in. in diameter.

The two rails referred to, and which serve to hold the rack together, are prepared from the same material as the ends to a size of about $1\frac{1}{2}$ in. by $\frac{3}{8}$ in.

The cutting of the holes for the tenons of these rails must be done with care to avoid splitting. The tenons measure $1\frac{1}{2}$ in. by $1\frac{1}{8}$ in. wide, and should be a good fit in the holes in the ends of the rack, and, the wedging-up pegs should be an equally good fit in their respective holes. When the rails are in place and pegged, the rack should be quite rigid without the rods.

These rods are of one size throughout, about $\frac{7}{16}$ in. in diameter and as long as required. They may be of polished hard wood or of light drawn tube (brass, copper, or steel). They should be perfectly straight, and with their ends cut square.

Double-tier Stand, Figs. 19 to 26.—This bookstand consists of a bottom and upper portion, made up separately and fixed together with screws from the underside. The stand may be made of deal, and enamelled or stained, but one of the cabinet hard woods finished in the natural colour

Bookstands, Racks and Troughs

would be preferable. The principal dimensions are given in the illustrations.

In making the stand, begin by preparing the legs, which are 1 ft. 10¾ in. long by 1⅛ in. square at the top, tapering to ⅞ in. square at the bottom. The rails A (Fig. 20) and B (Fig. 21) are 2½ in. deep by ¾ in. in section; the former being 1 ft. 9¾ in. long, and the latter 7¾ in. long, both between the

Fig. 19.—Double-tier bookstand

shoulders of the tenons. These rails are tenoned into the legs as shown in Fig. 22 at C, and on plan in Fig. 26. The bottom cross rails D (Fig. 21) are 4½ in. deep in the middle, by ¾ in. thick, shaped as shown in Fig. 23, and mortised and tenoned into the legs. The distance from the bottom end of the legs to the top edge of the rails is 9½ in. The shelves E are 4 in. wide by ¾ in. thick, the top edge being rounded. They stand at right angles to each other, and are tenoned as deep

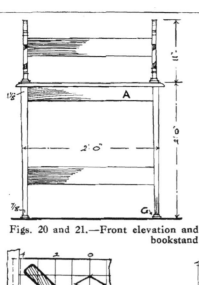
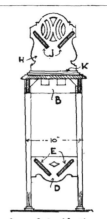

Figs. 20 and 21.—Front elevation and cross section of double-tier bookstand

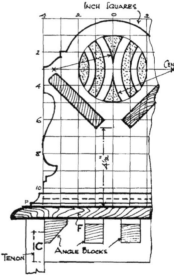

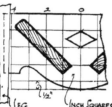

Fig. 23.—Detail of lower rails

Fig. 24.—Detail of feet to legs

Fig. 22.—Detail of upper part of bookstand

Fig. 25.—Tenoned end of shelf

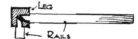

Fig. 26.—Top rails tenoned into legs

Bookstands, Racks and Troughs 11

as possible into the cross rails, joints similar to that shown by Fig. 25 being used.

The top F (Fig. 22) of the bottom portion of the stand is 2 ft. 1½ in. long by 11½ in. wide by ¾ in., the edges being moulded. The top is fixed in position with angular blocks as shown in Figs. 21 and 22. The bearers G (Fig. 20) at the bottom end of the legs are 2 in. square by ¾ in. thick, moulded round the edges, and tenoned to the bottom end of the legs as shown in Fig. 24.

The sides H (Fig. 21) of the upper portion of the stand are 10½ in. high by 8 in. wide by ¾ in.; they are shaped as shown at Figs. 21 and 22, and a small design is cut in the middle with curves set out from the centres indicated. The shelves J are 4 in. wide by ¾ in. thick, the top edge being rounded; they stand at right angles to each other, and are tenoned into the sides H, joints as shown by Fig. 25 being used. The feet K at the bottom of the sides are 9 in. long by 2 in. wide by ¾ in., moulded or chamfered round the edges, and tenoned to the bottom edge of the sides as shown in Fig. 24.

CHAPTER II

BOOKSHELVES

A Set of Dwarf Shelves, Figs. 27 to 29.—This set of shelving is intended for a recess, but is adaptable to other positions. Boarding about 8 in. by ¾ in. or ⅞ in. will be suitable, and when the heights have been settled to suit the books, etc., concerned, work may be begun by placing two uprights against the wall, as A and B (Fig. 28). These start immediately above the skirting, and between them, just about ¼ in. higher at the top than the skirting, is fitted a bottom shelf C cut along its edges to clear the skirting-mould as necessary. Fig. 29 shows how it is proposed to continue a new piece of skirting, to match the old as nearly as possible, across the front, small upright supports being fixed behind it.

On the other hand, the space at the bottom could be left open if preferred. Above the skirting level are three shelves, supported merely by means of pairs of moderately large

Fig. 27.—Dwarf bookshelves

Bookshelves

screw-eyes (as used for picture frames) fixed in the uprights in a horizontal position under either end of each shelf; this makes a surprisingly efficient support, equal to any possible load upon it, and is, in addition, much neater and easier than other methods, and it also allows the most rapid re-adjustment of the shelf-levels.

Above the top long shelf will be seen two 15 in. uprights D and E (Fig. 28) 12 in. apart, and screwed in position from below. Their tops are finished by means of a shelf as at

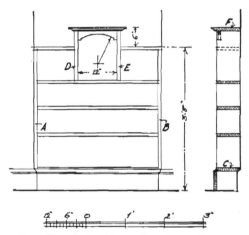

Figs. 28 and 29.—Front elevation and cross section of dwarf bookshelves

F (Fig. 29) fixed down, and either moulded or bevelled on the exposed edges, or alternatively finished with a small moulding planted on and mitred. A thin spandril piece shaped with a curve of $9\frac{1}{2}$ in. radius and small square ends, can be fixed about $\frac{1}{16}$ in. back from the front edges of the shelves, and the two small side shelves shown, should be nailed or screwed in position after being first of all supported on the ends of the upright sides at their outer extremes, and on two screw-eyes each in D and E as before mentioned.

Standing Cupboard with Shelves, Figs. 30 to 41.—This design can be modified or adapted in numerous ways, one such variation being suggested by Fig. 41, the total width being increased to suit. Work can best be begun by taking the two upright sides, cutting their top ends to the outline in Fig. 38, and then taking a semicircular piece $3\frac{1}{2}$ in. across out of their lower ends as at D (Fig. 32). Next, 5 in. up, carefully chisel out sinkings 6 in. by $\frac{5}{8}$ in. and $\frac{1}{4}$ in., and cut the ends of the bottom shelf as in Fig. 40 to fit these sinkings. This will hold the work at the bottom, and the top can be inserted in the same way. If preferred, however, it can be simply butted at the ends and nailed through the sides, as the latter will be tied in by the next part to be described. This consists of the piece B (Fig. 31), which should be set out by means of the central curve of 2-ft. 6-in. radius in combination with ends as shown in Fig. 36. It is screwed in position as at E in Fig. 32, with its bottom edge flush with the under-side of the top shelf, and its back-end edges slightly rounded.

Fig. 30.—Standing cupboard with shelves

The upright A (Fig. 31) and the two short shelves can easily be fixed with their ends housed as in Fig. 40, or merely butted, the back strip in Fig. 37 being added to prevent books, etc., getting too far back, and the strip C (Fig. 31) fixed $\frac{1}{16}$ in. back as a finish. The back and shelves for the cupboard call for no particular description. As shown in Fig. 31, the door consists of a single piece, having an oval shape pierced just a trifle larger than the sight opening of a simple gilt or oxidised photo frame, which is fitted over the hole, and either left with the glass clear or filled in with a picture. In Fig. 39 is an alternative form of door, composed

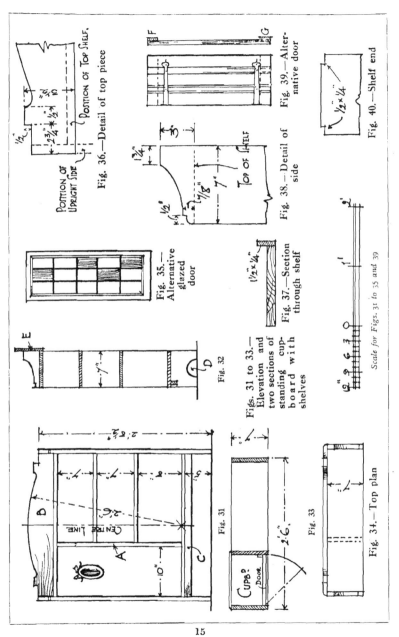

of alternate wide and narrow strips V-jointed, tongued together and held by two small horizontal pieces as seen in section at F and G; ornamental " strap " hinges as shown are very suitable for a door of this type.

The third design for the door (Fig. 35) consists of a rebated frame (which can be on the picture-frame principle if strongly secured at the mitres), filled in with rectangular leaded glazing. The spacing of this should be of about the proportion shown, as a pane nearly as wide as it is high does not look well. The leads should be fairly wide, and " bottle-ends " might be introduced at random. This glazing would cost about 1s. per superficial foot, or could be carried out in accordance with instructions given on a later page.

Collapsible Bookshelves, Figs. 42 to 49.—The illustrations show the construction of bookshelves that can be easily folded together for purposes of removal, etc. They are hinged together in such a way that, starting in Fig. 42 with the shelves open ready for use, the back rails A and B swing round when required from C to D in Fig. 48 flat against the sides as at E and F in Fig. 44, where the shelves are shown in the act of " collapsing," which continues till the position in Fig. 45 is reached, when they form a compact parcel, as sketched in Fig. 46. Sizes that will be found useful are given in Figs. 42 and 43, but they may be modified to meet requirements, and wood about ¾ in. thick will be suitable.

Fig. 41.—Alternative design for cupboard

Plane the several pieces of wood to the dimensions, curve the sides at the top and bottom as in Fig. 49. All the shelves are of the same length, but at one end of the top and bottom shelves, and at each end of the three intermediate shelves, are fillets, these varying in breadth, as indicated in Fig. 42, these figures are of course multiples of the assumed thickness of wood employed. The sides should be grooved to receive

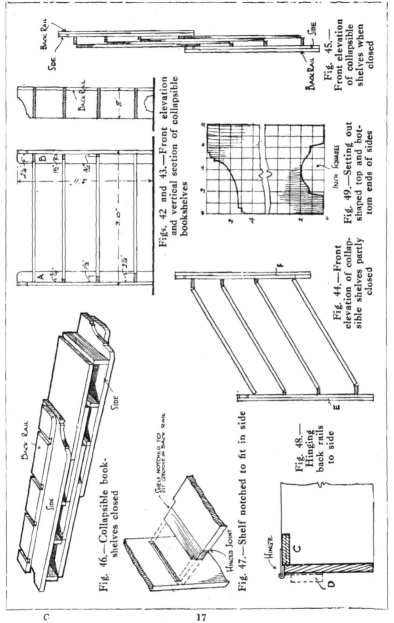

Figs. 42 and 43.—Front elevation and vertical section of collapsible bookshelves

Fig. 45.—Front elevation of collapsible shelves when closed

Fig. 49.—Setting out shaped top and bottom ends of sides

Fig. 44.—Front elevation of collapsible shelves partly closed

Fig. 46.—Collapsible bookshelves closed

Fig. 47.—Shelf notched to fit in side

Fig. 48.—Hinging back rails to side

the fillets as in Fig. 47, so that they may be firmly secured with glue and the insertion of a few fine screws ; but the left-hand side will not require grooving for the top shelf nor the right-hand side for the bottom shelf. The back rails as A and B (Fig. 42), have grooves formed in them, the depth of which is half the thickness of the wood. The backs of the shelves must be notched out to fit these grooves, and the fillets must be kept short so as to fit in the grooves (*see* Fig. 47).

The shelves should next be hinged. In the case of the top and bottom shelves one end will be hinged direct to the side, the other being hinged to the edge of the fillet. These hinges can be fixed on the under-sides of the shelves out of sight, one good hinge to each. The shelves and sides should be placed front edge downwards, and held together with a diagonal strip of wood at right angles to each other. Next the back rails should be accurately fitted to the back of the shelves, and the back rail and sides hinged together, as shown in Fig. 48.

Two pairs of hinges will be required, and they must have one half fairly long and the other cut down to the thickness of the wood as in Fig. 48. When the back rails are closed in position so that the shelves fit into the grooves, the whole will be found to hold rigidly together, but by opening the back rail, the whole will collapse and fold together, as shown in Figs. 44 and 45. A couple of screws inserted through each back rail into two of the shelves will prevent it from being pushed out of place by accident.

CHAPTER III

BOOKCASES AND CHINA OR CURIO CABINETS

Bookcase or Cabinet, Figs. 50 to 64. — This cabinet consists of a large compartment with glazed doors surmounting a couple of drawers, the whole being mounted on square-turned legs, and capable of many variations both in design and arrangement. For instance, the simple pattern of glazing bars seen on the right of Fig. 50 may be altered to one of the others given in this book, or the drawers could give place to longer legs supporting a case glazed in rectangular squares on front and sides as suggested in Figs. 60 and 61, or developed into more elaborate cabinets such as those shown by Figs. 62 to 64.

The carcase consists of sides, top, bottom, and back. An ordinary mould may be fixed to the top (as in Fig. 54). The shelves are 3 ft. 4 in. long, $8\frac{1}{2}$ in. wide, and $\frac{3}{4}$ in. thick. They should be fixtures—unless the bookcase is very solidly built. A good method, should adjustable shelves be preferred, is that known as the slip and rack (*see* Figs. 55 and 56). In this the movable slip A gives a firm support to the end of the shelf B which is cut to fit on it. The slip and rack should be about $\frac{1}{2}$ in. thick. A much superior contrivance, however, is to fit lengths of " patent adjustable shelving strip," obtainable through hardware merchants, and consisting of metal strips perforated at intervals to receive movable hooks, as shown in Fig. 67, of a later example. When this is completed fix in the upright that divides the drawers at the bottom of the case. The back consists of 6-in. by $\frac{5}{8}$-in. lining (*see* Fig. 57).

The door rails must be tenoned and mortised as shown in Fig. 59, and rebated. On the inside and at the bottom of the left-hand door fasten a small bolt ; on the other door fix a knob similar to that shown in Fig. 58, which will serve both as handle and fastener.

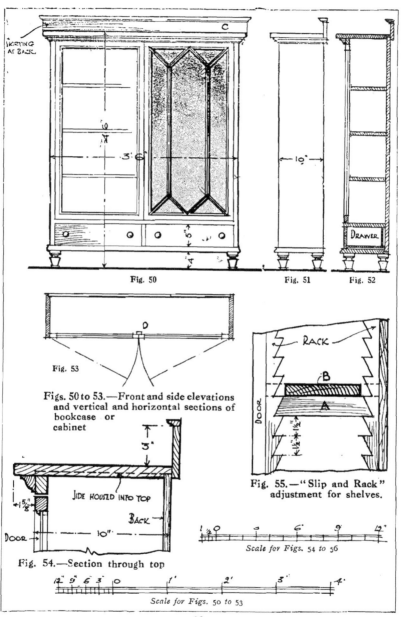

Figs. 50 to 53.—Front and side elevations and vertical and horizontal sections of bookcase or cabinet

Fig. 54.—Section through top

Fig. 55.—"Slip and Rack" adjustment for shelves.

Bookcases and China Cabinets 21

The drawers should be made next, and can be of the usual type (*see* page 34).

The feet are square-turned from 2½ in. wood. The best method is to fix them by means of two strong oak dowels in each foot.

The skirting C (Fig. 50) finished with a moulded capping,

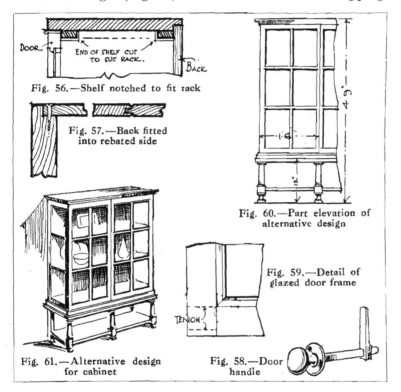

Fig. 56.—Shelf notched to fit rack

Fig. 57.—Back fitted into rebated side

Fig. 60.—Part elevation of alternative design

Fig. 59.—Detail of glazed door frame

Fig. 61.—Alternative design for cabinet

Fig. 58.—Door handle

as in Fig. 54, is sometimes desirable, as is also a strip along the inside of the left-hand door, as shown at D in Fig. 53.

If the wall against which the bookcase is to be placed is inclined to be damp, a space should be left between the back and the wall, through which the air can circulate, or, if it is known that the wall is damp, a better method is to make the back of the bookcase of zinc.

Furniture Making

Bookcase with Underneath Cupboard, Figs. 65 to 69.—A simple bookcase with a cupboard underneath is, here shown, and if made as described, to a width of 3 ft., can well be all in one piece. Should, however, a greater width be required, the case might be made in two sections—the

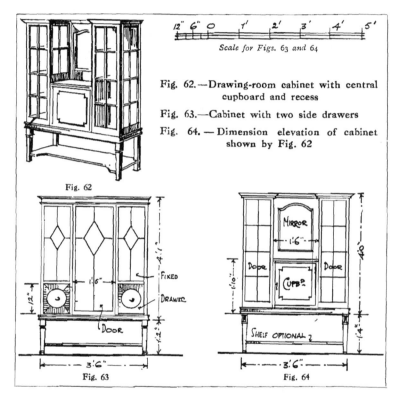

Fig. 62.—Drawing-room cabinet with central cupboard and recess

Fig. 63.—Cabinet with two side drawers

Fig. 64.—Dimension elevation of cabinet shown by Fig. 62

lower cupboard complete with its top A (Fig. 65) and the upper portion made independently and placed in position, with dowels at the ends and a few easily accessible screws. Among the most obvious ways of varying its appearance are the various designs made with the glazing bars, two of which are given in Fig. 65. The side view (Fig. 66) serves to show an alternative arrangement, in which the cupboard is in-

Bookcases and China Cabinets

creased 3 in. in depth and the bookcase reduced to 10 in. The height from the floor line to the top is 6 ft., the width outside the ends is 3 ft., and the depth from back to front is 11in.

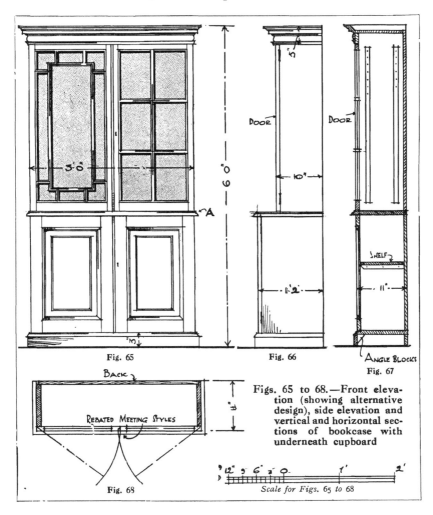

Figs. 65 to 68.—Front elevation (showing alternative design), side elevation and vertical and horizontal sections of bookcase with underneath cupboard

The lower part is enclosed by panelled doors, and the upper part by folding glass doors, the two parts being divided by a table shelf, having a moulding B (Fig. 69) along the front and returned at the ends. The skirting or plinth is also mitred along the front and ends. The cornice is shaped from a piece of stuff 3½ in. by 1⅜ in., and is supplemented by a ¾-in. by 2½-in. moulded frieze (Fig. 69), both being mitred in the usual manner.

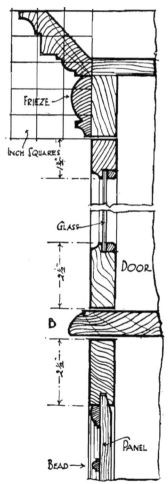

Fig. 69.—Detail through bookcsae cornice, etc.

The doors are made the full width of the case, hinged to the sides as shown, and the inside of the cupboard is fitted with shelves on small fillets, screwed to the sides. The inside of the bookcase is fitted with three or more shelves ; these should be movable, and can be dealt with as described for the first bookcase illustrated (page 20). The method shown in Fig. 67 is that of the latest metal strips.

In constructing the case, the sides are prepared and set out in pairs, the edges shot straight, and lines squared across to the dimensions. The back inside edge of each is rebated to receive the back. The ends are dovetailed or rebated to receive the top, and grooved 3 in. up to receive the bottom, and also 2 ft. 6 in. up to receive the table shelf. The top and bottom shelves are both alike, level with the edge of the sides, and the table shelf is moulded on the front edge, and cut long enough to mitre at each end to receive the two return mouldings on the side faces. The cornice moulding (Fig. 69) is worked, or a piece of ordinary architrave moulding may be used and mitred round.

Bookcases and China Cabinets

The doors are mortised and tenoned together, and moulded and grooved to receive the panels, which can be plain with just a chamfer on the framing or finished with mouldings and beads planted on, as in the lower part of Fig. 69. The upper doors are rebated, the glass being secured with beads or fillets mitred round and fixed with pins.

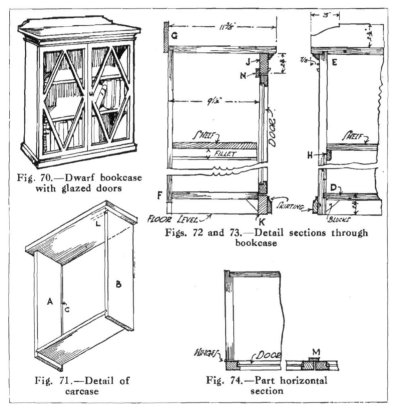

Fig. 70.—Dwarf bookcase with glazed doors

Figs. 72 and 73.—Detail sections through bookcase

Fig. 71.—Detail of carcase

Fig. 74.—Part horizontal section

Dwarf Bookcase with Glazed Doors, Figs 70 to 74.—This quietly designed little bookcase will be sufficiently explained by the various details shown on this page. Notice that the doors occupy the whole width of the front, the top being projected accordingly, also that the two sides go right down to the floor behind the small skirting. The suggested sizes are: overall width above skirting, 2 ft. 3 in.; height, floor to flat top, 2 ft. 11 in.; outside depth, including doors, 10½ in.

Cabinet Doors with Geometric Glazing-bars.—Several designs in this book will be found to include glazed doors with bars in diamond fashion or some other simple arrangement. In connection with these, the door about to be described should be of value to the reader, who is, however, advised to keep to a rather more restful arrangement in his actual work, the design being chosen mainly because it incorporates a number of different mitres.

The door stiles and rails shown by Figs. 75 and 76 are prepared from clean, straight-grained material, and finished 1¼ in. by ¾ in. The joints may be formed either with mortises and tenons, or dowels, and the moulding and rebate worked as at B (Fig. 76). The bars are made in two sections, the front part or astragal being prepared to intersect with the moulding on the stiles as at A (Fig. 76). The design of the door is set out accurately to full size (the centre lines of all the bars being first drawn), and the astragal is then cut and mitred together as shown in detail. Each joint is lettered in detail so as to correspond with the lettering in the elevation. When the whole of the design is finished, the joints are glued with the bars face down. Where the bars intersect with the stiles and rails, as at F, part of the end may be formed into a tenon and mortised to the stile and the whole glued up together.

Now take a piece of black tape slightly narrower than the width of the bar and glue to the back, completely covering the joints, and allow to stand until dry. Then prepare the backing, as shown in Fig. 78; this is ⅜ in. by ⅛ in., and where possible is notched together so as to allow it to be continuous over the mitred joints of the bar, and so strengthen them. In all cases the backing may pass over the joint a little and strengthen the mitre. When all is fitted, the backing is glued and permanently fixed with needle points into the bar. This backing forms the rebate for the glass, which is held in position by small beads. In order to make the joints of the backing additionally strong, a narrow

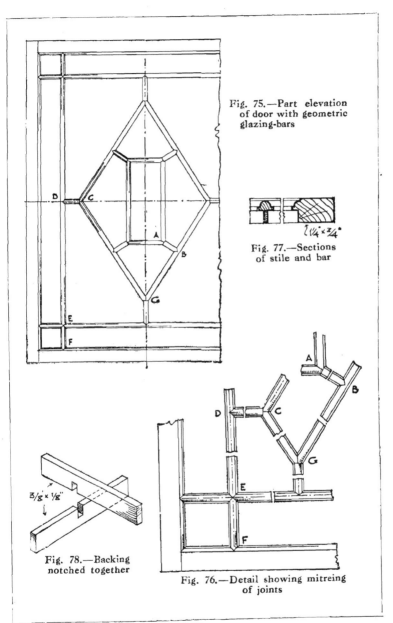

Fig. 75.—Part elevation of door with geometric glazing-bars

Fig. 77.—Sections of stile and bar

Fig. 78.—Backing notched together

Fig. 76.—Detail showing mitreing of joints

28 Furniture Making

piece of tape is glued to the sides, passing well over the joints.

Built-up or Sectional Bookcases, Figs. 79 to 95.—The great advantage of the sectional type of bookcase is that, as a library increases, so another division or "unit" may be added. The cases about to be described are easily made and require no elaborate fittings. As will be gathered from the drawings, the glass fronts are pivoted at the top to open outwards (*see* Fig. 83), and when raised to a horizontal position, slide into a compartment specially contrived for their reception (*see* Fig. 82). Figs. 81 to 84 explain the various portions required

The first figure is termed the cornice, and is detachable from the sections below, as is also the base or plinth in Fig. 84. Fig. 80 shows one section with the cornice and plinth. The width across the front is 3 ft., and the depth of the end at the narrow part is 12 in. (*see* Fig. 83), or a little less if desired.

Stuff 1 in. or $\frac{7}{8}$ in. thick is employed in the main, while the backs, etc., can be quite thin.

In beginning operations, first make a full-size drawing of the sections as follows : Start with the base line A in Fig. 84, and set out two vertical lines 12 in. apart. Then, with a pair of dividers or compasses, ascertain the various sizes, etc., in Figs. 89, 91, 92, etc.; some of these will be found figured on the drawings, or the scales may be referred to. Transfer the measurements full size to the working drawing, and so deal with all the different parts. Draw bottom B of the lower section, taking the thickness, etc., from Fig. 92. From this decide on the height of space required for the books. The lower section (Fig. 83) allows for 12 in., and the section above $9\frac{1}{2}$ in.

Next mark the position of the section top C. Insert a full-size copy of the rails D and E as in Figs. 91 and 92. Between the tops C allow for the space F equal to $\frac{3}{16}$ in. larger than the thickness of the doors, for clearance when they are lifted and pushed into this space while taking out books. Above the space F begin with the bottom of the upper section, and proceed as for the lower section. Note the line G in all figures represents the top point of each section.

Bookcases and China Cabinets

Next draw the cornice (Fig. 81), allowing the front H (Fig. 80) to drop $\frac{1}{8}$ in. lower than G; likewise the lower rail I (top of Fig. 91). The details of the plinth may now be put in. Let the doors stand back a full $\frac{1}{16}$ in. from the front

Fig. 79.—Built-up or sectional bookcases

edges of the ends. Half the front view (Fig. 80) may now be drawn, the horizontal lines of the cornice, doors, and plinth being obtained from the sections first drawn.

In beginning the construction, first make the sections, dovetailing the bottoms B to the ends as shown in Fig. 85.

The tops C (Figs 82 and 83), of $\frac{1}{2}$-in. stuff, are dovetail-grooved as in Fig. 93. Of course, this groove must not come through to the front. A back J (Figs. 82 and 83) of $\frac{1}{2}$-in. stuff is fitted in rebated ends, and fixed with screws, or $\frac{1}{4}$-in. 3-ply might be substituted. Two $\frac{3}{8}$-in. diameter dowels protruding about $\frac{3}{8}$ in. are fixed in the top of the section ends, as in Figs. 82, 83, 85, etc., and corresponding holes bored into the bottom of the ends.

Before the top and bottom of the sections are glued to the ends, a groove K (Figs. 82 and 83) must be made. This groove is for an iron or brass pin, shown by the dotted circle in Fig. 91 (*see also* Fig. 80, etc.). These pins should be put in half the thickness of the door down from the top edge, and may consist of screws with the heads filed off, leaving a projection of $\frac{3}{16}$ in. The groove, instead of coming out at the front, is turned upwards, as in Fig. 88, in order to drop the pins of the doors into position, the upper section of the cornice being tilted to do this. As by usage the pin would wear the bottom of the groove, and thus let the door down and interfere with its true hanging, a metal plate L (Fig. 91), and shown in Figs. 88 and 94, is fixed with a couple of countersunk screws. The lower side of the pin in the door will then ride on the top edge of the plate, which may be made out of a piece of sheet-brass or iron. The groove at the entrance should be the same size as the iron pin in the door, but farther inwards it should be wider, to avoid friction. In fact, for ease of running, the door should rest on the top C (Figs. 82 and 83) when pushed in as shown in Fig. 82. The space F (Fig. 83) should have a good application of powdered french chalk or blacklead, to help the easy sliding of the door.

In making the cornice (Fig. 81) the top may be housed into the ends as described for the top C (Figs. 83 and 93), the bottom dovetailed as in Fig. 85, and the front M have short tenons fitting into mortises going three-quarters through the ends. The back is continued above the top, and shaped as shown in Fig. 80. The moulding N is simply fitted between the ends.

The plinth (Fig. 84) need not have a top; the front por-

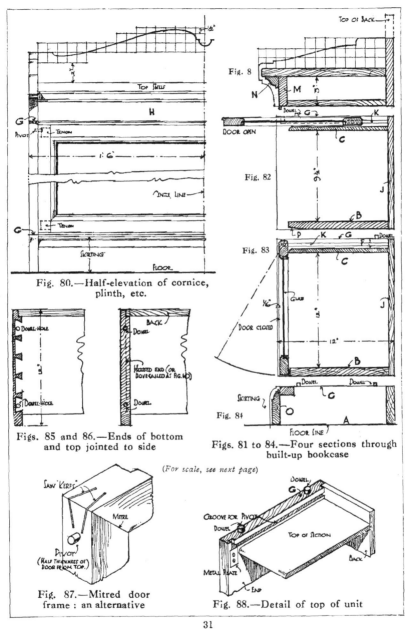

Fig. 80.—Half-elevation of cornice, plinth, etc.

Figs. 85 and 86.—Ends of bottom and top jointed to side

Figs. 81 to 84.—Four sections through built-up bookcase

(For scale, see next page)

Fig. 87.—Mitred door frame : an alternative

Fig. 88.—Detail of top of unit

tion o is tenoned into the ends the same as M (Fig. 81) Angle pieces, as in Fig. 90, are fixed in the corners.

The back is fitted as for the sections, and further secured with blocks. The skirting is fitted between the ends. The doors are tenoned and mortised together, and have moulded

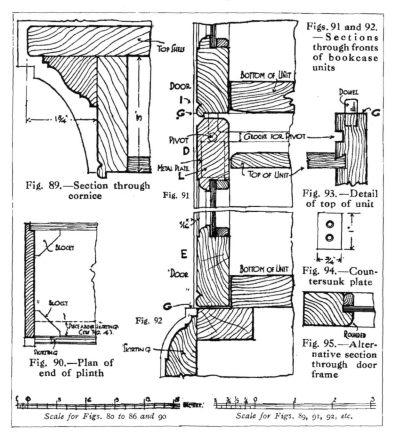

Figs. 91 and 92.—Sections through fronts of bookcase units

Fig. 89.—Section through cornice

Fig. 90.—Plan of end of plinth

Fig. 93.—Detail of top of unit

Fig. 94.—Countersunk plate

Fig. 95.—Alternative section through door frame

Scale for Figs. 80 to 86 and 90   Scale for Figs. 89, 91, 92, etc.

edges as in Figs. 91 and 92, which also show the fixing of the glass. Leaded glass of a light type would look very well, and can be obtained made to order for about 1s. per super foot.

A simpler method of forming the doors would be to use

Bookcases and China Cabinets

1½-in. by 1-in. stuff rebated and rounded as in Fig. 95, then mitred together and glued up. A piece of strong cord should be tied round, and eight small blocks inserted between the cord and the frame, gradually working towards the mitres until sufficient pressure is obtained to thoroughly close them. When the glue is hard, a couple of saw kerfs are run in the mitre dovetailing, and a slip of veneer glued in as shown in Fig. 87. If preferred, the glass can be fixed in with coloured putty to match the wood.

Figs. 85 and 86 show the positions of the dowels. The weight of the books will keep one section to the other; but for further security slanting screws may be driven from the upper face of the bottom into the ends beneath.

To prevent the doors from jamming when being pushed inwards, the bottoms or sections must be bevelled as at P (Fig. 82); also the front edges of the tops C should be rounded as shown.

To ensure the nice running of the doors in the space F (Fig. 83), the tops and bottoms B and C must be $\frac{1}{16}$ in. wider at the back than at the front.

A fillet is sometimes desired to keep the smaller books from going too far back, and a piece of cork lino makes an excellent bed for the edges of the books.

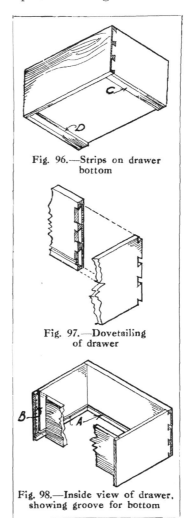

Fig. 96.—Strips on drawer bottom

Fig. 97.—Dovetailing of drawer

Fig. 98.—Inside view of drawer, showing groove for bottom

Drawer Construction.—A drawer will not be strong and will not fit and run easily, unless the work was very carefully set out. A commonplace drawer is shown by Fig. 96, this having a 1-in. front dovetailed to $\frac{1}{2}$-in. sides (*see* Fig. 97); dovetailing best resists the tendency to pull off the front when opening the drawer. A groove A (Fig. 98) should be worked round the lower edges of the sides and front to receive a thin bottom, which in most cases can be of three-ply wood slipped into the grooves from the rear and afterwards secured to the back piece, which, as shown in Fig. 98, stops at the top line of the grooves. This figure also shows how the back is rebated at each end to form a projecting tongue fitting into a vertical groove B. Two strips on the bottom, as at C and D in Fig. 96, will be useful to reduce the wearing of these upon the bearers on which they slide in and out. Rails and blocks should be fitted wherever possible inside the drawer space to act as guides, and there should also be a stop to prevent the drawer going the least distance beyond the front at which its face becomes flush with the surrounding framing.

It is usually advisable to make the drawer as a tight fit, and then to reduce it just sufficiently by planing, scraping, or glasspapering for it to run easily when moved with one hand only; and it will be found advantageous to have the wearing parts in oak.

CHAPTER IV

WRITING CABINETS AND BUREAUX

Writing Cabinet, Figs. 99 to 113. — A writing cabinet of modern design is here illustrated. In addition to the three external drawers, there is an interior stationery case, the whole forming a compact piece of furniture 4 ft. 6 in. high, 2 ft. 8 in. wide, and 1 ft. deep. Although the figured veneering greatly improves the appearance, it may be omitted. Should it be desired to modify the dimensions, it must be remembered that the surface of the flap when in position for writing should not be more than 2 ft. 6 in. or less than 2 ft. 5 in. from the floor. Either walnut or mahogany is suggested as suitable.

The cabinet is made in two parts which meet at A (Fig. 101), and are screwed together.

To make the lower part, four legs 2 ft. $4\frac{3}{4}$ in. long by $1\frac{3}{8}$ in. square are dowelled into the side rails, which are 5 in. by $\frac{7}{8}$ in. flush on the outside. The back rail (shown in section in Fig. 101) is $5\frac{5}{8}$ in. wide, and is also dowelled to the legs; but before gluing up, the rails must be rebated to receive the $\frac{1}{2}$-in. bottom, which is stub-tenoned to the legs and screwed into rebates. Beginning below the drawer, the legs taper to $\frac{7}{8}$ in. square, and at a distance of 5 in. from the floor they receive two $1\frac{1}{2}$-in. by $\frac{5}{8}$-in. rails to support the under-shelf. These rails are indicated by dotted lines in Fig. 102, and the same diagram shows a cross rail which is stub-tenoned between them. A couple of 3-in. by $\frac{1}{2}$-in. rails are dovetailed across the top of the legs, the joint used being shown in Fig. 104.

The drawer is dovetailed together in the usual way, with a front shown in detail by Fig. 111. This moulding is easily worked by means of a rebate plane and scratch stock, and if the rebated portion is veneered with cross-grained mahogany, and the centre part with "curl" mahogany as indicated in Fig. 100, a pleasing effect is produced. Fig. 112 is a detail of the ploughed slipping which is glued to the sides of the drawer to receive the bottom; this bottom, being extra wide, is made in two parts, and connected by a 1½-in. by ⅝-in. ploughed muntin shown in Fig. 105. Fig. 102 shows the ⅝-in. under-shelf fixed flush with back and sides,

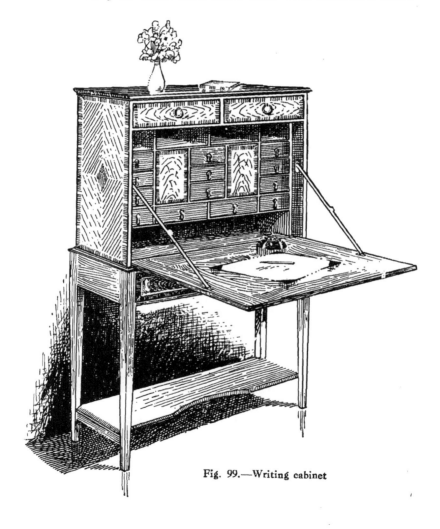

Fig. 99.—Writing cabinet

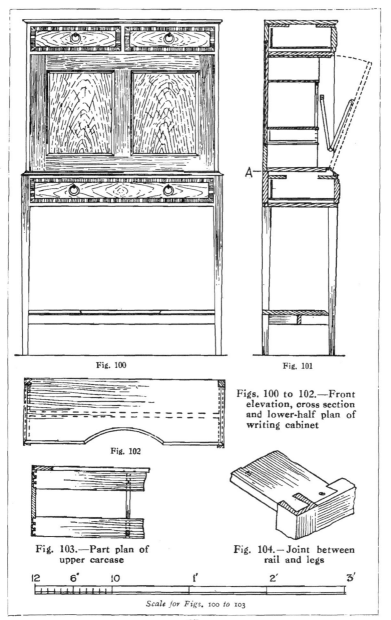

Fig. 100

Fig. 101

Figs. 100 to 102.—Front elevation, cross section and lower-half plan of writing cabinet

Fig. 102

Fig. 103.—Part plan of upper carcase

Fig. 104.—Joint between rail and legs

Scale for Figs. 100 to 103

but set behind the front legs, and shaped to a simple curve with a chamfered edge, as shown by Fig. 107.

To complete the lower stand of the cabinet a length of moulding about 5 ft. long by $2\frac{1}{2}$ in. wide is worked as in Fig. 108, then mitred, glued, and screwed round the sides and front, notching the back rail to receive it. The front strip of moulding is reduced to $1\frac{5}{8}$ in. and rebated (Fig. 110) in order to ensure free play for the writing flap.

The upper carcase is 30 in. wide, and consists of sides 2 ft. by 11 in. by $\frac{5}{8}$ in. rebated to receive a $\frac{3}{8}$-in. back, and having two 3-in. by $\frac{1}{2}$-in. top rails lap-dovetailed between them as shown in Fig. 103. A $\frac{5}{8}$-in. bottom $9\frac{3}{4}$ in. wide is also dovetailed to the sides, the front edge being rebated to receive the flap as shown in Fig. 110. Provision for the two upper drawers is made by housing a $\frac{5}{8}$-in. division 4 in. below the top rails, and inserting a vertical division of the same thickness in the centre. The latter piece will require a clamp tongued and grooved to its front edge, in order to show vertical grain. A $\frac{5}{8}$-in. top moulded to the section (Fig. 106) is screwed up through the top rails. In order to show a flush surface inside, a $\frac{5}{8}$-in. flush framed back is prepared with two panels, the bottom rail of the framing being $4\frac{1}{2}$ in. wide, the centre member or muntin 2 in. wide, and the other members 3 in. wide.

The stationery case is made separately, and placed in position after the carcase has been finished. Figs. 101 and 105 show the arrangements, which consist of four top divisions, a clear space of $3\frac{1}{2}$ in. at the bottom, and small drawers. The sides of the case are made $\frac{1}{2}$ in. thick; but all other parts are $\frac{3}{8}$ in., including the top, which is made wide enough to form a stop for the flap when closed (*see* Fig. 101). The drawer fronts should be about $\frac{1}{2}$ in. thick (*see* Fig. 109), all other parts of drawers being a bare $\frac{1}{4}$ in. The small cupboard doors may be made of dry mahogany $\frac{1}{2}$ in. thick, and to prevent warping it will be necessary to veneer them on both sides. A $\frac{5}{8}$-in. band of cross-grained mahogany and a "curl" centre veneer would be in harmony with the outside drawer fronts. A small inlaid check banding might be introduced, and the drawer fronts also afford opportunities for decoration.

Writing Cabinets and Bureaux

To construct the flap, a 2½-in. by ⅝-in. framing is mortised and tenoned together, having two panels flush on the inside with a small moulding mitred and glued into position as shown in detail in Fig. 110. This illustration also shows how the bottom edge of the flap is rebated and hinged

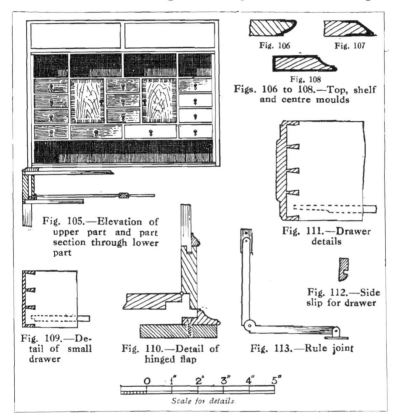

Fig. 106 Fig. 107
Fig. 108
Figs. 106 to 108.—Top, shelf and centre moulds

Fig. 105.—Elevation of upper part and part section through lower part

Fig. 111.—Drawer details

Fig. 112.—Side slip for drawer

Fig. 109.—Detail of small drawer

Fig. 110.—Detail of hinged flap

Fig. 113.—Rule joint

Scale for details

to fall and form a horizontal surface flush with the inside of the carcase bottom. A rule-joint stay (Fig. 113) is used to support the flap when open; but great care should be taken to ensure a level surface.

A suggestion for veneering the sides of the upper part is shown in the perspective view (Fig. 99). The handles of the lower drawer should be fixed exactly under those at the top.

A dull polish is a very suitable finish for a piece of furniture of this type.

Combination Writing-table and Cabinet, Figs. 114 to 120.—The combined writing-table and cabinet here shown is 4 ft. 6 in. high, 2 ft. 2 in. wide, and 1 ft. 2 in. deep. The top portion serves as a cabinet, enclosed by doors having leaded lights. Below the cabinet is a nest of pigeon-holes, and under this is a drawer, which, when partly drawn out, forms a rest for the writing-flap above. This panel should be of selected figure and grain. Near the bottom is a shelf for books, etc. Oak would be the best material to use, but the nest of pigeon-holes might look better in satin-wood or holly. The leading dimensions are given in the illustrations, Fig. 116 being a front elevation, Fig. 115 a transverse section through the centre. Fig. 116 shows alternative designs for the leaded lights of the cabinet, and additional suggestions will be found on other pages.

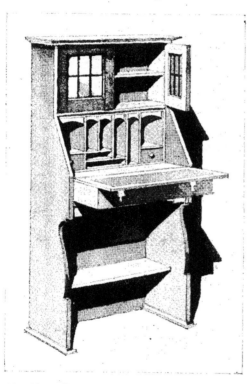

Fig. 114.—Combination writing-table and cabinet

First get out the two ends, which are 1 ft. 2 in. in the widest

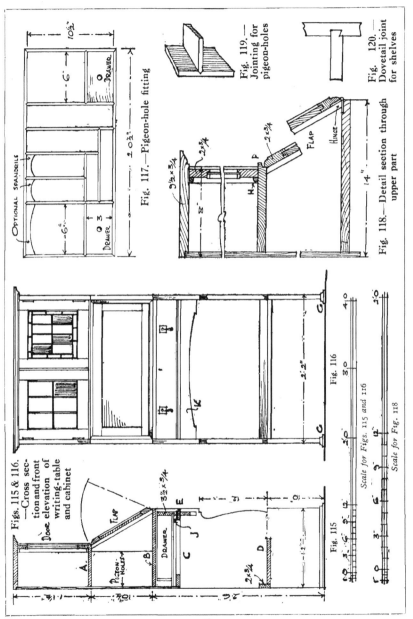

Fig. 117.—Pigeon-hole fitting

Fig. 119.—Jointing for pigeon-holes

Fig. 120.—Dovetail joint for shelves

Fig. 118.—Detail section through upper part

Figs. 115 & 116.—Cross section and front elevation of writing-table and cabinet

part, and therefore would have to be jointed up. As the upper portion of the ends is 8 in. wide, the best position for the joint would be in continuation of this width. Shoot the back and top and bottom edges, and mark the outline and the positions of the housings. Work a rebate on the inside back edges, for a length of 2 ft. $4\frac{1}{4}$ in. from the top. Next cut out the housings for A, B, C and D (Fig. 115), A, B and D being for preference dovetailed, as shown at Fig. 6, and c plain housed. The frame c is mortised and tenoned together in the usual manner. A hollow is worked on the front edge (*see* E, Fig. 115).

Having prepared the shelves A, B, D, and the framework C, cut their ends to fit into the corresponding housings, and work a scotia moulding on the front edge of the shelf A (*see* F, Fig. 118). The top of the cabinet should now be prepared, and housings cut to enable it to fit over the ends. The feet or bearers G (Fig. 116) are of $2\frac{1}{2}$-in. by 1-in. stuff, and should be secured to the ends with three stout screws from underneath; they should be chamfered or moulded, as shown.

The doors are tenoned and rebated to receive the leaded glass panels. The two meeting stiles are slightly rebated, and a bead is run along the face of one. A doorstop is shown at H (Fig. 118). The correct width for the writing-flap would be about 1 ft. $0\frac{1}{4}$ in. The frame is mortised and tenoned together. The inner surface of the panel should be a trifle below that of the frame if it is to be covered with real or imitation leather. If dispensed with, the panel should be flush. A thumb moulding is worked on the edges as shown. The flap, when closed, rests on two strips screwed to the ends (*see* Figs. 115 and 118). The drawer is constructed in the ordinary way. A narrow strip of baize should be glued along the top edge of the drawer front, to prevent the surface of the flap from being scratched when it is open, and two pieces J (Fig. 115) should be screwed to the framework D to prevent the drawer being pushed too far back. The rail K is 3-in. by $\frac{5}{8}$-in., and should be shaped as shown in Fig. 116.

The framework c (Fig. 115) and the shaped rail K should be blocked at the back angles as required. The back is made

Writing Cabinets and Bureaux

up of ½-in. boards grooved and tongued together. The nest of pigeon-holes is shown in elevation at Fig. 117; this is made separately and slipped in from behind, the depth from back to front being 6 in. Material ¼ in. thick should be used. The corners are mitred together, the **V**-ends of the division pieces fitting tight into corresponding grooves (*see also* Fig. 119). The bottom corners are fitted with drawers as shown.

A Bureau Bookcase, Figs. 121 to 129.—The bureau case illustrated is made up in two sections, which are constructed separately, and when complete placed one above the other and screwed together.

In the lower section a drawer is fitted above the cupboard and the space above the drawer is fitted with pigeon-holes, which are enclosed by a hinged writing-flap; this, when in use, is supported by slides at each end of the drawer, as in Figs. 127 and 128.

Fig. 121.—Bureau bookcase

The top section is in the form of an ordinary bookcase enclosed by glass doors, which can either be quite plain or follow some such design as that given.

The lower section should first be taken in hand. The

sides A (Fig. 123) are prepared from wood ⅞ in. thick, and the bottom B and the shelf C are ⅞ in. thick, dovetail-grooved into the sides, as at D, Fig. 128; they stand back ¼ in. from the front edge of the sides as shown in Fig. 127. The

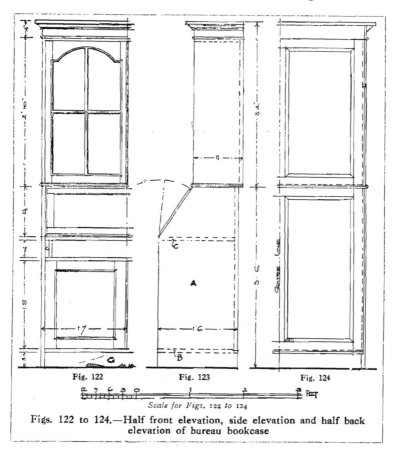

Figs. 122 to 124.—Half front elevation, side elevation and half back elevation of bureau bookcase

drawer rails (E E, Fig. 127) are 2½ in. by ⅞ in., stump-tenoned into the sides. The drawer bearer in Fig. 128 is 2½ in. by ⅞ in. grooved ⅛ in. into the sides and screwed. The top rails F (Figs. 126 and 127) are 3 in. by ⅞ in., dovetailed to the top edge of the sides. The back is framed, and panelled as in

Writing Cabinets and Bureaux

Fig. 124, with framework 2 in. by ⅞ in., and panels ⅜ in. thick grooved into its edges. The back is rebated into the back edges of the sides and bottom, and screwed to sides, rails, shelf and bottom. The strip G (Fig. 122) is cut from wood ⅜ in. thick and housed into the sides.

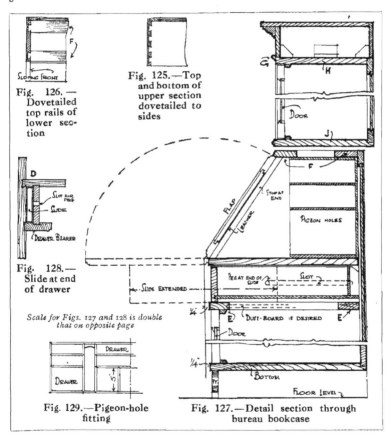

Fig. 126.—Dovetailed top rails of lower section

Fig. 125.—Top and bottom of upper section dovetailed to sides

Fig. 128.—Slide at end of drawer

Scale for Figs. 127 and 128 is double that on opposite page

Fig. 129.—Pigeon-hole fitting

Fig. 127.—Detail section through bureau bookcase

The framework of the cupboard doors is 2 in. wide by ⅞ in. thick; a bead is run round the inner front edges, and the back edges are rebated ⅝ in. wide by ¼ in. deep to receive the door panels, which are ¼ in. thick, and fixed with fillets. Fillet pieces are fixed to the bottom and the drawer rail, as shown at E in Fig. 127, to form stops. The doors are fitted with 1½-in. brass butt hinges and a catch fastener on the inside, and a lock.

The drawer is made up in the usual manner, a section being given in Fig. 127. The front is ¾ in., sides ½ in., back and bottom ⅜ in. thick.

The arrangement of the 4-in. by ½-in. pull-out slides, provided to support the flap when open, will be gathered from Figs. 127 and 128; in the latter is shown a false end or casing, separating it from the drawer-space, best fixed by slightly housing into the shelf and bearer. It should have a central slot cut as in Fig. 127, in which an oak peg let into the end of the slide fits loosely, thus preventing the slide from being drawn out beyond a distance of, say, 9 in. For a first-class job a dust board should be fitted between the drawer and cupboard as dotted.

The writing-flap is framed and panelled, and covered on the inside with leather. The framework is 2¼ in. by ⅞ in., mortised and tenoned together and moulded round the edges as in Fig. 127. The panel is ½ in. thick, grooved into the edges of the framework, and the leather covering on the inside is fixed with either glue or paste, and brought down over the edges of the panel as shown. The flap is fixed to the shelf C (Fig. 123) with a pair of 1½-in. brass butt hinges, and is fitted with a lock which locks into the front rail F (Fig. 127).

The pigeon-holes may be made up as shown in Fig. 129 and as described in the preceding design. This completes the lower section.

The cornice at the top is made up separately, and is kept in position by blocks, which are fixed to the top of the bookcase, over which the cornice drops as shown in Fig. 127, and the moulded fillet G should project sufficiently to cover the joint. The sides of the bookcase, the top H (Fig. 127) and the bottom J are ⅞ in. thick, and the top and bottom are dovetailed into the sides as shown in Fig. 125. The back of the case is framed as before. The shelves are ¾ in. thick, and can be supported as described on page 19 by means of the neat metal strips and movable pins now obtainable.

The framework of the glazed doors is of the following

Writing Cabinets and Bureaux

dimensions: stiles, 2 in. wide by $\frac{7}{8}$ in. thick, with top rails out of a $4\frac{1}{2}$ in. width. A bead is run round the inner front edges, and the back edges are rebated $\frac{5}{8}$ in. wide by $\frac{1}{4}$ in. thick to receive the glass, which is fixed in position with fillets. Stops should also be fitted as shown. The doors are hung and fitted as before described. The cornice is made up with $\frac{3}{4}$-in. sides and ends mitre-dovetailed together at the corners. The moulding is fixed with glue and screws.

CHAPTER V

OVERMANTELS AND MIRRORS

Overmantel with Cupboard, Figs. 130 to 134.—The illustrations on p. 49 show an overmantel designed as a portable piece of furniture. Beginning with a baseboard with a small moulding or bevel along its upper edge, there are at each end four uprights ($1\frac{1}{2}$ in. tapered to $1\frac{1}{8}$ in.), with small moulded bases mitred round. Those at the back are rebated for the square panelled framing against the wall. These uprights support a horizontal head (*see* enlarged section, Fig. 134), level with the top of the panelled back, and these two parts support the $\frac{3}{8}$-in. top shown. Round the whole is run a cornice mould, and in front below the head are two thin arch-pieces with diamond-shaped piercings.

The cupboard in the centre is made of $\frac{7}{8}$-in. stuff, the bottom being shaped, as on the plan, to form shelves at each side, and supported on two cut brackets. It projects sufficiently to stop the cornice to the sides, and has a similar cornice itself. The door is shown glazed with small leaded panes.

Two Overmantels of Architectural Character, Figs. 135 to 141.—This overmantel should be made to sizes to suit its particular position, more especially with regard to the length and projection of the existing mantelshelf on which it is intended to stand, and with which it should, if possible, correspond. The length, therefore, can be varied as necessary; but the height should be kept low in proportion, or the whole intended effect, which depends on the long, low appearance, may be spoilt. It is suggested that the work be executed in mahogany, brought to a dark rich tone and polished.

Alternative methods of carrying out the overmantel are given; but the elevation and general details are the same in both cases. The effect of the more elaborate method

Overmantels and Mirrors

can be gathered from Fig. 135, and the point in which the second method differs is that there is a considerable reduction of the projection.

The working drawings for both schemes are given, the front view being applicable to both. A detail to a larger scale, showing the intended mouldings and construction,

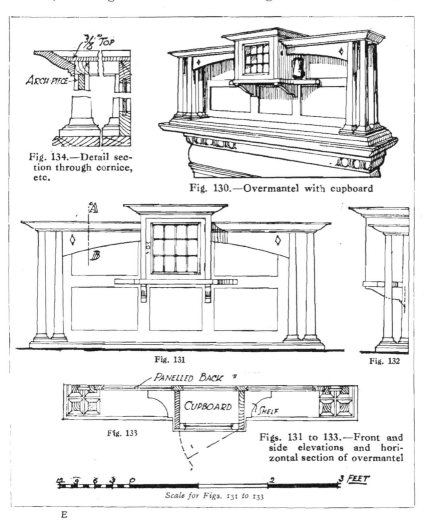

Fig. 134.—Detail section through cornice, etc.

Fig. 130.—Overmantel with cupboard

Fig. 131

Fig. 132

Fig. 133

Figs. 131 to 133.—Front and side elevations and horizontal section of overmantel

Scale for Figs. 131 to 133

is also given (Fig. 141); it is in the form of a section through the centre of the larger design, but in the main applies equally to the other.

Whichever arrangement is decided on, the best method of beginning the work will be to set out the whole full size, using as far as possible all the dimensions given. Such a drawing should comprise half the front elevation and the plan, a section through the middle, and an end view. This drawing will decide all the sizes of the different parts if these are altered from the illustrations, and will really simplify the work considerably.

Taking first the larger design, this is built up on a baseboard $\frac{5}{8}$ in. thick (c), raised about $1\frac{3}{8}$ in. from the mantelshelf by two fir bearers (marked with crosses) running the whole length. Round this base on three sides is mitred a moulding, rebated to fit in position. The next part to put in hand will be the back, which consists of a frame 1 in. or less thick, with upright ends, and horizontal top and bottom rails, halved together at the back. Notice that at the two bottom corners the sight-line or opening of the frame breaks down $\frac{1}{2}$ in. for a space 3 in. wide at each end. A slight chamfer is taken off the edge round the opening on the face, and at the back a $\frac{1}{4}$-in. rebate is prepared round the three upper edges; but in the middle of the bottom part this will have to be increased to 1 in. in width to permit the mirror to be rectangular in shape, instead of the difficult outline which will show on the face. Fig. 141 shows the ordinary $\frac{1}{4}$-in. rebate at D, and indicates at E the greater width necessary in the centre as just described. Mitred round the opening just away from the chamfered edge is a small moulding which will require careful work in fitting.

The bottom edge of the back should be grooved into the back of the base as shown in Fig. 141, and the upper part will eventually be made of deal of the same thickness tongued or dowelled along the top edge, to meet and fill in the top of the whole work. Two small solid plinth-blocks as at F, $1\frac{1}{2}$ in. high, are then fixed at the ends, and above these at the back are contrived out of, say, $\frac{1}{2}$-in. stuff, mitred at the angles, boxings 1 ft. $4\frac{1}{2}$ in. high, held together with blocks glued along

Overmantels and Mirrors

the internal angles, with one side housed into a groove in the back and the other wide enough to cover the end edge of the back-framing, all as shown at G. The total projection from the face of the wall to the front of these boxings is suggested to be 5 in. They partly support a long horizontal boxing of similar construction, forming the top of the structure, the front piece of which, H, is mitred at the angles and rebated and **V**-jointed to fit the soffit J, which is shown housed into the back framing. A light piece K forms a finish to the top, and should be grooved and rebated to fit the upright parts

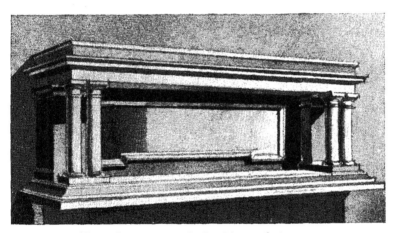

Fig. 135.— Overmantel of architectural character

below as shown; it has a small moulded edge. A cornice moulding 2 in. deep is fixed $1\frac{1}{4}$ in. up from the bottom edge of the front of this boxing.

The columns consist of round turned shafts $1\frac{3}{4}$ in. in diameter, with moulded caps, neckings, and bases, all as nearly as possible to match the outlines shown. They should each be turned out of one piece with the mouldings in the solid, and the shaft will look all the better if it is $1\frac{3}{4}$ in. across for one-third of the height up, and thence tapered very slightly to obtain the effect of a classic column. The square upper part of the cap (*see* L) had better be cut out of a separate piece and attached afterwards, and the columns may be

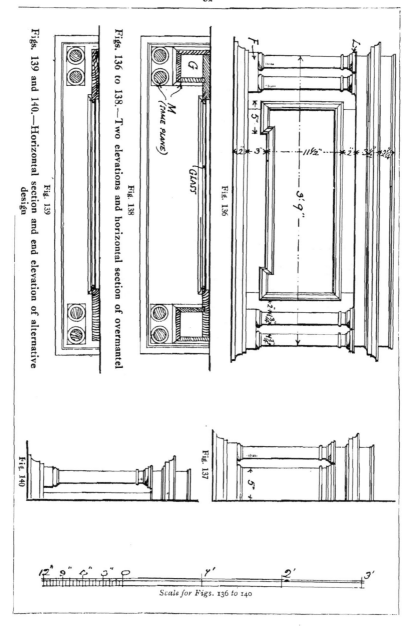

Fig. 136

Fig. 138

Figs. 136 to 138.—Two elevations and horizontal section of overmantel

Fig. 139

Fig. 137

Fig. 140

Figs. 139 and 140.—Horizontal section and end elevation of alternative design

Scale for Figs. 136 to 140

Overmantels and Mirrors

fixed with pegs through their centres at each end, in such positions that their outer edges line with the angles of the boxings as noted at M, which latter will be finished by the application of small mouldings specially worked to match those on the columns.

The second scheme (see Figs. 139 and 140) is similar to the first; with the exception that the boxings at ends G are dispensed with, and the 1-in. back framing extends to the edges of the outer columns, which are the same as before, although the plinth-blocks on which they stand are each only large enough to take the two columns. The base, top casing, and cornice moulding are similar, except that their projection is curtailed; but the mirror is precisely the same as before, and in fitting it should be well covered in at the rear to prevent discoloration.

Simple Modern - style Overmantels.—*First Example, Fig. 142.*—The first figure on p. 55 shows a type of overmantel that can always be depended upon to give a good effect, provided that, as noted in the preceding instance, similar proportions of width and height are maintained. It comprises a simple piece of framing in three panels with a small moulding on the solid, the heads segmental as shown or merely square, either the central one only or all the panels fitted with bevelled or plain mirrors, and per-

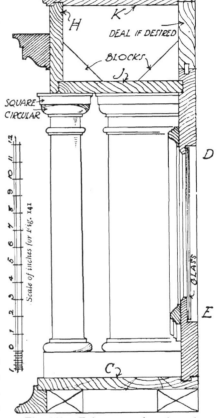

Fig. 141.—Enlarged section through overmantel

haps if the side panels are wood they can be fitted with well designed candle-sconces or electric light fittings. The small end pilasters (*see* Fig. 142), are intended to be square on plan, showing the same width on the side and being similar in detail to the columns in Fig. 141 ; the cornice also can follow this detail.

Second Example, Fig. 143.—The overmantel shown by Fig. 143 would look well in either a white finish or in polished hardwood. The cornice could be either plain or enriched with square dentils, etc. The suggested construction is that the framing be prepared, say $\frac{3}{4}$ in. thick, and the cornice, necking and plinth mouldings applied and mitred as necessary. The rebate for glass can be formed by fixing the inner moulding on the edges of the opening, leaving about $\frac{3}{8}$ in. at the back, mitreing it round the $\frac{1}{2}$-in. breaks shown on each side of the opening. These breakings of the moulding are very effective although they require careful manipulation. It will be noticed that as the glass will extend beyond the edge of the framing the corresponding portion of the framing on each face will need rebating, but that for the end 4 in. at each corner the framing will have a square edge on part of which the moulding will be planted.

Third Example, Figs. 144 *to* 146.—A more recent note is struck by this design, which should be carried out in oak. The 3-in. outer frame is secured together with slightly projecting oak pegs and the uprights project downwards about $\frac{3}{8}$ in. at either end. At the top is fixed a moulded shelf, shaped as indicated by the dotted line in Fig. 145 and finished with a couple of cut brackets as in Fig. 146. The frame is rebated to receive a sort of mount of $\frac{1}{4}$-in. oak, in which a segmental opening is cut and finished with a bevelled edge, and behind this a mirror, decorative picture, etc., can be secured. Unlike its predecessor, this overmantel should be suspended on the wall just over the fireplace instead of actually standing upon the shelf.

Two Hanging Mirrors, Figs. 147 and 148.—In the first of these examples the segmental top could be dispensed with if necessary, and the frame could be moulded or quite flat on the face in which latter case a band of Sheraton

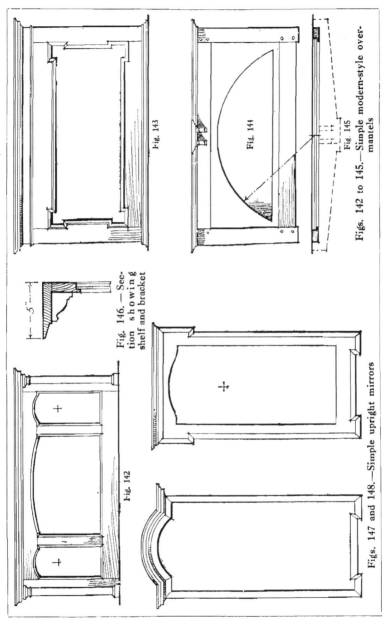

Figs. 142 to 145.—Simple modern-style overmantels

Fig. 146.—Section showing shelf and bracket

Figs. 147 and 148.—Simple upright mirrors

inlay along its centre would be quite telling. A composition moulding with "bead and reel" or "egg and tongue" enrichment would be particularly suitable. Much the same remarks apply to the next example (Fig. 148) which has an inner mount similar in substance to that in Fig. 144, and is, perhaps, best suited to a white treatment.

Upright Hall Mirror and Rack, Figs. 149 to 154.—No more appropriate material than figured oak could be selected for this upright mirror, and it might be stained to any shade of green or brown or merely wax-polished. The sizes adopted emphasise the long narrow appearance, which is always very effective; but they could easily be varied.

A suitable thickness for the whole of the work would be $\frac{3}{4}$ in., and the first portion to prepare would be the frame round the mirror. It consists first of two uprights each 2 ft. $5\frac{1}{2}$ in. long, which can have a rebate worked down their inner back edges for a distance of 1 ft. $11\frac{1}{2}$ in. from the top, that is, to within 6 in. of the extreme bottom edge, the outer corners of which are slightly rounded off as shown.

The top horizontal rail A (Fig. 150) is rebated along its lower edge, and has its ends worked as shown in Figs. 152 and 153 to form a halved joint with the uprights. This joint will have to be screwed, and has been adopted as an easy method; but, of course, it would be an improvement in the class of work to employ a joint not relying entirely on extraneous fixing, such as the dovetailed form of halving.

The lower rail is 6 in. wide, rebated and halved as shown in Figs. 152 and 153. For the top shelf, which has a chamfer $1\frac{1}{2}$ in. wide along its front and side edges, a piece as shown 1 ft. $3\frac{1}{2}$ in. by $5\frac{1}{2}$ in. should be employed. It is intended to be screwed down on to the top edge of the framing, and to have the two brackets added afterwards. They can be accurately set out from Fig. 154, in which each square represents 1 in., into which the actual work should be divided.

A couple of hooks screwed on the bottom rail are sure to prove useful; but care should be taken to obtain tasteful patterns.

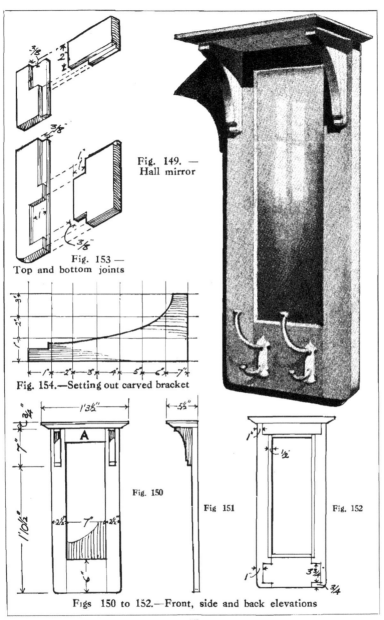

Fig. 149. — Hall mirror

Fig. 153 — Top and bottom joints

Fig. 154.—Setting out carved bracket

Figs 150 to 152.—Front, side and back elevations

Horizontal Hall Mirrors and Racks, Figs. 155 to 159.
—These two designs are of the same class of work as the upright mirror just described, and without their pegs could be adapted as modern overmantels, especially with

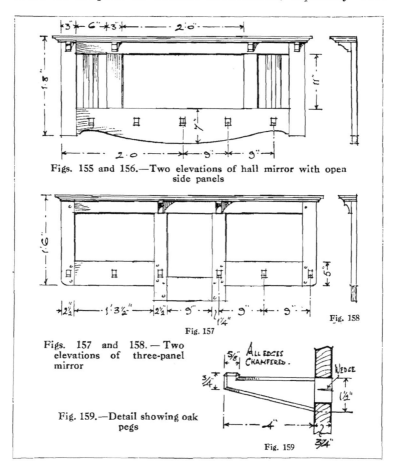

Figs. 155 and 156.—Two elevations of hall mirror with open side panels

Figs. 157 and 158. — Two elevations of three-panel mirror

Fig. 158

Fig. 157

Fig. 159.—Detail showing oak pegs

Fig. 159

suitable pictures in the side or central panels. Both are very simply framed and finished with shelves and cut brackets, and it is suggested that oak pegs, shaped, housed and wedged as in Fig. 159, be employed in lieu of metal fittings. The

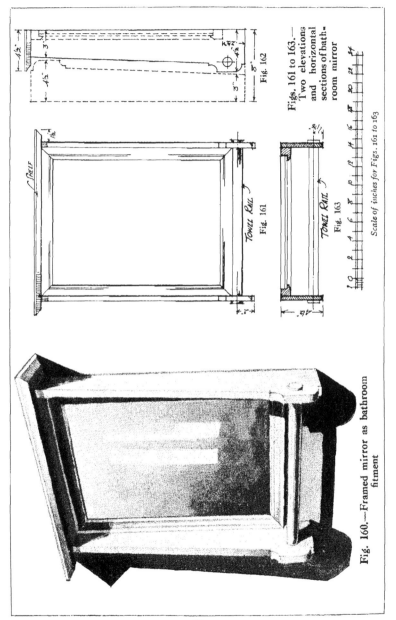

Fig. 160.—Framed mirror as bathroom fitment

Figs. 161 to 163.—Two elevations and horizontal sections of bathroom mirror

rack shown by Figs. 157 and 158 might well have a central mirror flanked by coloured prints, or mirrors at each side with a plain central panel on which an aneroid barometer, circular gong or set of brushes could suitably be mounted.

Converting Framed Mirror into Bathroom Fitment, Figs. 160 to 163.—A mirror in an ordinary picture frame can be readily turned into a useful fitting especially suitable for the bathroom or lavatory. First of all two side pieces about $\frac{3}{8}$ in. or a little more in thickness, $4\frac{1}{2}$ in. wide, and $2\frac{1}{2}$ in. longer than the outside length of the frame, should be cut out to an outline resembling that in Fig. 162, which also shows by the dotted lines on the left how the two can be economically prepared from one piece of wood $7\frac{3}{4}$ in. or 8 in. wide. These two pieces are fixed one on each side of the frame, and a third piece is then fixed along the top as a shelf. This latter has a bevelled edge on its three exposed sides as shown, and can suitably be $4\frac{1}{2}$ in. wide and $1\frac{1}{2}$ in. longer at the ends than the width of the frame.

A circular wooden rail of about 1 in. diameter will be required to complete the fitting, and should be fitted with its centre about 2 in. up and $1\frac{1}{8}$ in. back from the front edges. To make a sound, lasting job it will need careful fixing. One method would be to take the ends through circular openings a shade larger in circumference, and then to fix hardwood discs on them, sufficiently large to prevent their return through the holes as shown. Another way would be to fix projecting oak dowels or pins in the rail ends, projecting either into or through suitable holes in the sides prepared with a brace and bit. In the last two cases the rails can be left loose enough to revolve.

In the event of a towel rail not being required, this treatment of a mirror could still be adopted, and a shelf $4\frac{1}{2}$ in. wide placed immediately under the frame.

As a finish for the whole, white enamel would be eminently suitable, and in hanging the fitting care is necessary in arranging the small "wall-plates," which should be screwed to the frame itself.

CHAPTER VI

Enclosures to Unsightly Mantels

VERY often an inferior mantelpiece is to be found in a position where it is not desired to incur the expense and trouble involved in replacing it with a more suitable design. In such a case, one of the enclosures shown in this chapter might be adopted, either with or without the overmantel,

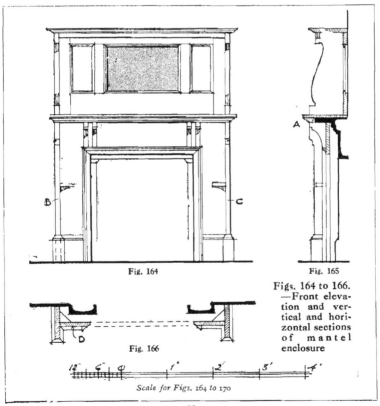

Fig. 164

Fig. 165

Figs. 164 to 166.—Front elevation and vertical and horizontal sections of mantel enclosure

Fig. 166

Scale for Figs. 164 to 170

which could also be used independently of the mantel framing.

First Example, Figs. 164 *to* 166.—The smallest of these designs is built up round the existing jambs and shelf without interference with them—an important point in the case of a tenant's fitting. The overmantel will speak for itself, and the mantel will be seen to consist, first of a wide shelf, resting upon the old one, and thickened out with a moulding as at A, Fig. 165. This shelf links up with two uprights, B and C (Fig. 164), shaped at the top and finished with a skirting next the floor. Between them is a plain lining D (Fig. 166) taken as close as may be considered safe to the fire, having an architrave moulding and two sets of cut brackets, also two small curved shelves in the angles. The whole of the work could be in 1-in. stuff, finished as required.

Fig. 167.—Mantel enclosure with shelves

Second Example, Figs. 167 *to* 170.—The next enclosure is on a rather larger scale than its predecessor, and comprises two uprights, E and F, shaped as in Fig. 169 and connected by a top shelf and two lower ones, G and H, the last resting upon the old shelf. The top compartment is divided into three parts, with a shaped spandril to each and a comparatively large cornice moulding. The next stage of the work has a piece of framing moulded and rebated to receive a mirror, and rebated into the

Enclosures to Unsightly Mantels

sides of the uprights, and two small shelves are fixed in the angle as shown. The bottom portion has a shaped rail J (Fig. 168) and moulding, under the shelf edge and in front of the old shelf, and a plain lining with moulded architrave and skirting. In such a case, a gas or anthracite

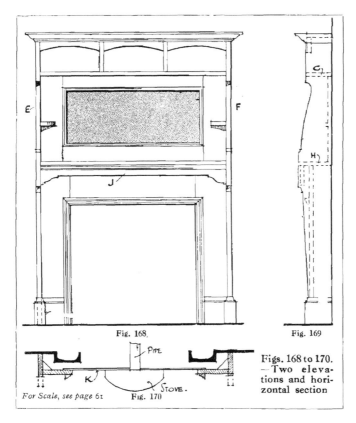

Figs. 168 to 170.—Two elevations and horizontal section

stove might well be fitted against a plain filling of sheet iron or preferably slabbed-up tiles K (Fig. 170), through which the stove pipe would be passed.

Third Example, Figs. 171 to 173.—Another design, having a similar object, is illustrated by Fig. 171. In this case a light piece of oak framing is set out as shown in small panels, complete with top and cornice and a small shelf on three shaped brackets just above the opening. It can be relied upon for a good effect in suitable surroundings.

Fourth Example, Figs. 174 and 175.—A similar idea in a reduced form is shown in Fig. 174; it is merely a plain boxing to the existing mantel, and with suitable mouldings

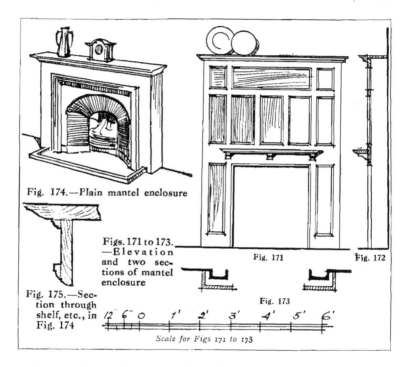

Fig. 174.—Plain mantel enclosure

Figs. 171 to 173.—Elevation and two sections of mantel enclosure

Fig. 175.—Section through shelf, etc., in Fig. 174

Scale for Figs 171 to 173

and attention to its proportions it can be made to look very well, especially if the curb can be made to fit against the plain faces as shown.

Any of the enclosures shown in this chapter might be secured in position by means of a few of the brass wall-plates generally employed for overmantels, etc.

CHAPTER VII

CLOCK CASES

Mantel Clock Case with Side Shelves, Figs. 176 to 180.
—This case can be executed in any wood to hand, and fretwood could be used for a small clock.

Many suitable clocks are obtainable, or one already possessed can be adapted if its case is of no value ; or a small circular clock might be arranged simply to stand on the upper shelf, behind the circular opening. A French movement or pendulum clock could easily be accommodated by cutting a suitable slot in the upper shelf shown. The most satisfactory course is to obtain a movement that can be screwed in position from the rear, and to which the dial and glass may be attached from the front. The method of fitting depends on the particular type of movement selected, but at the same time there is little difficulty in the matter.

The illustrations are to a scale suited for a dial 3 in. in diameter, and any marked difference in this measurement should be accompanied by a proportionate increase or decrease of the other sizes.

The case is suggested to be mainly out of $\frac{3}{8}$-in. stuff, although the shelves at the top might well be $\frac{1}{2}$ in. thick, while the parts at the back forming the box could be reduced. The front is wholly cut out of one piece to the outline shown in Fig. 176, including the side brackets, the curved top being part of a circle $2\frac{1}{2}$ in. in radius, and enclosing a circle to suit the diameter of the clock employed. Below this an opening is cut slightly smaller than the door shown. The front measures $6\frac{1}{2}$ in. across the bottom, and the straight sides taper in slightly to 6 in. width under the shelves, while its extreme width across the shaped brackets is 8 in., and a piece $3\frac{1}{2}$ in. by $\frac{1}{4}$ in. is cut out of the bottom edge. The two shelves on a level with the clock are next prepared out of $\frac{1}{2}$-in. stuff, and with a chamfer along three sides as shown ;

their net sizes are 3 in. on the face and about $4\frac{1}{2}$ in. front to back; they require slots, to be carefully cut out, in order to fit round the curved top portion of the front, and will ultimately have shaped brackets under them at right angles to the front corresponding with the shaped projections on the sides of the front.

The box at the back is formed chiefly by two upright sides reaching from the bottom to the under side of the mounted shelves (a height of $8\frac{1}{2}$ in.), which they help to support. They are rebated for a light back to the lower part, which forms a box. The top and bottom of this box are formed of horizontal pieces fixed on small fillets secured to the sides as shown in the section, which has been taken through the case behind, looking towards the front. This section will explain the boxing in of the clock. The whole when accurately fitted should be glued and bradded together. The inside angles can be greatly strengthened by gluing strips of wood along them.

The $\frac{1}{2}$-in. thick stuff might be employed for the door, which measures $3\frac{1}{2}$ in. across and begins 2 in. up from the bottom. Its curved top follows the circle of the dial, and round the whole edge is worked a chamfer $\frac{1}{2}$ in. wide. Very small hinges are desirable, and if any difficulty is experienced in providing a suitable catch, a small brass knob turning on its own spindle, and fitted with a strip of metal bent as shown in Fig. 178, should be quite sufficient for the purpose.

A Hanging Wall Clock, Figs. 181 to 188. — The type of wall clocks shown, is not nearly so well known as the usual bracket or mantelpiece clock, or the grandfather long-case clock. For use in a hall it is especially suitable, and if made of lighter proportions it can be used to advantage in any of the living rooms of a house.

The inlays should correspond to those in the rest of the furniture so far as materials are concerned; but it is quite legitimate to vary the design of the inlaying in a small piece of this character. Ebony, satinwood, or boxwood are the usual inlaying woods for use in conjunction with mahogany, and in the event of the latter wood being used for the ground-

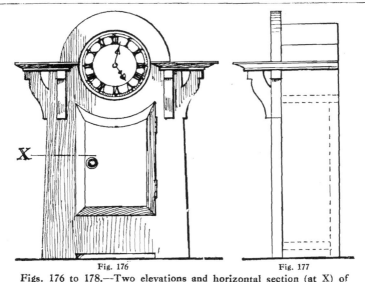

Fig. 176   Fig. 177

Figs. 176 to 178.—Two elevations and horizontal section (at X) of clock case with side shelves

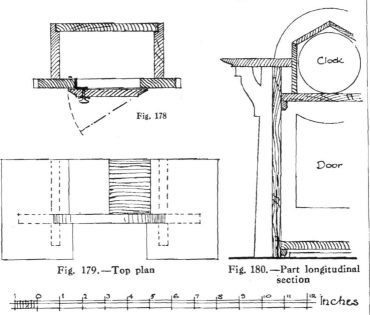

Fig. 179.—Top plan   Fig. 180.—Part longitudinal section

work of the case, the diamond inlay could well be of satinwood with mosaic stringings of ebony and boxwood.

Should the clock be destined for use in a hall, where oak predominates, it could be made of this material, omitting the

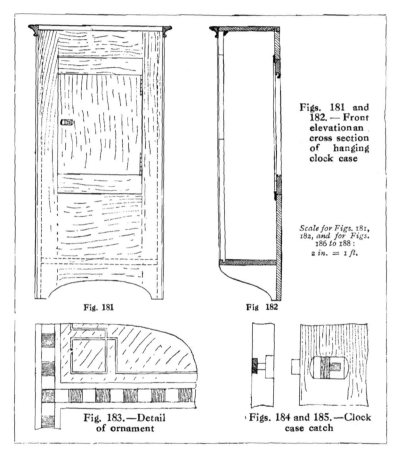

Figs. 181 and 182. — Front elevation an cross section of hanging clock case

Scale for Figs. 181, 182, *and for Figs.* 186 *to* 188 :
$2 in. = 1 ft.$

Fig. 181

Fig 182

Fig. 183.—Detail of ornament

Figs. 184 and 185.—Clock case catch

broken inlay corners on the front. The mosaic stringing could be of holly and ebony, with a rosewood or ebony diamond inlay. Another suitable treatment is ordinary oak for the case with brown or pollard oak for the veneering on the front. The ends and plain parts should be stained

Clock Cases

darker, and the whole finished by slightly polishing to fix the colour, and then rubbed with turpentine and wax until a suitable surface is obtained.

For use in rooms where a lighter treatment is essential, satinwood, inlaid with tulip wood, ebony and silver grey

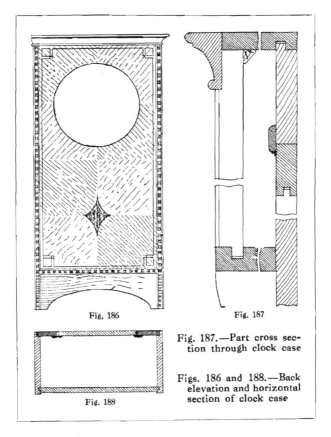

Fig. 186

Fig. 187

Fig. 187.—Part cross section through clock case

Figs. 186 and 188.—Back elevation and horizontal section of clock case

Fig. 188

wood, can well be employed. The latter material also is quite fine for a very delicate treatment, in which case purplewood and ebony can well be used for the inlaying.

The front elevation of the case gives general proportions. To make the clock case, all the wood should first be cut out and then planed up to width and thickness. The ends should then be squared off and the bottoms shaped as indicated. A top and bottom are then squared off. The bottom is slip-dovetailed between the ends, and the top is lap-dovetailed down. Both the ends should then be related to receive the back, as indicated in the sectional plan (Fig. 188). Grooves must then be worked on both ends and the bottom to receive the rebated front piece. These grooves must be very carefully made and can be easily worked with an ordinary scratch-stock, with a piece of steel projecting just the size of the groove required. Corresponding barefaced tongues are then made on the front piece and fitted to the grooves. This box part can then be separated, and the inlaying on the edges proceeded with; this should be followed up by veneering the front (see Chapter VIII.).

A back is then prepared as indicated in Fig. 186. It will be seen that a small clamped door is made to fit into a framed-up back. This is prepared as shown, and screwed into the rebates of the ends, the top edge preferably being tongued into the underside of the top. This detail is also illustrated in Fig. 187. To form a rebate to receive the back door, small slips, or fillets, are glued to the back of the frame as shown.

Figs. 184 and 185 show how a small catch, having the advantage of being flush outside, can be made. A small slot is cut at the back of the door, into which is fitted a small sliding piece of hardwood which acts as a bolt. A wider slot is then cut in the front as shown, and is stopped at each end. A third slot is then cut right through the two small slots, which enables a thumb-piece to be attached to the bolt. This thumb-piece should be exactly the size of the larger rectangle, and it may be moved from right to left accordingly as the bolt is required to be operated. When the door is hinged to the frame, a small mortise or hole is cut to receive the bolt.

The cornice moulding is the next part to be dealt with. This should preferably be worked on the edge of a board with a rebate plane, hollows and rounds as near the section shown as possible. To complete the moulding, a scratch-stock should be prepared, with a cutter exactly corresponding to the reverse of the section. Good hard, crisp wood

Clock Cases

should be used, which allows the moulding to be accurately scratched. The case can then be rebated at the top as shown in Fig. 187. The moulding is mitred and glued round, and when dry the top can be levelled off.

Cutting the front to receive the clock itself should be left until last. The movement, when purchased, will be found to have a rebate at the front underneath the bezel. Two

Fig. 189.—18th-century English clock

brass straps are attached with long set-screws at the back. The front of the case is cut out to receive the movement, which is then carefully inserted. Two small holes are next bored through the back frame. A couple of washers are necessary to prevent the screw-heads biting into the wood of the frame. The set-screws can then be inserted and screwed into the L-shaped ends of the straps, which securely fixes the whole movement. Two small brass looking-glass plates should be attached at the sides or at the top. Another can be introduced with advantage underneath the bottom; these serve for fastening the case to the wall. It is important to note that the clock case should have a bezel opening at the front for the necessary winding. If a striking movement is required, two small brass frets should be fitted in holes cut in the sides of the case, with coloured material at the back.

Eighteenth - century English Mantel Clock, Figs. 189 to 197.—The accompanying illustrations show an authentic clock of English workmanship, made probably about the end of the eighteenth century, and of a design often sought after. The case was found, on examination, to be of oak, with a thick mahogany veneer over the whole of the outside, while a simple design is inlaid in some white wood on the front, comprising a marginal line and a lozenge under the dial, which latter is of polished steel, and is furnished with an indicator showing the day of the month, changing automatically at midnight. The numerals and maker's name, " George Pyke, London," are written in very graceful style, and the hands are very delicate in outline. On each side of the case is a Gothic panel, fitted with a brass fret backed with dark red silk, while just above is a brass drop-handle, now nearly corroded through.

The back, which is quite as carefully finished as the front, has a semicircular-headed glass door fitted with a small lock, which gives access to the movement, the exact position of the back plate of which is shown by the dotted lines on the back view (Fig. 193). The space below is empty, while above in the spandrel of the arch is just sufficient space for the gong. The movement is also indicated by dotted lines on the plan (Fig. 192), which further shows the two brass angles suporting the back plate (A B), and secured through each side with screw and nut just above the handle, as on the side elevation. Two arrows in Fig. 193 serve to give the centre and radius for each of the curves with which the outline is obtained. In Fig. 196, which shows how the work was built up, the piece marked c acts as a kind of stiffening next the back door, the rebates to take the glass and cover the joint round the edge of which are formed simply by an over-

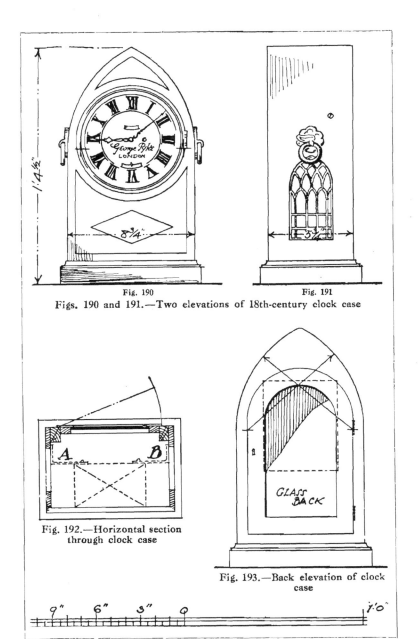

Fig. 190

Fig. 191

Figs. 190 and 191.—Two elevations of 18th-century clock case

Fig. 192.—Horizontal section through clock case

Fig. 193.—Back elevation of clock case

lapping of the veneer. The glass is now held on the inside by a few small brads only, although the brass fret is still secured with small, neat slips of wood inside, while the veneer projects sufficiently to hold it on the front. The joint shown at D (Fig. 196) is assumed, but very possibly the work is really dovetailed. On the left of the last detail mentioned is one cutting through the base of the clock case, showing veneer on oak, and having a mahogany cavetto moulding.

In the example, the sides, where they curve over to meet at the top of the arch, are built up of wedge-shaped blocks, seemingly simply butting one against the other, their upper surfaces being worked to the required curve and veneered. With a modern reproduction, however, solid mahogany, walnut, or rosewood are more likely to be used, so that this method will not be suitable, and it is therefore suggested that the work be carried out as shown in Fig. 194, where a number of saw-cuts at close and regular intervals enable the sides to be bent over sufficiently, the precise curve being obtained by fixing them to curved blocks or centres underneath, as noted. Then also it will be best to have the vertical joint between the front and each side running up the angle, unless the clock is a very small one, and accordingly a joint similar to the one shown in Fig. 195 is advocated; this will need some patient fitting round the curved head, but it will be found to give a far more satisfactory result than if the joint shows elsewhere.

The remaining parts of the work call for no especial comment. The back will probably be simplified in carrying out, and, as previously mentioned, the total size should be in a similar proportion to the size of the dial employed, and while pleasing little ornaments can easily be made on these lines to take the cheap miniature clocks so often met with, yet the case properly made on a larger scale will deserve a worthier timepiece.

Grandfather Clock Case, Figs. 198 to 218.—The design of the long or grandfather clock, here illustrated, is in some ways more refined than that of many genuine old models. The case may be made in mahogany, walnut, or

Clock Cases

oak with equal suitability, of the best type, selected for good figuring. The concealed parts can be of cheaper hard wood or well seasoned pine. The workmanship can be either very simple with plain mouldings, etc., or it

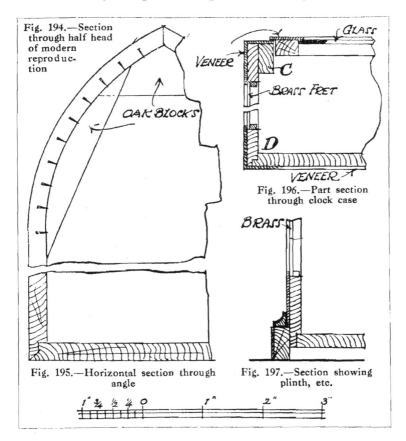

Fig. 194.—Section through half head of modern reproduction

Fig. 195.—Horizontal section through angle

Fig. 196.—Part section through clock case

Fig. 197.—Section showing plinth, etc.

can be elaborated very considerably, especially if the "faking" idea is entertained.

Among the optional enrichments, etc., are the curved top and turned vase terminals, which, if used, can be plain or beaded and fluted, as in Fig. 215, the flutings to the coved cornice A (Fig. 211), the inlaid banding at B in Fig. 199, and such things as bead-and-reel carving round the door and lower panel, square dentils to the main cornice, etc. The quartering of the door with veneer as shown is also optional, but is strongly recommended. In short, the work can be elaborated by carving or inlay to any extent; but the two methods should be employed separately, rather than in conjunction.

First secure the actual clock or " movement," which should be fitted with a dial of between 10 in. and 12 in. in diameter, the case being adjusted slightly to the opening required. An old specimen might be picked up, and should have gong, weights, and pendulum complete. The dial should be of distinctly old style, if possible, and rather elaborate hands would be quite in keeping. Two stout metal strips will be required securely bolted to the plates of the movement, one at each side, adjusted to suit the exact space; bent at right angles and drilled ready for screwing to the inside faces of the case, in a position accessible for removal on occasion. The weights and pendulum merely work in the boxing or "shaft" of the case.

Fig. 198.—Grandfather clock

These clock cases being rather large, the present example is constructed in two portions for convenience in moving, the shaft fitting into the capping of the plinth, and being, of course, secured with screws put in on the slope from the inside. The base or plinth is fully shown in Figs. 202 to 205, and has a framed front $\frac{7}{8}$ in. thick consisting of $2\frac{1}{2}$-in. stiles, 2-in. top rail

Clock Cases

and 4-in. bottom rail (all seen in Fig. 205), into which a $\tfrac{3}{4}$-in. panel is rebated $\tfrac{3}{8}$ in. deep, as in Figs. 202 to 205. This panel has quadrant corners of $\tfrac{5}{8}$ in. radius and a small hollow (or a carved bead, etc.) worked round its edges. Note that

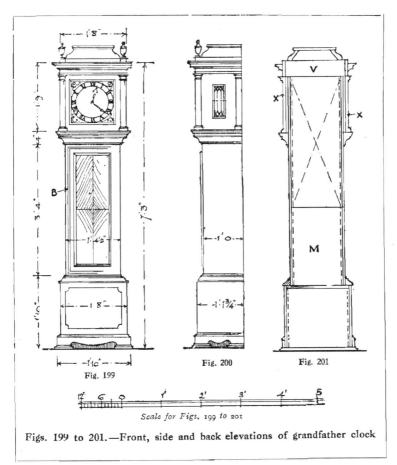

Figs. 199 to 201.—Front, side and back elevations of grandfather clock

the stiles project 1 in. below the rail at c in Fig. 204. The front is "mitred and rebated" to plain sides 1 ft. $1\tfrac{3}{4}$ in. by 1 ft. $6\tfrac{7}{8}$ in. high as at D (Fig. 202), and secured with angle blocks, which should be used plentifully throughout the job.

78　　　　　Furniture Making

A rectangle about 6½ in. by 1 in. is cut out of the bottom of the sides E (Fig. 205), and their back edges, together with the top edges of both sides and front, are rebated ½ in. for plain square ¾-in. top and back pieces as shown. The top is then completed by the addition of a 2-in. by 2¼-in. moulding F (Fig. 205) mitred and screwed along the front and sides. Next a ⅝-in. by 2¼-in. skirting is shaped and fixed to the stiles and rail as in Fig. 204, mitred, returned and shaped on the sides, and finished with a ⅝-in. by 1-in. moulding as at G. The whole plinth can then be inverted, and completed by the addition of ⅞-in. feet moulded where shown, the front ones being 4¾ in. square (H, Fig. 203), and one continuous piece used at the back J (Fig. 203) and K (Fig. 205).

The shaft will be found quite a simple portion of the work, and consists of ⅞-in. front and sides, the former having 3-in. stiles, 5¼-in. bottom rail L (Fig. 204), partly concealed by the plinth moulding, and 9-in. top rail as noted in Fig. 206. Only a 3-in. part of this latter rail is exposed, and it might accordingly be built up with hard wood for the bottom part only. The door is ⅞ in. thick, rebated ⅜ in. by ½ in. to fit the opening, the ½ in. just allowing sufficient space for the hinges. Its edges are moulded as in Fig. 209, and it is quartered on the face and fitted with lock and key. The stiles are mitred and rebated as before to plain sides 12 in. by ⅞ in. of the same length, rebated to receive a ⅝-in. back, the lower two feet or so of which M (Fig. 201) can be fixed. At a distance of 2½ in. above the top edge of the door is fixed a 2⅜-in. by 4-in. coved cornice (see Figs. 208 and 211) preparatory to the work on the head of the case.

Fig. 208 probably offers the most lucid explanation of the remaining work. In it at N is seen the top of the shaft side, with the coved cornice applied on its face, and at O a ¾-in. side measuring 1 ft. 1½ in. by 1 ft. 9¾ in. high. This is seen also at O in Fig. 210, where N indicates the side of the shaft on plan at the lower level seen in Fig. 211. In fixing, one piece is lapped against the other for a distance of 2 in. and screwed. In Fig. 210 the side is shown mitred and rebated with a front framing Q ¾ in. thick, measuring 1 ft. 6 in. across the front and moulded round the opening, the exact size of which is

Clock Cases

regulated by the dial. The top rail of the framing is extended to the same height as o o in Fig. 208, the whole being finished with a ½-in. top as there shown.

The finishings of the head (which, it may be pointed out, overhangs ¾ in. at the back as at R in Fig. 207) can next

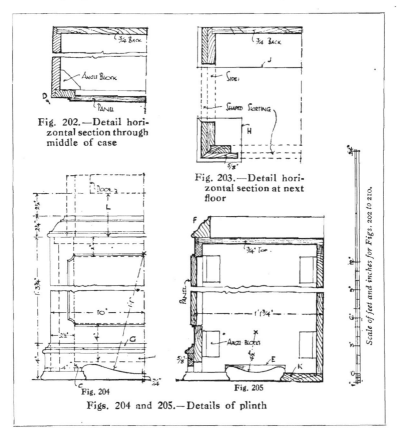

Fig. 202.—Detail horizontal section through middle of case

Fig. 203.—Detail horizontal section at next floor

Figs. 204 and 205.—Details of plinth

be put in hand. First there are four columns turned out of 2½-in. square stuff (unless the caps are turned in separate pieces from the shafts) to the contours in Fig. 211, keeping the ends square as noted and making all the mouldings quite small. The shafts should be turned to 1¾-in. diameter for the bottom third of this height, and tapered to 1½ in. at the top in the remaining two-thirds. From two of these columns rather less than a quarter circle should be cut (*see* s, Fig. 210 and plan in Fig. 211), so that they will accurately fit the corners of the head just above the coved cornice, and project immediately above their bases 1 in. from the general face, thus showing as practically complete columns. The two other columns should be cut off flush on one side as at T in Fig. 207, and applied next to the wall, while a 1¾-in. by 1-in. architrave with small necking and a 3-in. by 2-in. cornice, as in Figs. 208 and 211, should be applied and mitred round the three sides, as shown in the various illustrations. The " blocking course " which surmounts the cornice U (Fig. 208) can then be added, flush with the top and 1 in. thick at the sides, but set back to ¾ in. thick on the front for all except the end 1¾ in. where it forms a base for the vase (*see* Figs. 206 and 213). Of course, if it is decided to omit this vase, the break would also disappear.

Perforations are usually provided in the sides of the head in order that the sound of the gong may not be muffled; and to meet this requirement the sides can be fitted with tiny louvres set in a 3-in. by 9-in. opening edged with a beaded strip about 1½ in. by ⅜ in., as in Figs. 207 and 210, or in the more orthodox manner shown in Fig. 214. This is designed for a brass fret backed with deep red silk, bordered with a small moulding not exceeding ⅝ in. in width and slightly rebated. It can readily be set out with the dimensions given, keeping the tracery $\frac{3}{16}$ in. wide, or it can be adapted for fretwood.

If the curved top above the cornice is desired (say for a position where the clock is seen a good deal from above, as, for instance, in a staircase hall), it can be built up with a mitred moulding as dotted in Fig. 208, rebated at the top for a thin cover-board, and filled in flush at the rear. It is shown in detail in Fig. 215, where the dotted rectangle indicates the square piece from which the moulding must be worked. The terminal is also seen, and the optional enrichments shown have previously been mentioned. The cornice portion of the head can be filled in at the back with a plain fixed board V (Figs. 201 and 212), its ends being

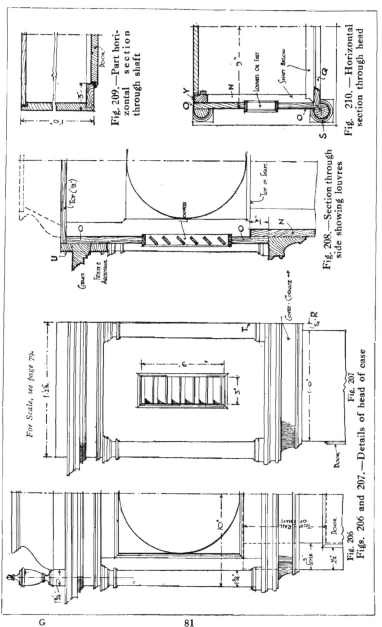

Fig. 209.—Part horizontal section through shaft

Fig. 210.—Horizontal section through head

Fig. 208.—Section through side showing louvres

Fig. 207

Figs. 206 and 207.—Details of head of case

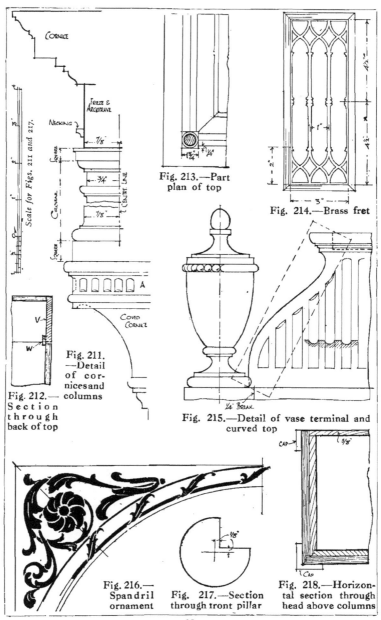

Fig. 213.—Part plan of top

Fig. 214.—Brass fret

Fig. 211.—Detail of cornices and columns

Fig. 212.—Section through back of top

Fig. 215.—Detail of vase terminal and curved top

Fig. 216.—Spandril ornament

Fig. 217.—Section through front pillar

Fig. 218.—Horizontal section through head above columns

Clock Cases

covered by the cornice, etc. It will serve to tie the work securely together. The lower portion of the back (marked with a diagonal cross in Fig. 201) should be in one piece, either solid or panelled, fitted into rebates at the sides and against a fillet w (Fig. 212) at the top. The head at x in Fig. 201 will require making out to meet this back by means of small pieces as at y in Fig. 210, turn-buckles being provided at the top and bottom to keep it in position. Small fillets should be provided to cover all joints in order to exclude dust, especially if the clock is a good one.

Clocks of the type concerned are wound simply by pulling down one of the weights, so that the glass over the dial can be fixed on the inside by means of a plain rebated strip. In most cases this should also take a mount of some sort to fill in the spaces between the front framing and the dial. This could be of thin wood with a bevelled edge, or might be formed of Bristol board or sheet metal painted to such a design as that in Fig. 216, say in dark steel-grey on a grey ground, or in gold-bronze on grey, in order to get an effect approximating to that of the old models.

CHAPTER VIII

Veneering and Inlaying as a Decorative Medium

Stringings or Bandings.—Fig. 219 illustrates various stringings or mosaic bandings, and Fig. 220 shows the method of building them up. A sheet of thick veneer is obtained to act as a groundwork on which the mosaic work is glued. Supposing the colour scheme to be black and white; three thicknesses of veneer glued up, holly wood outside, with a centre of ebony veneer. When thoroughly dry, one end is planed true, and lengths can then be cut off with a circular saw to coincide with the design. The centre part of the square is also cut from this piece, and for the outside parts it is necessary to prepare material with ebony outside, cutting them off when dry to the required length. A long strip A (Fig. 220) is then glued to the ebony veneer groundwork. Next B is glued against this, then C, and so on, until about 3 ft. is completed. If this gluing has been carefully effected, the surface will only require toothing, and then veneering with the ebony veneer.

It will readily be seen that the grains all run in one direction, parallel to the edge illustrated, and when this has been planed true, the bandings can be cut off to the thickness of a stiff veneer with a circular saw. All the bandings illustrated have been executed on these principles. Those with an oblique pattern entail more work, though not unduly difficult if a tilted block be arranged on the saw.

Coloured Woods.—The colour treatment of these lines is important, and, generally speaking, should be obtained through the use of naturally coloured woods, owing to the unsightly effects of wood stains on many artificially-dyed woods. For red, sandal, granite, purple, and the many varieties of rosewood supply a charming selection. There is also tulip wood of a pink tone. Browns can be obtained from Russian oak, amboyna, yew, and thuya burrs, and

Veneering and Inlaying

various mahoganies. An effective light-speckled brown is peculiar to the wood of the plane tree, and is especially suitable when used in combination with satinwood. American

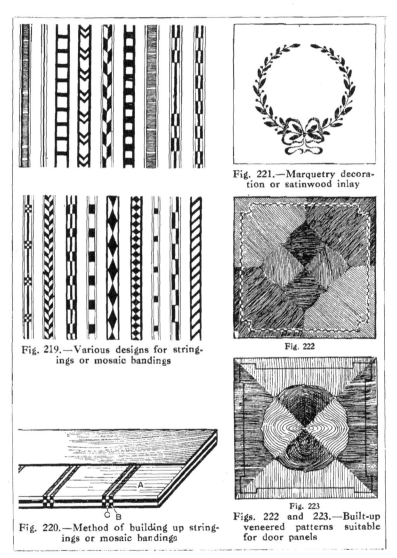

Fig. 219.—Various designs for stringings or mosaic bandings

Fig. 220.—Method of building up stringings or mosaic bandings

Fig. 221.—Marquetry decoration or satinwood inlay

Fig. 222

Fig. 223

Figs. 222 and 223.—Built-up veneered patterns suitable for door panels walnut also supplies numerous shades of brown with a purplish tinge—English with black streaks, French and Italian of a colder brown tint. Snakewood is particularly rich in colour, reddish brown, and the speckled appearance of this wood, resembling snakeskin markings, makes it suitable for use in small squares or diapers. Very bright yellows are obtained from both varieties of satinwood, blacks from ebony and coromandel, the latter with dark brown stripes; white from holly; and flesh colour from sycamore, chestnut, and boxwood. With such a range of naturally coloured woods as enumerated above, artificial dyeing is superfluous, for no artificial process can obtain the richness of colour or grain exhibited by the natural woods.

Inlaid Drawer Front.—The design given in Fig. 224 shows the application of inlaying to a drawer front, and is effected by first veneering with mahogany and then gauging the requisite margins, removing the veneer with a heated file and a chisel. The stringing is then glued in position and the cross banding united and glued round, rubbing the bands with a hammer. It is a general principle with veneered work to protect the edge from splitting, which is likely to occur when pushing in a drawer. To obviate this, small square lines are glued into the corners, and form sufficient protection for the veneer. Very effective decorative treatments are possible by the insertion of a richly figured centre-piece, as illustrated in this example. The veneer should be placed between two thin pieces of wood, cutting and filing them to the desired shape; it is then cut into the drawer front and carefully glued down. When dry, one of the thin templates is temporarily pinned down, and acts as a guide when cutting in the surrounding line, which is best accomplished by scratching with the sharpened end of an old file.

Marquetry Effects.—Fig. 227 shows the application of marqueteried decoration. Marquetry cutting is economical, for six, or even eight, designs can be produced with one cutting, and there is not the necessity to cut each unit separately into the groundwork; but if only one or even two designs are required, they can be accomplished by tracing the design on suitably coloured woods, cutting the various

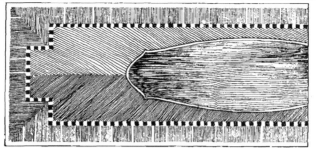

Fig. 224.—Veneered and inlaid drawer front

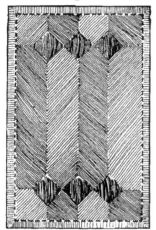

Fig. 225.—Veneered panel: Two mahoganies or two walnuts

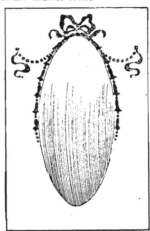

Fig. 226.—Satinwood ellipse, husks and ribbon inlaid into mahogany

Fig. 227.—Veneered and inlaid drawer front

shapes with a small fretsaw, and then cutting them into the groundwork with carving gouges, having as a guide a tracing of the design gummed to the groundwork. Fig. 221 is an application of the principle explained in connection with Fig. 227.

Other Inlay Designs.—Fig. 222 shows a rich treatment obtained by the judicious use of contrasting veneers, and Fig. 223 illustrates a variation. The centre part of each design is composed of four parts. Richly figured wood should be used, and four pieces are then fixed between thin wood, and cut and filed to shape. They can then be separated, and simply opened out each way to form the centre part. This is then glued down to strong paper, and the outside portions fitted up to shapes, gluing each piece down as fitting is completed; then when dry veneer as a whole with the paper uppermost. This is easily removed with a toothing plane when the glue is thoroughly dry.

To inlay the line shown in Fig. 223, a scratch-stock (Fig. 232) is necessary. A is the stock which holds the steel cutter, B an adjustable fence which is moved according to the margin required, and C is the adjusting thumbscrew. The stock is operated from the edge of the panel with the fence pressed close to it, and the grooves are routed down as required.

To execute the inlaid edges or corners shown in Fig. 225 the design should first be drawn on stiff paper, fitting the veneers and lines to the various shapes, gluing them down to the paper. When the whole design is complete it is glued down and levelled off as previously described. Bearing in mind the necessity for a square edging, a piece is made up as illustrated in Fig. 228 if a mosaic edging is required, otherwise an ordinary $\frac{1}{8}$-in. square line is used. Only one veneer is required to hold the pieces together, and strips can then be cut from this and glued to the panel edges, removing the veneer when quite dry. This could also be utilised as an inlaid line, with black line each side of the mosaic, as is illustrated.

An infinite number of combinations is possible by the application of the above processes and principles.

Veneering and Inlaying

Veneers.—Apart from the strip veneers used in inlaying, veneers are of two classes, " knife cut " and " saw cut," the latter being generally thicker than the former. They may be obtained in almost any kind of wood.

Veneerer's Tools.—These include the veneering hammer, a special kind of saw, and a few cauls. The hammer (Fig. 231) has a wood head and handle, a zinc blade fitting into the head, and being secured with two screws while the handle is wedged in position. The blade of the saw (Fig. 230) is about 6 in. or 7 in. long, and the teeth should not be too large, and should not be given much set. Cauls are used to give a direct, even pressure, for which purpose they are heated and cramped over the veneers. The cauls retain the heat better if made of zinc about $\frac{3}{16}$ in. thick; but if this is not readily obtainable, some stout pieces of board may be used instead.

Laying Veneer.—The surface on which the veneer is to be laid must be perfectly level. Brush over it some thin glue, working it well into the grain and allowing it to dry. The veneer must be cut to shape, and for straight cuts the saw (Fig. 230) and a straightedge should be used, while a fine fretsaw may be used for circular cuts. The caul to be used is heated in front of a fire, and the cramps and other necessary appliances should be at hand. The surface should be slightly warmed, and the glue should be well boiled and fairly thin. Rapidly coat the surface with glue, and lay the veneer in position, holding it down by inserting a few brass pins round the edges. These should only be driven in half way; and they may then be turned over, care being taken not to embed them in the veneer. The surface of the veneer should next be covered with paper, and the heated caul should be quickly cramped in position over the veneer (*see* Fig. 229). It is not the quantity of glue used that makes good joints, but rather the expulsion of the surplus. Systematic cramping is, therefore, of the utmost importance, and a beginning should invariably be made in the middle. Cramps are next added on each side of the middle cramp until the veneer is firmly pressed down, and the edges should be watched to see that the surplus glue is being forced out. The work should stand for twelve hours before removing the cramps. Having removed the cramps and caul, the temporary pins may be withdrawn, and the surface cleaned up with steel scraper and glasspaper.

For curved surfaces the veneer is cut, the surface glued, the veneer placed in position, and the surface of the veneer rapidly damped with hot water to render it more pliable. It may then be well rubbed down with the veneering hammer, working the hammer from the centre. In this method the use of cauls will not be necessary; but it might, perhaps, be found an advantage to pass a hot iron over the surface to heat the glue. Great attention should be paid to the edges of the veneer, and they should either be pinned or cramped down. This method may also be employed in the case of laying a small piece of veneer to a flat surface. Cauls for curved work must be an exact reverse of the surface on which they will be pressed.

A common trouble in laying veneer is the formation of blisters, caused by the glue having become chilled, or by an air bubble. To remove a blister, a small slit should be cut through the veneer with a very sharp chisel, and the surface of the veneer over the blister should be well damped. A hot flat-iron should be worked over the damped surface, and should it be necessary some fresh glue may be inserted through the slit. Carefully work all the surplus glue through the slit, and cramp down with a hot caul.

Veneer Inlaying.—Very effective inlaying is accomplished by means of veneers. Having set out the design full size on a piece of paper, the pieces of wood to make up the design are cut out (with fretsaw or in some other convenient way) to the shape required. The pieces are then fitted together to form the complete design, and then glued direct to the paper pattern, and glue is also worked in between the edges of the veneers. Another piece of paper is then glued over the top, and the whole is cramped between two pieces of board until the glue is dry. The inlay is then removed, and the piece of paper at the back on which the design was originally marked is stripped off. The inlay is then placed in position on the groundwork, and is scribed round the edges with a

Veneering and Inlaying

marking or scribing point. The wood in the groundwork must next be cut away to a sufficient depth to receive the inlay, care being taken to work exactly to the scribed lines. The cutting is accomplished with chisels and gouges, and a

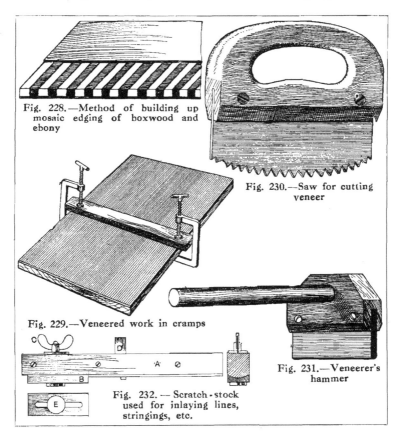

Fig. 228.—Method of building up mosaic edging of boxwood and ebony

Fig. 230.—Saw for cutting veneer

Fig. 229.—Veneered work in cramps

Fig. 231.—Veneerer's hammer

Fig. 232.—Scratch-stock used for inlaying lines, stringings, etc.

router would also be found most useful in removing the surplus wood. The inlay is then glued in position, and cramped until the glue is set, when the surface is cleaned off with scraper and glasspaper.

CHAPTER IX

HALL FURNITURE

An "Armoire" Hall Fitment, Figs. 233 to 239A.—
With very small halls it is a difficult matter to provide
neat and suitable accommodation for clothes, etc., which
will be decorative; although, where a small square hall is available, it is comparatively easy to get away from stereotyped forms. The stand for a narrow hall, however, requires more effort to produce a satisfactory type. Probably the best arrangement in large houses is to have an antique or modern "armoire," similar to a wardrobe, fitted up with pegs, etc., with a special tray and rail at one side to accommodate umbrellas and sticks. In houses and flats of small size a good adaptation consists of a simple cupboard like a wardrobe without doors.
In place of doors a rail is provided at the top, from which a pair of curtains is suspended. If the material is selected with due regard to colour and to the wood employed, a pleasing result can be obtained at moderate cost.

Fig. 233.—"Armoire" hall fitment

An adaptation of the "armoire" idea is the hall stand, here illustrated. This is more elaborate than the suggestion

Hall Furniture

before outlined, but would be a successful treatment where space is available. It will be seen that this is a combination piece, providing a chest, seat, cupboard, and hanging space with doors. The seat part is really a chest with lift-up lid, which is particularly useful as a receptacle for travelling rugs,

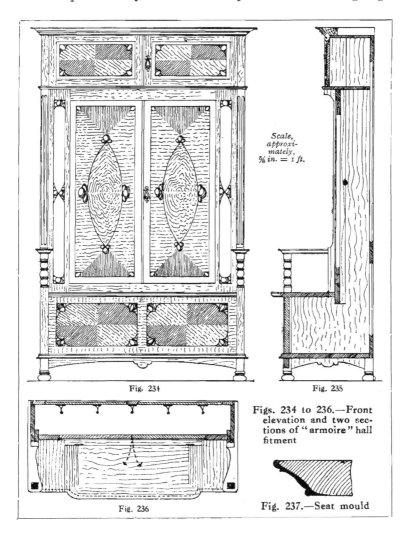

Scale, approximately, ⅝ in. = 1 ft.

Fig. 234. Fig. 235.

Figs. 234 to 236.—Front elevation and two sections of "armoire" hall fitment

Fig. 236.

Fig. 237.—Seat mould

etc. The cupboard above the seat serves as a hanging space, and, as will be seen, it runs through into the chest part in order to obtain the maximum of hanging space. The interior of this part should also be fitted with an umbrella rack and tray, whilst a small mirror can be fixed in the centre at the back.

The decorative treatment of this stand is chiefly effected by means of " quartered " and patterned veneered surfaces. The corner parts (enlarged details of which are shown) should be carved, and if left rather duller than the rest of the work when polishing a fine effect would be obtained.

In the end sectional view (Fig. 235) the main constructive features are shown. The pilasters, as shown in Fig. 234, are the same thickness as the ends, and fluted. To obtain this it will be necessary to make up both the carcase ends by gluing on a piece of $\frac{5}{8}$-in. stuff, the outline of which will be seen in Figs. 235 and 236.

A panelled back is advisable. Four panels should be introduced with bead-and-butt flush on the inside. It will be necessary to rebate the panels on the front sides.

When the ends have been prepared to the outline shown in the section, the bottom of the top cupboard can be tenoned between them. The bottom should also be attached in like manner, then a wide board, clamped at each end, should be dowelled between the legs, which is to receive the seat frame and flap. Reference to the sectional view (Fig. 235) shows that the two long doors are hung inside a frame, the latter being mortised and tenoned, then dowelled between the carcase ends, and screwed behind the chest seat frame.

The seat frame is made in three parts, one narrow piece being mortised and tenoned between two wide end pieces (*see* Fig. 236). The seat itself, moulded as in Fig. 237, should have two end pieces clamped on with mortise and tenon joints. The shape of the arms is shown in plan, and reference to Fig. 233 and the plan will show that the arms are cut away to butt against the pilasters and run across the ends. For this reason the arms are made with moulded edges, and the part running across the ends is little more than the actual moulding. The bottom

Hall Furniture

of the stand is finished by mitreing mouldings across the ends, making them intersect with the front moulding, which is worked on the solid.

Next a spanrail can be fitted underneath the front edge.

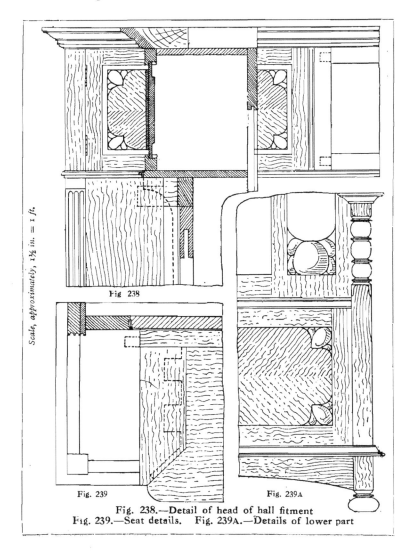

Fig. 238.—Detail of head of hall fitment
Fig. 239.—Seat details.   Fig. 239A.—Details of lower part

Both the front feet require square material larger than the actual legs, and therefore the feet are made separately and pinned into the legs. In Figs. 235 and 238 the cornice moulding is shown, the hard wood moulding being backed up with pine.

An enlarged detail of the small top doors is given in Fig. 238, these being mortised and tenoned together as shown on the right of the diagram. A $\frac{1}{2}$-in. panel is then introduced, and this acts as a base or groundwork to receive a flat tablet as shown in the enlarged section. The tablets should be prepared from $\frac{5}{16}$-in. stuff, then veneered with a quartered pattern and squared up to size, so as to leave the margin shown. After they have been glued down and are thoroughly dry, the corner parts can be set out and carved in low relief, the design being modelled as indicated and cut perfectly smooth.

The large doors encasing the hanging cupboard are made with clamped ends, and are then veneered with the 4-in. device only. The necessary relief is given to this part by rebating the margins round, and then the corners may be carved up as with the small door panels. The pointed centre parts are both executed as separate tablets, both being veneered with curl mahogany as shown before they are cut to the required outline, which comprises also the carving shown executed as before. Almost identical practice is essential for the pilaster tablets.

Stand for Narrow Hall, Figs. 240 to 246. — The next hall stand is designed for use in a narrow hall. Its main feature (*see* Fig. 241) is a panelled back part based on Elizabethan work, so that oak will be the most suitable wood to use. The main support is derived from two side stiles, with a centre muntin running right through from top to bottom. These are made about $\frac{1}{4}$ in. thicker than the rails and inside panelling, which permits of the frieze moulding being " broken " or mitred round as a decorative feature.

The back is not difficult to construct if considered as two separate panelled frames tenoned between the uprights. At the bottom two narrow rails are provided to form a tie

Hall Furniture

for the uprights. With regard to the panelled device, the rectangular centre parts of the frame are first cut out and planed up, and then mortised to receive the short connecting

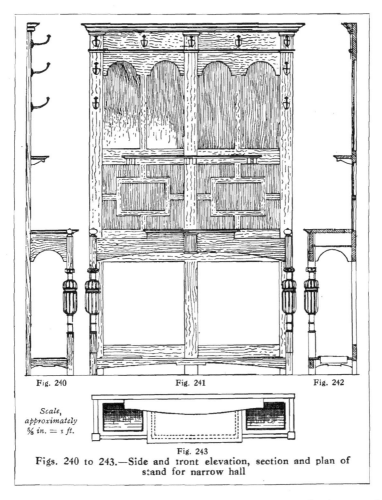

Figs. 240 to 243.—Side and front elevation, section and plan of stand for narrow hall

rails. This part of the work is done at the beginning, and then the various pieces are rebated and mitred up. For additional strength the rectangular frames are made with

H

tongued mitre joints. At the top of the back two wide rails are necessary, tenoned between the uprights.

Next the semicircular shapes to form the heads of the panels can be cut out and then the rebates of rails and muntins; but it will be found a good plan to groove the uprights only, the panels may then be slipped into the grooves, and lowered into the rebates when the frame is finally fitted up. If this method of construction is followed, long and short shoulder joints will be necessary for all the connections with the exception of the rails into the uprights.

The sectional view in conjunction with the part elevation in Fig. 245 shows the arrangement of the cornice, which should be made in two sections to economise material, and if glued up and levelled off on the back before being glued round, a saving of labour will be effected. The frieze moulding and the small mouldings under the cornice can then be fitted.

A detail of the legs is given in Fig. 244. These should be cut from solid stuff, if possible. A wide front rail is then tenoned in together with a bottom rail. The top rail should be set out and cut to the outline shown in Fig. 241, and then the front frame cleaned up and glued together. Two rails at each end fix the front frame to the back. These are fitted and cut to shape, and then glued up with two cross rails (*see* dotted lines in Fig. 243), slip-dovetailed between the front and back frames to form a box. A three-ply bottom $\frac{1}{4}$ in. thick should be grooved into the cross rails, etc.

Fig. 246 shows a detail of the small centre tablet with simple moulded finish, and also the hinging piece of the top.

At the bottom a shelf should be cut in between the legs and screwed through the rails, blocking it underneath for additional security. This shelf is cut to receive the dull black zinc drip-pans shown in Fig. 244, these pans being made with wired edges which act as flanges.

An armour-bright or oxidised brass finish is suggested for the pegs, or suitably designed wooden pegs, which may be made of oak to exactly match the framing, similar to those on page 397 might well be employed.

Modern-style Hall Stand, Figs. 247 to 260.—The hall stand shown on pages 100 and 101 is of a design that is suitable

Hall Furniture

for constructing in oak, mahogany, ash, or walnut. It consists of two sides conveniently fitted with hat and coat hooks; a back fitted with a bevelled-edge mirror, and a bottom part made up with four drawers, two on each side,

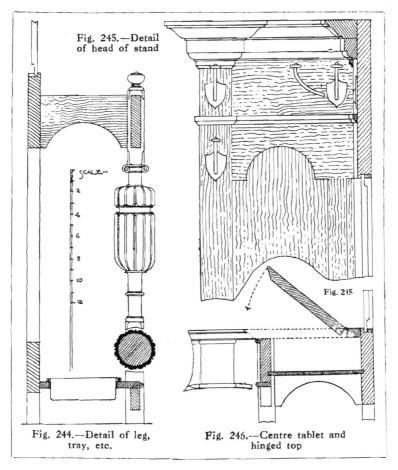

Fig. 245.—Detail of head of stand

Fig. 244.—Detail of leg, tray, etc.

Fig. 246.—Centre tablet and hinged top

the centre space between the drawers being fitted up for the reception of walking-sticks and umbrellas. The dimensions are shown in the illustrations.

The sides (Fig. 249) should first be prepared; they are

Furniture Making

1 in. thick, cut to the shape shown. The bottom is 1 in. thick, dovetail-grooved or housed into the sides. The upright divisions next to the umbrella space are 1 in. thick, dovetail-grooved or housed into the bottom. The cross rails seen in Fig. 257, which connect the divisions and provide for the reception of sticks and umbrellas, are of the sizes shown in Figs. 253 and 254, which also give details of the light balusters or laths and the two small pierced diamonds in the top rail shown in Fig. 248. All these parts should be stump-tenoned together, and the space should be subdivided by means of a longitudinal rail about $\frac{1}{2}$ in. by $1\frac{1}{2}$ in. and a small transverse rod as in Fig. 258.

The framework at the top of the drawer divisions is made up with a front rail as shown in Fig. 255. The cross rails under the drawer fronts are 2 in. wide by $\frac{3}{4}$ in. thick, stump-tenoned into the sides. The drawer runners may be 1 in. wide by $\frac{3}{4}$ in. thick, fixed with screws. The tops over the drawers are 1 in. thick, with plain or chamfered edges and rounded

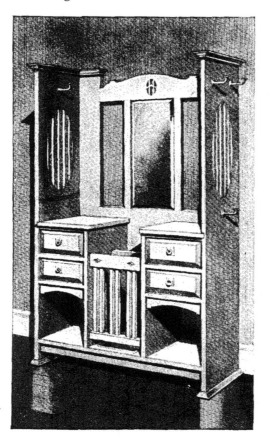

Fig. 247.—Modern-style hall stand

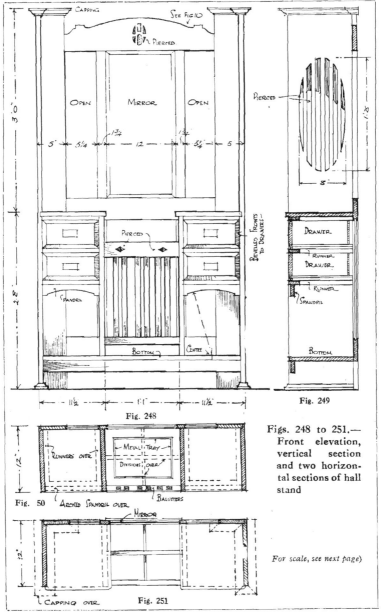

Figs. 248 to 251.—Front elevation, vertical section and two horizontal sections of hall stand

(For scale, see next page)

corners. They should be grooved $\frac{3}{16}$ in. into the sides, and fixed with screws from underneath.

The back is of $\frac{3}{4}$-in. stuff framed together as in Fig. 252. It is rebated into the back edges of the sides as shown in Fig. 255, and fixed with screws. The side stiles are $4\frac{1}{2}$ in. wide, the

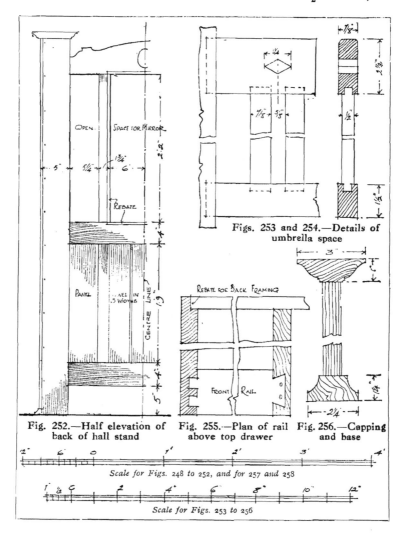

Fig. 252.—Half elevation of back of hall stand

Figs. 253 and 254.—Details of umbrella space

Fig. 255.—Plan of rail above top drawer

Fig. 256.—Capping and base

Scale for Figs. 248 to 252, and for 257 and 258

Scale for Figs. 253 to 256

Hall Furniture

top rail being 6 in. wide in the centre, shaped and pierced in accordance with Fig. 260. The centre and bottom horizontal rails are 4 in. wide, and the centre stiles are 2 in. wide. The

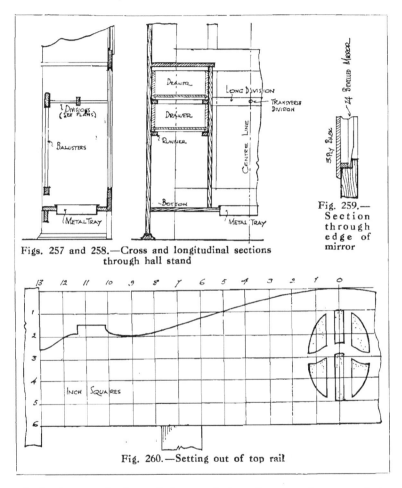

Figs. 257 and 258.—Cross and longitudinal sections through hall stand

Fig. 259.—Section through edge of mirror

Fig. 260.—Setting out of top rail

whole is mortised and tenoned together, and grooved to receive the panels, which are about ⅜ in. thick, chamfered off a little at the back to suit the grooves. The framework is rebated as required to receive the bevelled-edge mirror, which is fixed with beads to the framework, and is protected at the back with a backing of three-ply fixed to the framework as shown in Fig. 259. The moulded capping is worked as shown in Fig. 256, moulded round the edges as shown, and fixed with screws from the top. The same figure also gives a detail of the chamfered or hollow-moulded bases to the ends shown in Figs. 248, 249, etc. The sides can be housed into these or merely fixed with screws as before.

The drawers are made up in the usual manner, the sides being dovetailed into the fronts, and grooved for the backs; the bottoms are grooved into the sides and fronts. The fronts are $\frac{3}{4}$ in. thick, chamfered about $\frac{5}{8}$ in. as shown, the sides $\frac{1}{2}$ in. thick, and the backs and bottoms $\frac{3}{8}$ in. thick.

The shaped spandril pieces underneath the drawers are cut from wood $\frac{3}{4}$ in. thick, and are 2 in. deep at the ends. They are secured to the sides and upright divisions with glued blocks on the inside, and the centre of their curve is indicated on the right-hand side of Fig. 248. The piece under the front edge of the bottom is cut from wood $\frac{3}{4}$ in. thick, and fixed in the same way.

The metal tray or drip-pan is 10 in. long by 7 in. wide. It is fitted into the bottom as shown in Figs. 257 and 258, a hole being cut in the bottom to receive it

A Small Hall Fitment with Cupboard, Figs. 261 to 269.—This fitment includes a low cupboard, covered by a lift-up seat, a space for hanging coats, etc., and above a small cupboard with an open recess on each side. The appropriate material in most cases would be oak, say $\frac{5}{8}$ in. thick, while, if economy must be studied, the back might be constructed of pine.

The main supports consist of the two sides, each 1 ft. wide and cut to the outline shown in Fig. 262. They are rebated to take a light panelled back between the points A and B (Fig. 263), the alternative being V-jointed boarding; while the spaces at the back above A and below B will be filled in with boarding in any case. A panelled front should be prepared to go below the seat (as c, Fig. 263), housed into grooves in the sides, and having a bottom rail 5 in. or 6 in.

Hall Furniture

wide, with about $2\frac{1}{4}$ in. for the others. This part should be fixed $1\frac{1}{2}$ in. back from the front edges of the lower parts of the sides, and a small moulding planted on next the floor. Small bearers as at D should be fixed on each side level with the top edge of the panelled front, and also a piece at the back as at E (Fig. 267), this being provided to receive the hinged seat,

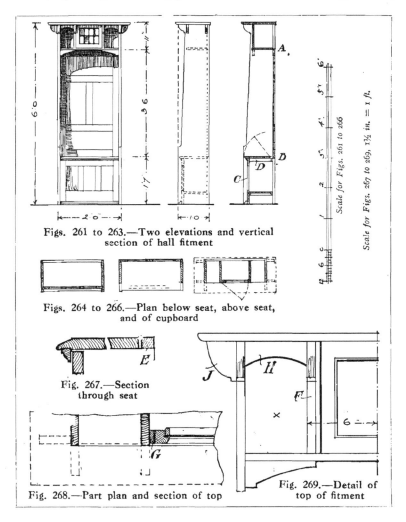

Figs. 261 to 263.—Two elevations and vertical section of hall fitment

Figs. 264 to 266.—Plan below seat, above seat, and of cupboard

Fig. 267.—Section through seat

Fig. 268.—Part plan and section of top

Fig. 269.—Detail of top of fitment

which is intended to have a moulded edge and a small moulding housed into it below.

A shelf 3 ft. 6 in. above the seat is fixed between the sides. It might be supported on small fillets fixed against the sides, and has simple brackets as in Fig. 269, where may also be noticed an upright piece F, corresponding with the outline of the sides. This, with its fellow on the other side, forms the top cupboard; two small fillets will be required, as G (Fig. 268), to take a door of the usual type, which would look well with leaded glazing; or small oak bars would do.

Two arch pieces as at H struck from radii of 5 in., and also four brackets of the outline at J (Fig. 269), will be required for fixing to the recesses and at the sides (*see* upper part of Fig. 262) after the top has been put on. This last projects $3\frac{1}{2}$ in. on the three exposed sides, and about $\frac{3}{4}$ in. along the back, and its edge can be rounded as shown or finished with a small moulding planted on. Hooks can be fixed to the back framing if desired, or can be of the revolving three-way variety, screwed into the under side of the upper shelf. Additional hooks can be fixed to the sides, inside and out.

Corner Stand, Figs. 270 to 277.—This may be constructed from pitchpine and varnished. The finished thickness of the rails (Figs. 274 and 277) should not be less than $\frac{7}{16}$ in., and the front legs may be cut from board $1\frac{3}{4}$ in. wide and $\frac{7}{8}$ in. thick finished. Care must be exercised in cutting the oblique mortices. A full-size plan should be made and the dimensions marked off from it to the material. Then square the ends and edges of the legs, set the bevel to an angle of 45°, mark two lines on each end representing the width of the mortices, set the marking gauge to the face ends of the lines, and scribe from them; this will give the diagonal or face widths of the mortices. A small gauge, similar to a bevel, could be made from a thin piece of hard wood; if small enough to enter the mortices it would be useful for correcting purposes. There are three tenons on the upper rail (*see* Figs. 274 and 275) and one on the bottom rail which is shaped as shown in Fig. 270 next the floor. The back leg is in two parts, each $1\frac{5}{8}$ in. by $\frac{7}{8}$ in. mitred, and finally glued together. The top and bottom side rails

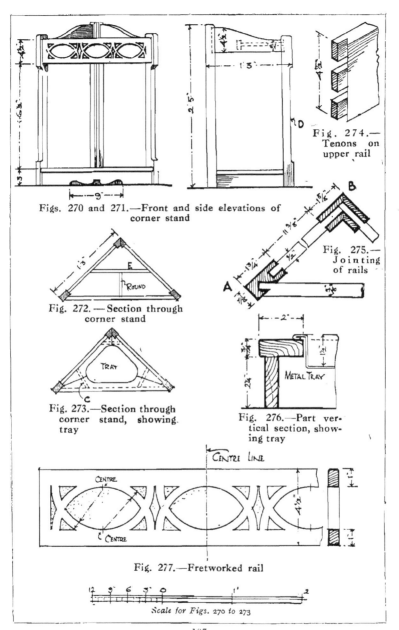

Figs. 270 and 271.—Front and side elevations of corner stand

Fig. 274.—Tenons on upper rail

Fig. 272.—Section through corner stand

Fig. 275.—Jointing of rails

Fig. 273.—Section through corner stand, showing tray

Fig. 276.—Part vertical section, showing tray

Fig. 277.—Fretworked rail

Scale for Figs. 270 to 273

are framed to the uprights as at A and B (Fig. 275), the former being shaped as shown in Fig. 271. See that the shoulders fit well to the legs; then remove the top front rail, and space it out for the fretwork which can readily be done on reference to Fig. 277, the pattern consisting of a series of semicircles interlacing. Beginning at the centre, make a template of cartridge paper similar to Fig. 277. After the fretting is finished fix the parts with fresh hot glue.

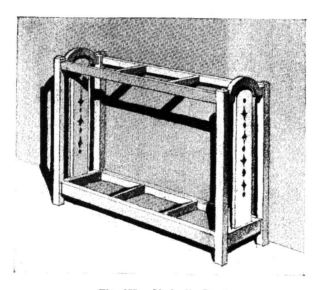

Fig. 278.—Umbrella Stand

Next fit the lower shelf as in Fig. 273, which shows a plan of the under-side of the base. The shelf is formed of three boards ¾ in. thick, glued and bradded to the rails and mitred at the angles; three fillets as at C are shown, and to stiffen the mitre extra blocks may be glued under the joint. When the glue has set, trim off the top and the space for the drip tray; the latter must be made to order and should lift out easily and be given a coat of enamel paint. The projecting angles of the lower shelf should be rounded off slightly as in Fig. 276, as should the tops of the three legs where shown,

Hall Furniture

the two front ones being further sunk slightly on the face as at D (Fig. 271). A cross rail E (Fig. 272) should be tenoned into position together with a small round division

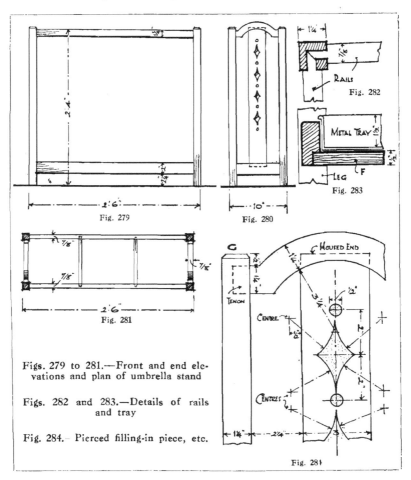

Figs. 279 to 281.—Front and end elevations and plan of umbrella stand

Figs. 282 and 283.—Details of rails and tray

Fig. 284.—Pierced filling-in piece, etc.

shown at right angles to it in the centre, kept high up in order to meet the solid margin of the front rail.

Straight Umbrella Stand, Figs. 278 to 284.—The dimensions of this stand are: 2 ft. 6 in. long over the posts by 10 in. deep and height from floor to top rail 2 ft. 4 in. The stand is divided into three equal spaces by the two small cross rails as shown in Fig. 281. First prepare the four posts and square them up to $1\frac{1}{4}$ in. by $1\frac{1}{4}$ in. and mortice for the top and bottom rails, which are $1\frac{1}{4}$ in. by $\frac{7}{8}$ in. and 2 in. by $\frac{7}{8}$ in. respectively. The top rails are formed out of 3 in. by 7 in. to the curved outline shown in Fig. 284, and set out from the centre-point given; they are housed to receive the top of the filling-in piece shown in Fig. 280, which is also housed at the bottom; it is 3 in. wide by, say, $\frac{3}{8}$ in. and can be pierced to the design shown, a geometric setting out for which will be found in Fig. 284. Tenon the rails to the posts, keeping the latter $\frac{1}{8}$ in. in advance of the rails. Fig. 283 gives a section of the bottom rails, which are rebated to receive the $\frac{1}{2}$ in. pine bottom F, which is fitted and fixed with screws to the bottom rails. The two cross rails, $1\frac{1}{4}$ in. deep by $\frac{7}{8}$ in. thick, are fixed to the two long top rails with short rebated tenons, for example, tenons about $\frac{3}{4}$ in. wide formed in the centre of the $1\frac{1}{4}$-in. width of rail. When the stand is cramped up, the posts can be finished off with a chamfer as at G (Fig. 284), and the various exposed angles should be rounded off as in Fig. 283. The zinc pan fits between the bottoms rails, and is divided into three spaces. It is shown in section in Fig. 283 and must be made to order. When finished, the stand would look well stained lightly and dull polished. Of course, a similar stand could be made without the ornament at the ends if desired, or the design could be varied by employing turned legs.

High-back Hall Seat, Figs. 285 to 292. — This depends for a satisfactory appearance solely on straightforward construction and pleasing proportions. In length it might be varied from 3 ft. to 5 ft., according to requirements, the middle course of 4 ft. being adopted in the example as probably the most convenient dimension in the majority of cases. The two upright ends A and B (Fig. 292) are each 11 in. by 1 in. by 3 ft. $3\frac{1}{4}$ in. long. (These thicknesses are the sawn scantlings before planing.) The ends are connected by the seat C, 12 in. by 1 in. and 3 ft. 11 in. long, each end of which

Hall Furniture

should be cut away in order to leave a projecting piece as at D in Fig. 291, 8 in. long, ½ in. wide, and starting 2 in. back from the front edge as figured. This projection should be housed securely into a groove cut in the end piece, the top being arranged 1 ft. 3 in. up from the bottom end of the latter, and the back edges of seat and ends agreeing with each other. When in position the front corners of the seat will project 1 in., and should be rounded off to a quadrant E

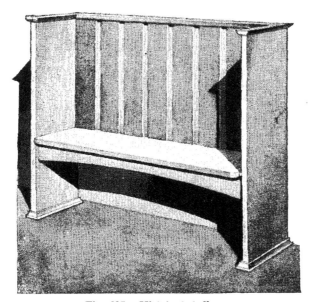

Fig. 285.—High-back hall seat

(Fig. 291); or, if preferred, the projection might be increased a little; or, on the other hand, dispensed with completely.

The two rails F and G (Fig. 292) might be $2\frac{1}{2}$ in. by 1 in. and 3 ft. $11\frac{3}{4}$ in. long, and should have their ends rounded off as at H (Fig. 291), so as to be quite inconspicuous from the front or side. These rails are seen also at the top and bottom of the back in Figs. 287 and 290, and are indicated by the horizontal dotted lines in Fig. 286. They require to be strongly screwed to the back edges of the ends, which are

Furniture Making

thereby braced considerably. The lower of the two rails should also be secured to the back edge of the seat.

The back boarding can be of ordinary V-jointed boarding, or, as shown, boarding 5 in. wide grooved down the edges to take the wide oak fillets or tongues about ¼ in. thick and showing 1½ in. on the face, thereby giving a very good effect

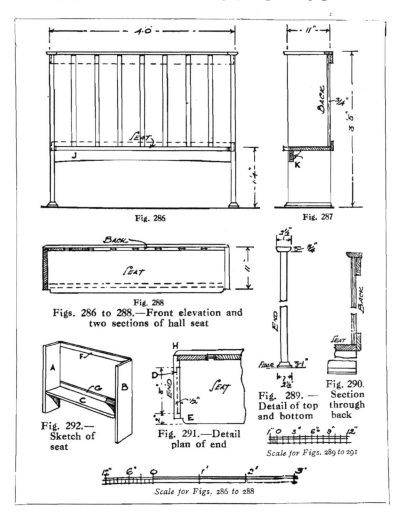

Fig. 286

Fig. 287

Fig. 288

Figs. 286 to 288.—Front elevation and two sections of hall seat

Fig. 292.—Sketch of seat

Fig. 291.—Detail plan of end

Fig. 289.—Detail of top and bottom

Fig. 290.—Section through back

Scale for Figs. 289 to 291

Scale for Figs. 286 to 288

Hall Furniture

(*see* Figs. 285 and 291). An alternative would be to fit a panelled back having, say, three or four upright divisions; but this would be departing somewhat from the simple character of the work involved. The back is intended to be fixed vertically to the two rails; or it could be slightly sloped by introducing a fillet 1 in. or so wide along the bottom edge, and fixing the boarding to this instead of direct to the rail. It would be advantageous to let the back into a rebate along the inner back edges of the ends as shown at II (Fig. 291).

A slightly curved spandril-piece as at J (Fig. 286), $3\frac{1}{2}$ in. by $\frac{3}{4}$ in. and 3 ft. 10 in. long, should be fixed under the front of the seat, $\frac{1}{16}$ in. back from the edges of the ends, and secured by means of small blocks at the back as at K (Fig. 287) The tops of the back and ends are finished simply by means of a $2\frac{1}{2}$-in. by $\frac{3}{4}$-in. plain capping, with its exposed edges rounded off to a quadrant as in Figs. 289 and 290. The feet of the two ends should have $2\frac{1}{2}$-in. by 1-in. pieces $11\frac{3}{4}$ in. long, as in the same two figures, firmly screwed on from below and splayed or moulded on their sides and front ends, the backs being cut off flush in order to allow the work to go close against the usual skirting board, which the back of the capping will probably overhang.

The space below the seat could be enclosed, the seat then becoming the hinged top of a long narrow box

CHAPTER X

AN EIGHTEENTH-CENTURY HALL SEAT

Semicircular Hall Seat, date about 1800 ; Figs. 293 to 307.—The small hall seat described in this chapter is to be seen at South Kensington Museum. It is of highly polished very dark mahogany, and the general effect taken as a whole is far more important than the details of the design, which, in any modern work based on this example, may be somewhat simplified, as will be explained later. Undoubtedly the features that create the charm of the work are the semicircular seat plan and the carved ornament on the back. The quaint ornaments along the bearer under the seat, however, might be better omitted.

The difficult part of the work will be the proper formation of the outer framing which forms the curved panelled back, more especially that surrounding the side panels. The craftsman can produce an interesting result of a more modern type by forming the upper corners as in Fig. 302, this consisting of plain work curved on plan only, and not as shown in the photograph (Fig. 293), which is in part curved both on plan and in section. Observe also that in both the modern adaptation and the old example the actual panels are curved on plan only, being quite straight in vertical section, although sloping back slightly. From this it will be understood that the roll or turned-over effect of the sides as seen in the photograph is produced by the shaping of the top of the framing. Then, again, the panels might be omitted, and their spaces filled with upholstery if preferred, and the legs simplified to plain tapered forms, or kept as shown, but without the flutings.

For convenience in describing this piece of furniture, the seat may be divided into two parts, namely, those portions respectively below and above the level of the actual seat. This last is perfectly flat, about $\frac{3}{4}$ in. thick and all in

An Eighteenth-century Hall Seat

one piece, although two might be cross-tongued together to make up the size. It has a rounded edge projecting 1 in. all round, and on plan it is a trifle less than a semicircle.

The framing under the seat has four legs, the front ones ornamented on their front faces as shown in Fig. 297, and similarly on the outer side in each case, except for the little

Fig. 293.—Mahogany hall seat, English, about the year 1800

carved leaf pattern, which is replaced by three short flutings as in Fig. 295. (This carving was, seemingly, applied afterwards, and, oddly enough, is a little out of centre with the leg, as may be noticed in Fig. 294, although this is corrected in Fig. 297.)

The front legs are of 2-in. by 2-in. material, tapering to $\frac{3}{4}$ in. square near the floor, and with slightly projecting bands left on as shown. The flutings taper slightly in width and are of semicircular section; they occur only on the front legs, the back two being merely tapered and a little stouter than those in front. All four are 1 ft. $4\frac{3}{4}$ in. long, and will require to be framed up with horizontal bearers as indicated on the right-hand half of Fig. 296, the curved ones A and B being finished about 2 in. by 2in., cut to the required slight curve, and tenoned into the legs. The front bearer is $3\frac{1}{2}$ in. deep, and consists, as indicated in section in Fig. 297, of a mahogany face about $\frac{3}{8}$ in. thick and a deal bearer behind 2 in. thick. The mahogany front was probably not jointed into the leg, and it may have been necessary to add the little carved panel in the one-sided manner previously noted, in order to cover the butt joint. Accordingly it would be as well to let it in a little way, keeping it $\frac{1}{8}$ in. back from the face of the legs. A simplification of the ornament to the bearer has already been advocated, and if Fig. 302 is followed the carving might be on the solid, and the surrounding oblong and the narrow projecting strip along the top carried out with veneer. The whole should be very cleanly cut.

The bearers should be tenoned securely into the uprights, three extra bearers as at C and D (Fig. 296) serving to support the centre of the seat and to tie the framework together. Triangular brackets are fixed next to the joints as shown in Fig. 295; and when it comes to fixing the seat, this should be done by means of "buttons" fitting into grooves in the bearers to allow for possible slight shrinkage, as indicated at E (Fig. 297).

To execute the back exactly as in the example will require much skill and care. The oval portion consists of a piece of framing 2 in. thick at the bottom, tapering to 1 in. at the top, the back surface being vertical and all the slope going

An Eighteenth-century Hall Seat

on the front as in Fig. 303. Round the inner edge on the front is worked a small ovolo on the solid, and the back is rebated, the panel being secured in position with a bead. It will be noted that the increasing thickness of the rebate

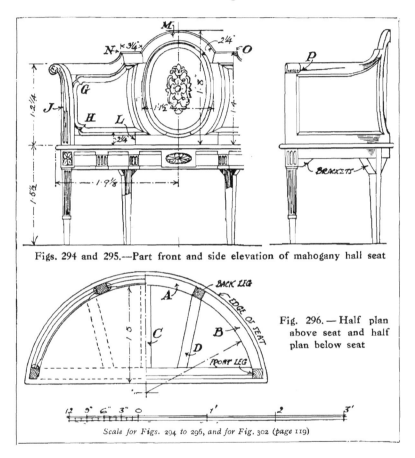

Figs. 294 and 295.—Part front and side elevation of mahogany hall seat

Fig. 296.—Half plan above seat and half plan below seat

Scale for Figs. 294 to 296, and for Fig. 302 (page 119)

makes the bead (which is flush at the top) to set in about an inch at the bottom (*see* F, Fig. 303), the edge of the framing being rounded off at this point as shown.

The panels should be as thin as possible, in order to prevent difficulty in bending them to the slight curve they each present on plan, it being remembered that in section they only slope backwards, taking no part in the roll or turn-over of the sides, this being confined entirely to the top of the framing. The panels have a sunk bevel about $1\frac{1}{4}$ in. wide round their margins, and are fixed with the grain vertical. In the original, small pieces are fitted into the front angles of the side panels to form points or " cusps " as at G and H (Fig. 294); but this device is omitted in favour of a plain mitre in Fig. 302.

The part of the framing marked J in Fig. 294 will need to be cut out of a piece of $3\frac{1}{2}$ in. by 3 in. about 1 ft. 3 in. long, as in Fig. 299, which is divided into inch squares for simplification of the setting-out. (Note: This figure and the section, Fig. 298, are shown on their sides). After cutting to this outline, the face is splayed off slightly as marked by crosses on the section through the same part (Fig. 298). The exact outline and flutings can then be set out as in Fig. 297, keeping the central part almost straight, so as to avoid bending the panel, and putting all the curve into the top 3 in. or 4 in. Take the dimensions given from the left-hand edge, thus leaving a narrow margin, which is worked back about $\frac{1}{4}$ in. and rounded off as noted on Fig. 298 and shown at K (Fig. 301), the object being to combine thickness of material with a light appearance from the front. It will be seen that this projection gradually dies out in the sloping surface above. The two semicircular flutes are filled to a height of 6 in. with a small bead, and allowance should be made for the little carved flower on the wreathed end. This is not very sharply modelled, probably because of its rather prominent position. The small moulding and the rebate required along the inner edge will present no difficulty, it being remembered that the rebate increases in depth as it descends in Fig. 303.

The old example is worked differently; but it will be best to form the bottom rail of the back in three lengths with tenoned joints as at L (Fig. 294), this enabling them to be cut out of much lighter stuff; their curve on plan must be accurately set out. They should be worked to the same section as the part shown at F (Fig. 303), rebated and moulded as before. Note that the bottom $\frac{1}{4}$ in. is intended to be housed

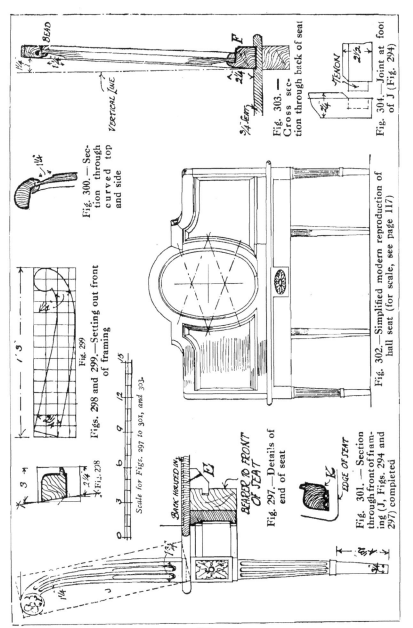

Fig. 300.—Section through curved top and side

Fig. 303.—Cross section through back of seat

Fig. 304.—Joint at foot of J (Fig. 294)

Figs. 298 and 299.—Setting out front of framing

Scale for Figs. 297 to 301, and 303.

Fig. 302.—Simplified modern reproduction of hall seat (for scale, see page 117)

Fig. 297.—Details of end of seat

Fig. 301.—Section through front of framing (J, Figs. 294 and 297) completed

119

into the seat. Fig. 304 shows how the ends of this built-up rail should be tenoned into the upright ends, and the moulding mitred to fit.

The oval should next be set out, and carefully worked to taper in thickness until the top part becomes only 1 in. thick, giving a slope of $1\frac{1}{4}$ in. on the front, as in Fig. 303. The short horizontal lengths marked $3\frac{1}{4}$ in. on Fig. 294 will need to be prepared for framing up with the rest. The top piece M could be in two with a central joint if desired, a thin strip being fixed round the top from N to O to finish off the edge (*see* top of Fig. 303).

The remaining member is the top to each side, which has a rounded surface or roll. This will require to be cut out of a piece 3 in. by 4 in. high and 1 ft. 6 in. long, as in Fig. 306. It must be tenoned to the other parts, and afterwards carefully worked in such a way that starting at N (Fig. 294) 1 in. in thickness, it widens out into a full curve meeting the wreathed end of the front piece. The photograph (Fig. 293) should make the meaning of this clear. In the example the part next to the line of the joint with the front is in section as in Fig. 300, this accounting for the break in the line shown at P in Fig. 295. The beaded slip at the top of the back is continued on the solid a little past N, and gradually dies out in the curve of the roll.

When ready, the framing should be housed $\frac{1}{4}$ in. deep into the seat (*see* Figs. 297 and 303), and fixed with several long oak dowels, especially where it comes immediately over the legs, and in addition screwed through the rebate and seat well into the bearers below. The panels can then be prepared with the bevelled margins $1\frac{1}{4}$ in. wide, and fitted and bent round to the slight curves necessary. They can afterwards be beaded in position. Lastly, the carving should be executed in accordance with Fig. 305, and applied on the face of the panel. The balls as at R, and perhaps that in the centre also, appear to have served to conceal screws. This ornament is boldly and sharply cut, the centre being of about 1-in. projection, and all the edges standing well out. The ground is slightly punched all over. Fig. 307 shows the carving on the front bearer.

An Eighteenth-century Hall Seat 121

After the foregoing, the modernised version in Fig. 302 will be easy to follow, but the seat will rather suffer if the carving in the centre of the back has to be omitted. The

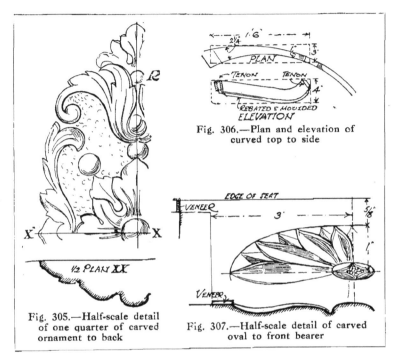

Fig. 305.—Half-scale detail of one quarter of carved ornament to back

Fig. 306.—Plan and elevation of curved top to side

Fig. 307.—Half-scale detail of carved oval to front bearer

centres used for striking the ellipse are indicated, as also the suggested joints on the right-hand half of the figure. The plan is practically the same as in Fig. 296.

CHAPTER XI

Two Old Chests

Flemish Cupboard or Credence, Figs. 308 to 315.—The oak cupboard or credence of Flemish workmanship here illustrated dates from the latter part of the fifteenth century, and possesses qualities of vigorous design and invention not always found in more recent times. The craftsman may make a copy of it, or he may regard it simply as a guide in the production of a different design.

The actual cupboard consists of a single compartment supported on stout legs, the ends each having two panels decorated with the well-known linen-fold pattern, while the front has a pierced tracery panel at each end, seemingly for ventilation. In the middle, separated by an upright rail, are two doors, each out of a single piece of oak with the grain vertical, and strengthened with long iron strap hinges. These doors have boldly incised diamond panels filled with carved portraits, presumably of the master and mistress of some long-forgotten household. The diamonds are out of the centre in order to accommodate large lock-plates. That the old craftsman had no mean sense of proportion is obvious: Observe how, when the cupboard was virtually complete, he added the carved apron along the front under the bottom rail, in order to get a satisfactory balance. And imagine how poor would have been the effect had this been omitted.

The question of carving the various parts must be left for individual decision, but it can be readily simplified or left out; the tracery might be deleted in favour of the linen-fold pattern, and the diamonds might be plain sinkings.

The whole of the work is secured by means of oak pegs, and it will be seen that the sizes given are rather on the heavy side. The cupboard may be taken as consisting of four plain legs $3\frac{3}{8}$ in. by $1\frac{3}{4}$ in. and 2 ft. $10\frac{1}{8}$ in. long. The ends (*see* Fig. 310) have two horizontal rails tenoned between them,

Two Old Chests

the top one C $2\frac{7}{8}$ in. by $1\frac{1}{2}$ in., and the lower one D $2\frac{1}{4}$ in. by $1\frac{1}{2}$ in., slightly splayed along its upper edge; a middle rail, $2\frac{3}{4}$ in. by $1\frac{1}{2}$ in., moulded along both edges (as at E, Fig. 314) is also fitted, the whole being grooved to take the linen-fold panels. The front and back have similar rails at the same levels, the back, of course, being square and arranged to take a panelled or boarded filling-in as preferred; while the lower

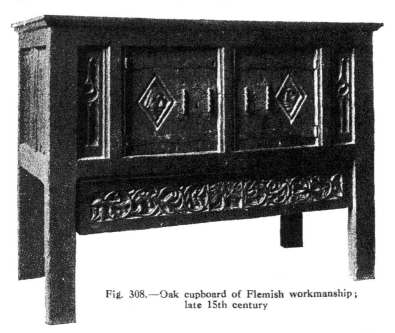

Fig. 308.—Oak cupboard of Flemish workmanship; late 15th century

rail in front is both splayed and moulded, a 6-in. by $\frac{3}{4}$-in. carved apron being ultimately fixed under it.

The pierced tracery is on a geometrical basis, set out from centre lines as in Fig. 314, where the section on plan will be noticed, the small cusps or points being extra to this. The bottom or sill finishes with a wide splay, and the small pointed arches at the top are based on equilateral triangles.

In comparison with the heavy sizes of the other parts, the top is rather thin, say $\frac{5}{8}$ in.; but it has a moulding fixed under its projecting edge as shown. A similar thickness might

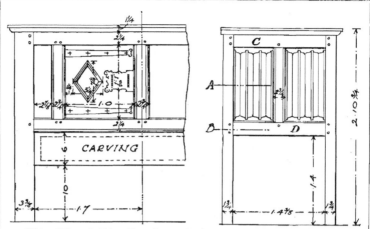

Figs. 309 and 310.—Part front elevation and end elevation of Flemish cupboard

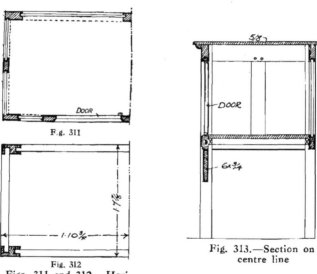

Fig. 311

Fig. 312

Figs. 311 and 312.—Horizontal sections at A and B (Fig. 310)

Fig. 313.—Section on centre line

Scale for Figs. 309 to 313, ¾ in. = 1 ft

Two Old Chests

be employed on small fillets (marked with tiny diagonal crosses in Fig. 313) to form the bottom of the cupboard.

Fig. 315 shows a variation on the cupboard, in which the same appearance gained by the carved apron is produced

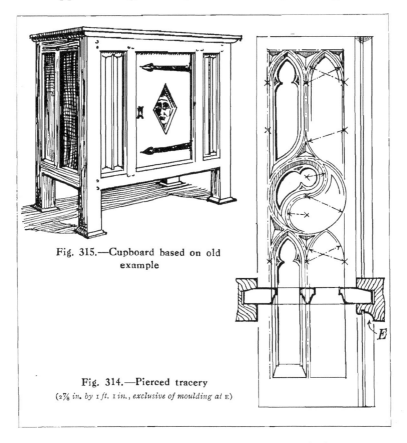

Fig. 315.—Cupboard based on old example

Fig. 314.—Pierced tracery
(2⅞ in. by 1 ft. 1 in., exclusive of moulding at E)

by taking the cupboard nearer the floor. This is a sketch suggestion for a smaller piece of work, having a central door flanked by linen-fold or tracery panels. Another possible variation would be to treat the work as a chest, omitting the legs entirely, but perhaps putting a skirting round the bottom and introducing a third narrow panel between the two square ones in Fig. 308, and, of course, putting a lift-up top instead of doors.

A Chest Rug Box, Figs. 316 to 322.—This chest is made in oak, roughly finished externally, with pegs driven through the various tenoned joints, and the whole stained to a dark dull colour in order to simulate the effect of work dating from Tudor times, but without the distressing surface ornament so often employed. The edges of the framing next the panels are worked with mouldings and splays on the solid in the mediæval manner.

The chest consists of four pieces of framing with rails, etc., finished about $\frac{7}{8}$ in. thick, and with panels as shown in Figs. 316 and 317, the tenoned joints being secured with two oak pegs each. A small ovolo moulding is worked along the edges of each panel, stopped where shown at the top, and dying out on a splay worked on the bottom rail as at A (Fig. 316). The horizontal joint runs through the small moulding as at B, this being the traditional method. A slightly different finish for the edges of the panels, and one also founded on old work, is shown in Fig. 322, where the ovolo runs right out against the edge of the top rail, while the latter has simply a stopped chamfer. At the back the three panels intended to be formed can suitably have square edges, and at each corner the upright "stiles" project downwards about $\frac{5}{8}$ in. to form feet, which might either serve to conceal small castors or to receive "domes of silence," if desired. The various panels can either be quite thin or they may be rebated as at D (Fig. 322) in order to present a flush internal face.

When the four pieces of framing have been prepared to size, they should be rebated as at E (Fig. 321) in order to take a wood bottom; and when this has been made ready, the sides should be mitred together as at F (Fig. 322), this joint being far more practicable than concealed dovetailing.

For the lid or top, a piece of framing $\frac{3}{4}$ in. thick and large enough to overhang the box 1 in. on three sides is prepared, mitred and tenoned as G (Fig. 319) at the angles, and has rounded angles and a small moulding under to fit round the box as at H (Fig. 322). The top is filled in with a panel flush on the top, having a small V-shaped sinking all round,

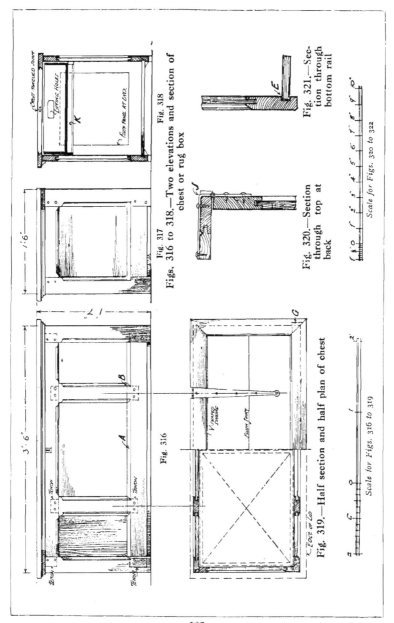

Fig. 317
Fig. 318
Figs. 316 to 318.—Two elevations and section of chest or rug box

Fig. 320.—Section through top at back

Fig. 321.—Section through bottom rail

Fig. 316

Fig. 319.—Half section and half plan of chest

Scale for Figs. 316 to 319

Scale for Figs. 320 to 322

as in Fig. 322, and in two widths with a joint longitudinally down the centre, this joint being cross-tongued.

Hinges of a fairly rough quality and similar to what are termed " cross-garnets " may be employed, and if, as is proposed, they are required to show on the top of the box, they must be very carefully heated and bent to a right angle as at J (Fig. 320). Specially wrought iron hinges of a slightly decorative character would be eminently appropriate. A small chain or strap will probably be of service, if arranged so as to prevent the lid falling back too far.

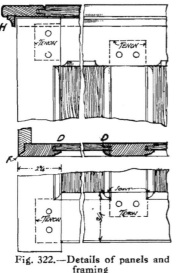

Fig. 322.—Details of panels and framing
(*For scale, see preceding page*)

It is suggested that instead of carrying the old-style appearance to extremes, the interior should be finished with a natural surface and slightly waxed, this being cleaner than if stained dark; while $4\frac{1}{4}$ in. down from the top edge, a small fillet as at K (Fig. 318) is fixed all round the box, in order to support two light wooden square trays, indicated by the internal dotted lines in the right-hand portion of Fig. 319, intended to contain small articles. Holes may be cut in the tray sides as noted in Fig. 318 for lifting. In fitting the trays together, the pieces could be mitred and secured with fine wire brads.

CHAPTER XII

MUSIC STOOLS

As with so many other examples in this book, the designs given in the present chapter are open to all sorts of minor alterations; thus the stools can be : (*a*) of single or double length ; (*b*) with fixed seats or hinged tops concealing music-boxes; (*c*) with upholstery confined within the exposed upper edges of the frame or taken over its top into a slight rebate on the side (as at A, Fig. 328).

Simple Music Stool with Box Seat, Figs. 323 to 329.—This is a straightforward piece of work, which if desired could be produced in the smaller size without the underframing between the legs; if, however, it is extended to the duet length (that is, 2 ft. 6 in. or 3 ft.) this addition would be necessary and could be curved as in Fig. 323, or it could be straight as in Fig. 327, or as shown elsewhere in this book. For the larger size, also, it is not unusual to employ an extra pair of legs in the centre. In the completed stool, illustrated, simple inlaid banding has been introduced on the sides, and ornament of this description can be carried very much further, although it is always advisable to maintain if possible a similarity in general finish between the stool and the piano. The necessary dimensions for setting out will be found incorporated in the figures.

The stool as here illustrated has $1\frac{1}{2}$ in. square legs, tapering below the box to $\frac{7}{8}$ in., connected at the top by $4\frac{1}{2}$-in. by $\frac{3}{4}$-in. rails forming the sides of the box and tenoned into the legs as in Fig. 329. If these joints are made sufficiently strong, the inner angle of each leg can afterwards be cut away as indicated by the dotted lines, but if there should be any question as to the strength of the work or the wood employed, this need not be done. The bottom of the box is formed with a piece of three-ply or other thin stuff fixed from below as at B (Fig. 325), with its edges rounded and set

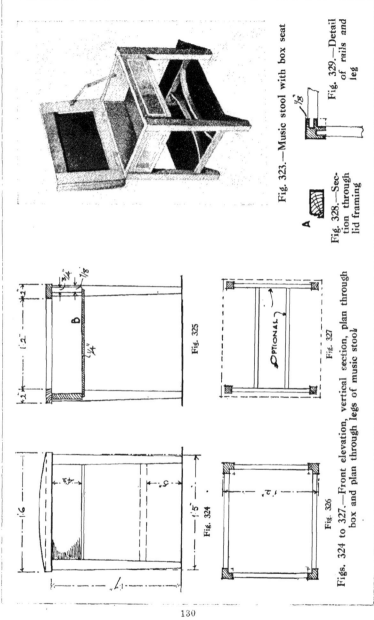

Fig. 323.—Music stool with box seat

Fig. 329.—Detail of rails and leg

Fig. 328.—Section through lid framing

Figs. 324 to 327.—Front elevation, vertical section, plan through box and plan through legs of music stool

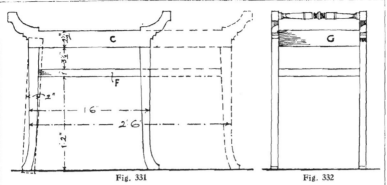

Fig. 331   Fig. 332

Figs. 331 to 333.—Two elevations and part plan of music stool with arms

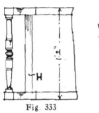

Fig. 333

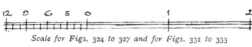

Scale for Figs. 324 to 327 and for Figs. 331 to 333

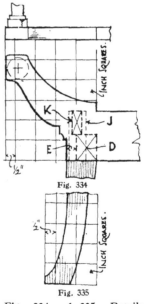

Fig. 334

Fig. 335

Figs. 334 and 335.—Details of shaped arm and leg

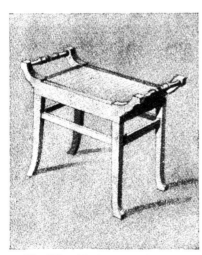

Fig. 330.—Music stool with arms

back a little, so that they may not be apparent. The lid consists of an open frame of 2-in. by $\frac{7}{8}$-in. stuff, mortised and tenoned (rather than merely halved) together and hinged in position, with corners slightly rounded and top edges rebated as in Fig. 328 for the covering material. Under the webbing of the seat should be stretched a piece of tapestry or plain material in order to present a neat finish when the box is open. Either a chain, or for preference a brass " rule-joint stay " should be fitted in order to prevent the lid going too far back.

A Single or Double Stool with Short Arms, Figs. 330 to 335.—This is a more fanciful design which might, in suitable surroundings, be finished in flat white enamel as in the case illustrated. It consists of two top rails c (Fig. 331) of the required length, and about 1 in. thickness, which could be cut out of one piece $8\frac{1}{2}$ in. wide to the design in Fig. 335, all edges being finished square both in the rails and legs. The latter are each cut out of 2-in. by 1-in. stuff as dotted on the left-hand side of Fig. 331 to the curves shown in Figs. 331 and 335, and tenoned about $1\frac{1}{4}$ in. deep into the rails as at D, leaving $\frac{5}{8}$ in. at E. As at F, the legs are connected on all four sides by a 1-in. by $\frac{5}{8}$-in. plain square rail, or this might be arranged at a lower level and made rather more elaborate, as suggested for the first example. End rails as at G and H, 1 in. by $2\frac{1}{2}$ in. square, will also be necessary; their positions are indicated by the thin dotted lines at J (Fig. 335), while the thicker ones marked K indicate the tenon by means of which they should be secured in position. The curved ends or arms of the top rails are connected by means of rails, round-turned out of 1-in. or $1\frac{1}{4}$-in. stuff to some simple outline, and tenoned or dowelled in position, thus completing the frame ready for the upholsterer, whom it is suggested in this case might very suitably finish his covering material with a row of oxidised nails round the top rails.

Duet Stool with Shaped and Moulded Ends, Figs. 336 to 341.—This is a larger piece of work than its predecessors and can be made to any required length. Its ends consist of $1\frac{3}{8}$-in. square legs tapered and shaped, filled in with a $1\frac{1}{4}$-in. by $\frac{3}{4}$-in. rail L and three upright laths

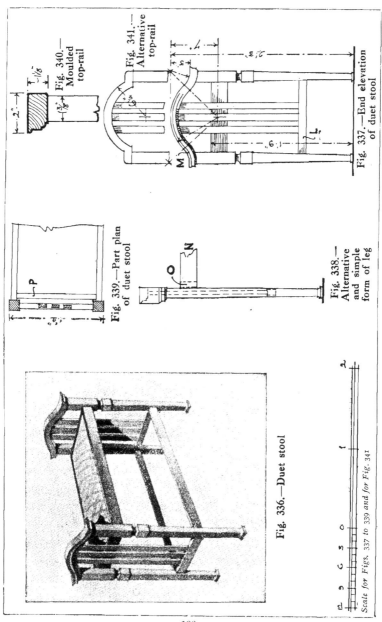

Fig. 340.—Moulded top-rail
Fig. 341.—Alternative top-rail
Fig. 337.—End elevation of duet stool
Fig. 339.—Part plan of duet stool
Fig. 338.—Alternative and simple form of leg
Fig. 336.—Duet stool

Scale for Figs. 337 to 339 and for Fig. 341

1 in. by $\frac{1}{2}$ in. slightly housed top and bottom. The top rail M is set out from three centres (Fig. 337) and moulded on the front and ends as in Fig. 340, but finished flat with rounded angles on the inside. The two rails necessary could be cut out of one piece $6\frac{1}{2}$ in. wide, or of course built up in several sections if preferred. Should the moulded work to them present difficulties or too great an expense, they might be reduced to the form shown in Fig. 341, the legs in each case being stub-tenoned into them. The legs themselves also might be simplified as in Fig. 338. The seat-rail N in the latter figure is $2\frac{1}{2}$ in. by 1 in. tenoned in position, and a transverse rail as at O (*see also* P, Fig. 339) will be required to take the upholstery, which must of course be kept clear of the upright laths to the ends.

CHAPTER XIII

Music Cabinets

Cabinets with Drawers and Trays, Figs. 342 to 354.—
The general arrangement of a useful music cabinet is here shown. It is capable of accommodating quite a quantity of music, any of which is readily accessible for use, and it can be varied in many ways (*see* sketches A and B, Fig. 354). Modifications could easily be made in order to match a piano; it would not be necessary to depart from the general arrangement or proportion; the introduction of some inlaying or carving, similar to the piano panels, for instance, could be effected in the doors and drawers, although the cabinet would look very well without the various carved ornaments shown. The trays afford good accommodation for the

Fig. 342.—Music cabinet with drawers and trays

usual paper pieces, whilst the drawers provide for bound volumes, etc. The insides of the doors are treated decoratively, and it is a good plan to use a light-coloured wood for veneering the insides of the doors. If a mahogany exterior polished a dark colour is decided on, the inside can very well be polished natural colour. Another suitable treatment would be to polish the trays and interior natural colour, and to introduce satinwood for the insides of the doors. If a coromandel or ebony exterior is decided on, satinwood is again a suitable colour combination, whilst a walnut exterior, with boxwood for insides of doors, gives a pleasing

Figs. 343 and 344.—Two elevations of music cabinet

effect. For a rosewood exterior, a walnut interior is satisfactory. For the purpose of this article it is assumed that the exterior is to be of mahogany, with satinwood inside the doors.

Fig. 351 shows that the ends are framed together, a thick pilaster being used at the front for decorative purposes. This can be inlaid or sunk on the face as in Fig. 343, and really acts as a stile, with a thinner one at the back equal

Music Cabinets

to the thickness of the rails. This should be framed up as for an ordinary door frame, and the panels, after being veneered and cleaned up, have the edges bare-face tongued, and are put in the frame previous to gluing up. Work of this description should have the mouldings and panels

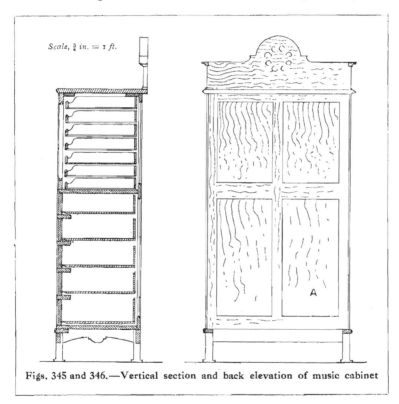

Figs. 345 and 346.—Vertical section and back elevation of music cabinet

properly polished before it is glued up, or otherwise muddy corners are inevitable, and if shrinkage should take place, part of the unpolished panel comes out of the groove.

The method of connecting the two top rails is shown by Fig. 348. The rails are dovetailed into the end grain of the stiles, and cut into the straight grain of the rails, afterwards being screwed as shown for additional security. The carcase bottom would also be dovetailed at the front and back into the end grain of the stiles, and the rail should be rebated all through to receive the bottom, which is screwed up in a similar fashion to the rails. A solid bottom is essential for the cupboard part, and this can be securely attached to the end frames by tenoning into the stiles, the frame being trenched across to hold the middle part of the cupboard

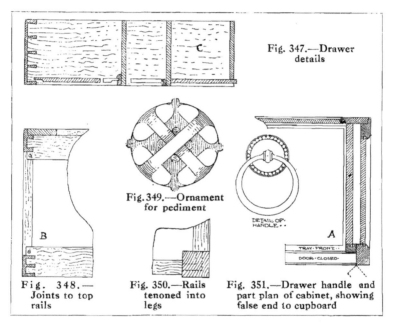

Fig. 347.—Drawer details

Fig. 349.—Ornament for pediment

Fig. 348.—Joints to top rails

Fig. 350.—Rails tenoned into legs

Fig. 351.—Drawer handle and part plan of cabinet, showing false end to cupboard

bottom. The drawer rails should also be tenoned between the pilasters or stiles.

The panelled back A (Fig. 346) is rebated into the framed-up ends. Fig. 345 shows the bead and butt-jointed panels, which yield a flush surface on the inside of the cupboard. Fig. 347 shows the constructive details of the drawers, which should measure about 1 ft. 10 in. by 12 in. internally, and also indicates alternate methods of "slipping" the sides in order to obtain a better running surface on the bottom. For convenience in use, it is better to employ falling fronts

Music Cabinets

to the drawers, which can be contrived as in Figs. 352 and 353, where the brass plate shown at D is screwed at the end of a separate drawer front E where indicated by a thick line, while the piece at right angles is screwed to the side as at F in

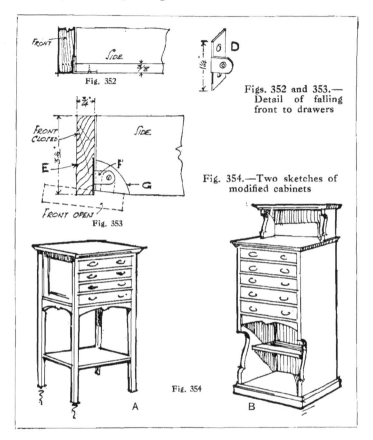

Figs. 352 and 353.—Detail of falling front to drawers

Fig. 354.—Two sketches of modified cabinets

such a way that when opened the front falls automatically to the position indicated by the dotted lines in Fig. 353. In order to avoid projections, the surface of the side is reduced about $\frac{1}{16}$ in. to the line G to give the movement free play, and the bottom edge is splayed off as shown.

After the drawers have been made and fitted on the

necessary runners, the fronts should be planed down level with the front edges of the carcase. They can then be withdrawn, and the quartered veneering proceeded with. Some simple carved detail might be executed in the centre of each drawer front, such as is suggested in the illustrations. Cocked beads should be made, and fitted round the edges. A good plan is to make the top bead the full width of the top edge of the drawer front, the side and bottom beads being made about $\frac{3}{8}$ in. wide and rebated into the front. When the drawers are finally fitted and stopped, the fronts should be in the same line as the carcase edges, the projecting bead breaking the joint and giving a refined appearance to the work.

The doors are clamped and veneered, and the carved decoration shown should be executed if required by first tracing the outline of the carving, and then gluing the tracing down to a piece of $\frac{1}{4}$-in. Cuba mahogany. This outline should be cut with a fret-saw or band-saw, and then the resultant shape can be glued down to the veneered doors. When quite dry, carving can be proceeded with, in low relief only, in harmony with the general treatment. The veneers for the inside of the doors would be laid at the same time as the fronts. If properly done there is little danger of the doors casting or twisting. Cocked beads are also introduced round the edges, with a double one at the centre in place of the usual astragal moulding which conceals the meeting joints of the two doors. The hinges should be cut into the doors, and should coincide with the cocked bead, being exactly flush and level when finished.

False ends must be fitted in the cupboard part in order to allow the trays to pass the doors when they are withdrawn. The construction of one false end is shown at Fig. 351. A $\frac{3}{8}$-in. piece is tongued into a thicker front piece, and slips are put across the back part to act as bearing pieces when the false end is screwed to the framing. The dotted lines indicate the position of the door when open, and it will be seen that when the tray is withdrawn it will easily clear the hinged edge of the door. The trays themselves should be of as light material as possible; $\frac{1}{4}$ in. for sides and

Music Cabinets

fronts rounded and shaped as in Fig. 345 and three-ply bottoms would be suitable if carefully fitted together.

The stand part of the job is made quite separate from the rest, and the legs are cut from $2\frac{1}{2}$-in. stuff. After the rails have been tenoned into the square legs, all the legs can be cut to the shape shown, and then carved or recessed about $\frac{1}{8}$ in. deep as indicated. Shaping the rails should be proceeded with after they have been glued between the legs, otherwise they will be weakened considerably, and not be able to stand the pressure exerted when cramping up. The moulding is mitred round, and stiffens the shaped rails. A few blocks should then be glued in the inside angle, which also adds to the general strength of the stand.

The pediment is fairly straightforward. The mouldings would, of course, be cut from solid material in the first instance, and then moulded prior to being mitred and glued into the face of the pediment. This is a much more economical method than that of cutting the mouldings out of thick material, and then gluing them down to the top edges of the pediment. An enlarged detail of the ornament for this part is shown in Fig. 349. Part of this is cut out or pierced after the veneering has been done, and then the front part is carved up as indicated in the enlarged detail.

Finally, it should be said that oxidised-silver finish in the fittings is admirable, and that the polishing of this piece would present a fine effect if slightly dulled with pumice powder to take away the glossy effect.

Music Cupboard, Figs. 355 to 362. — This cabinet or cupboard is not difficult to make. Oak would be a very suitable material, and the sides, top, and back can be $\frac{3}{4}$ in. thick, as can also the door and surrounding frame. At each angle is a post $1\frac{3}{4}$ in. square, rebated to receive the angle of the carcase. This rebate facilitates the construction of the corners, as the meeting pieces need only be butt-jointed or mitred, and the necessity for complicated dovetailed joints is dispensed with. The top should be cut to receive the ends of the posts, although this is not absolutely indispensable and, if properly housed, great strength and rigidity are ensured.

On the lower parts of the corner posts is introduced a

little turning, while in the square blocks just above the turned feet, mortices are cut to receive a shelf, which may be ½ in. to ⅝ in. thick, which will be found useful in practice.

The sides are framed and panelled or they could be each in one flush piece. As it is improbable that the back will be seen, it can be left plain.

Fig. 355.—Music cupboard

The lower part of the cabinet is finished with a small moulding planted on all four sides, as will be found clearly shown in Fig. 362.

The door is framed with mortice-and-tenon joints, and is rebated for the lead lights. Lead cames about ⅜ in. wide give a good effect, and various patterns of wood bars could

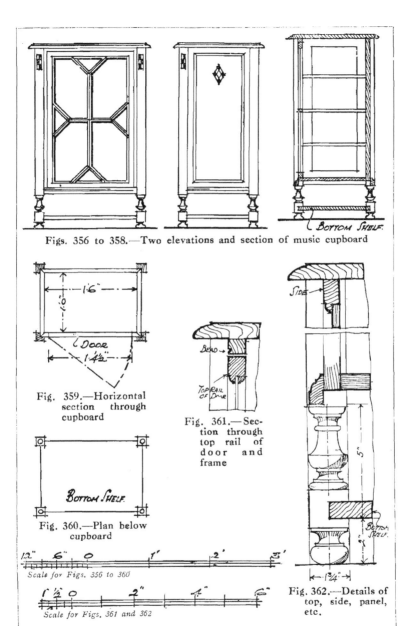

Figs. 356 to 358.—Two elevations and section of music cupboard

Fig. 359.—Horizontal section through cupboard

Fig. 360.—Plan below cupboard

Fig. 361.—Section through top rail of door and frame

Fig. 362.—Details of top, side, panel, etc.

Scale for Figs. 356 to 360

Scale for Figs. 361 and 362

be employed, one such being suggested in Fig. 356 on the preceding page. The shelves are ½ in. thick, and may be secured to fillets on the sides.

The optional inlay shown on the front of the corner posts and on the side panels is of holly and ebony.

The door is hung with small brass butts, and has a turnbuckle fastening with swivel drop handle.

Modern - style Music Cabinet, Figs. 363 to 373.—This small piece of furniture is an example of the style of design that aims at producing a pleasing effect by means of simple forms and construction, combined with good proportions, rather than by enrichment.

Fig. 363.—Modern-style Music Cabinet

Four legs constitute the main supports, 1¼ in. square at the tops, and each having its two inner sides vertical. The other sides, however, are tapered in to ⅞ in. square near the floor, where curved feet may be formed of nearly the full 1¼ in. square as shown; but the result will be almost as good, and the work much simpler, if the taper is merely continued down to the floor. The legs are 2 ft. 9 in. long, with extra at the tops for tenoned joints into two horizontal bearers 1¼ in. square which run along the front and back edges of the top as at D on the front view, or as shown in section at E E (Fig. 366). These bearers have an extreme length of 1 ft. 10 in., with shaped ends as shown at D. Two legs are tenoned into the front and two into the back bearers 1 ft. 2¼ in. apart; and then 8 in. up from the floor, 1-in. square

Music Cabinets

bearers F (Fig. 364) and G (Fig. 366) are fitted with tenoned joints.

The sides are next prepared with similar bearers showing a length of 11¼ in. at the same level, and one 1¼ in. square at the top connecting the front and back bearers with the

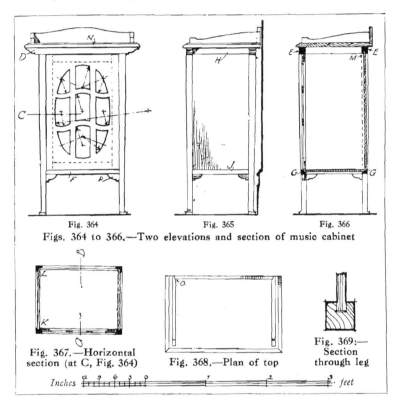

Figs. 364 to 366.—Two elevations and section of music cabinet

Fig. 367.—Horizontal section (at C, Fig. 364)

Fig. 368.—Plan of top

Fig. 369:— Section through leg

shaped ends (*see* H and J, Fig. 365). All these parts are jointed into the legs, completing the loose carcase of the cabinet, which must not be joined up until the framework has been rebated and grooved, in some cases like a panel and in others like a picture-frame (all as indicated by the section and plan, Figs. 366 and 367), to receive the sides, which should be put in first, fitting into a groove at K and a

K

rebate at L. These side panels fit into a groove in the top side bearers, and a rebate about $\frac{3}{4}$ in. wide and $\frac{1}{2}$ in. deep in the bottom bearers.

The back is then prepared and fitted into a groove in the back bearer (*see* M in Fig. 366) and rebates along the three other edges. The bottom piece is next tightly fitted into the remaining parts of the rebates in the sides and back, and also into a narrower one along the front, and serves to keep the side and back panels in position at their lower ends, while their tops cannot move from the grooves prepared for them. These parts may suitably be about $\frac{3}{8}$ in. in thickness and the whole can be firmly fixed together at this stage.

A $\frac{5}{8}$-in. shelf with simple moulded edge on three sides and measuring 1 ft. $10\frac{1}{2}$ in. by 1 ft. $3\frac{1}{2}$ in. over-all is next secured on top of the upper set of bearers (*see* N, Fig. 364), overhanging about $\frac{7}{8}$ in. at the back. Grooves are worked 1 ft. 7 in. apart along the sides, and a rebate along the back edge, to receive curved back and side pieces to complete the top in conformity with the design. These pieces are shown in detail in Figs. 372 and 373, and require rebating together as at O in Fig. 368. The back rises $3\frac{1}{2}$ in. in the middle, while the sides are not more than $2\frac{1}{4}$ in. at their higher ends.

Six shaped brackets $2\frac{1}{2}$ in. long by $1\frac{1}{2}$ in. high (Fig. 370) are fixed under the junction of the lower bearers with the legs, as at P (Fig. 364), finishing the whole except for the door, which latter may have a front all in one piece, 1 ft. $11\frac{1}{2}$ in. by 1 ft. $2\frac{1}{4}$ in. and from $\frac{3}{16}$ in. to $\frac{3}{8}$ in. thick, as convenient (fretwood might be used). The openings are marked out with compasses or with string as described for the oval table in Chapter XXV, using a centre line along and across the door, on which the outer ellipse may be set out. It measures 1 ft. 7 in. and 11 in. greatest length and breadth, the small ends being set out from points 5 in. above and below the centre, and the long sides from points 1 ft. 1 in. to the right and left of the centre of the door. The ellipse may then be divided vertically with two upright bars $1\frac{1}{8}$ in. wide and a little less than 3 in. apart in the centre, and crossed from side to side with two bars each set out from three centres, as indicated in Fig. 364. The middle curve of the upper

Music Cabinets

bar is struck from the centre of the door with the smaller radius of 4 in., and given this, it might be simplest to leave the other small curves to be set out on the work, taking the illustration as a guide. Of course, these curves can be set out freehand if preferred.

The compartments are fretted out, and the front edges slightly rounded. A frame at least $\frac{1}{2}$ in. thick, preferably of

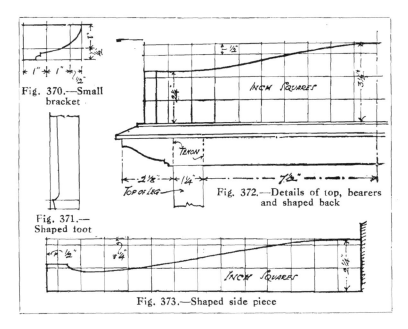

Fig. 370.—Small bracket

Fig. 371.—Shaped foot

Fig. 372.—Details of top, bearers and shaped back

Fig. 373.—Shaped side piece

oak and as wide as possible, is prepared with halved joints at its corners, and cramped round the inside of the door as a stiffening, as indicated by the dotted lines in Fig. 364. A piece of glass is then fitted behind the front of the door, either in a rebate in the frame or, better, with small glazing beads.

Shelves will be required on small fillets screwed to the sides, dividing the cabinet into compartments for piano pieces, duets, songs, etc., as desired. These shelves can be quite thin, and either fixed or made to slide.

CHAPTER XIV

Draught-screens, Fire-screens, and Easels

Four-leaf Screen, Figs. 374 to 378.—Four folds or divisions make the more usual form of draught screen, although three may sometimes be preferable; and the height in each case should be about 5 ft. 9 in. or 5 ft. 6 in. The framing used should be at least $\frac{7}{8}$-in. thick. Taking first a four-fold design as shown in Figs. 374 and 375 (or, to be precise, one having four leaves, but three folds), each compartment consists of two upright stiles 2 in. wide for the outsides, into which two rails 6 in. deep are tenoned, one next the floor and the other 4 ft. 6 in. up, forming, when the top rail has also been fitted, two wide panels, the edges of which should be rebated. The lower panel is filled in with three equal widths of light panel stuff or three-ply, and a flat or rounded fillet (Fig. 377) fixed over the joints. The top rail to each of the outer leaves is the same width as the upright sides, and the outer corners are rounded; but to the inner leaves the top is 4 in. wide, cut to the curve shown, the middle of which can be struck with a radius of 5 ft. 6 in.

The top panels are filled in with plain rebated bars to form diamonds in two cases and small squares in the others, being subsequently filled with glass, held in place by means of beads, which are also employed in the lower compartments, being fixed round the thin panels just described before the fillets are planted over the joints. The glazing bars need to be tenoned into the sides, and halved together where they intersect, as in Fig. 378. The fixing beads will look well if projecting slightly as indicated on the details, which show a rebate formed on the square frame by bradding a bead all round one side, the panel or glass being then inserted and secured with a similar bead on the other side.

Three-leaf Screen, Fig. 379.—Whereas a width of 2 ft. for each leaf will be found quite enough for the larger

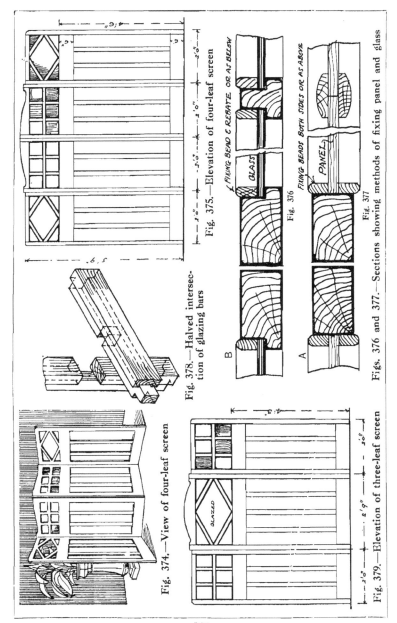

Fig. 375.—Elevation of four-leaf screen

Fig. 376

Fig. 377

Figs. 376 and 377.—Sections showing methods of fixing panel and glass

Fig. 378.—Halved intersection of glazing bars

Fig. 374.—View of four-leaf screen

Fig. 379.—Elevation of three-leaf screen

screen already described, the triple pattern (Fig. 379) might well have the centre compartment wider. In this case the diamond might be placed in the middle, the curve in the top rail above it being struck with a radius of 2 ft. 4 in., and the panel below being divided into four parts. The proportion also will be improved if the wide rail under the glass is 3 in. lower than in the first pattern as shown.

As an alternative, the lower parts might contain compo-board covered each side with artistic canvas, on top of which the fillets would be applied as before.

Special screen hinges are sold for the purpose of folding both to back and front, or for a single movement ordinary butts would suffice.

Fire-screens, Figs. 380 to 382. — The fire-screen shown by Fig. 380, can easily be made from 1-in. square framing, tenoned or halved together, tapered and rounded where shown and filled with plain glazing bars and clear or obscured glass, or alternatively with thin laths over a backing of silk or other coloured material.

Fig. 381 shows a similar screen, each leaf having two rebated panels, the lower of which is filled in with a pleated silk curtain with or without glass, while the narrow top panel has a fretwork pattern set out with compasses as in Fig. 382, and very accurately cut from three-ply mahogany, etc. Often these screens are made with the curtain easily detachable, so that in winter the fire may be seen through the glazing, which will, however, screen off much of the heat.

Lead-glazed Fire-screen, Figs. 383 to 385. — The third design of fire-screen is of the non-folding class, and consists of a simple frame as before, with the sides tenoned into shaped legs $1\frac{1}{4}$ in. thick, as in Fig. 384, and a moulded capping at the top. The narrow panel under this capping is similar to the one in the previous example, but without the complete circles there shown, and the lower panel is intended to receive plain or decorative leaded glass (*see* page 286 for instructions) or a piece of bevelled clear plate, which can have a curtain or not as preferred.

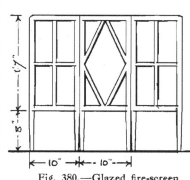

Fig. 380.—Glazed fire-screen

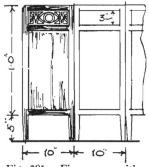

Fig. 381.—Fire-screen with fretwork and pleated silk

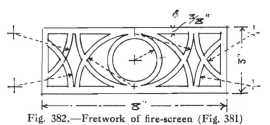

Fig. 382.—Fretwork of fire-screen (Fig. 381)

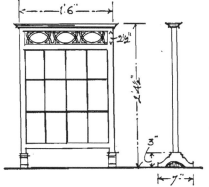

Figs. 384 and 385.—Lead-glazed fire-screen

Fig. 383.—Lead-glazed fire-screen

Drawing-room Easel, Figs. 386 to 390, and Fig. 396.—The easels illustrated in this chapter are suitable for supporting pictures and engravings, and can be used also as portfolio stands. They may be made of ordinary pine, kauri pine, or whitewood, painted, enamelled, or gilded. If preferred, mahogany, stained and polished, or oak, fumigated or stained green and polished, or American walnut may be used. As a preliminary it is advisable to get out a full-size drawing of half of the design. For the first easel shown (Figs. 386 and 387) the following sizes will be suitable: Outer stiles, 1$\frac{3}{8}$ in. wide at the top, tapering to 1 in. (front view), and 1 in., tapering to, say, $\frac{3}{4}$ in. for the side view. The pediment A is $\frac{3}{4}$ in. thick. The rails B and C can be about 1 in. or $\frac{3}{4}$ in. The terminals D are the same in section at the bottom end as the top of the outer stiles. The two central upright rails should be a shade thinner than B and C, about 1 in. wide on the face and 1$\frac{3}{4}$ in. apart. To enable the ornamental brackets to be copied correctly, enlargements spaced in squares are shown in Figs. 388, 389 and 396. The same number of squares should be copied on to the full-size drawing. To transfer the patterns on to the wood, previous to cutting with the saw, prick through the outlines with a thick needle, or make a tracing of the pattern and paste it on the wood.

In constructing the easel, the pediment and rails are tenoned into the outer stiles as in the details; but must not go through to the outer side. To avoid weakening the stiles, the pediment and bottom rail are connected with double tenons (*see* Figs. 388 and 396). The inner stiles are slightly tenoned into the rails. To break the joint of the terminals D square pieces E (Fig. 388), $\frac{3}{4}$ in. thick, with rounded edges, are fixed on the top ends of the stiles. These may be nailed on, and the dowels on the terminals will further secure them. To get the correct angles for the shoulders of the cross rails, place the rails in position on the working drawing; then place the outer stiles over them, and mark with a chisel or sharp-pointed marker. The shoulder on the other side of the rails is obtained by squaring across the edges and then connecting the two lines. A $\frac{1}{4}$-in.

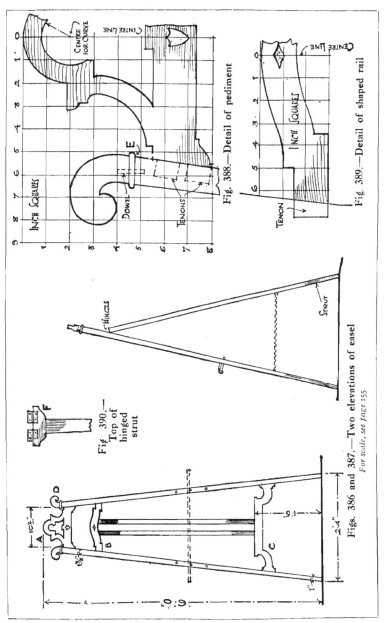

Fig. 388.—Detail of pediment

Fig. 389.—Detail of shaped rail

Fig. 390.—Top of hinged strut

Figs. 386 and 387.—Two elevations of easel
For scale, see page 155

chisel will do for the mortices. The shaped parts must be cut with the fretsaw, after the mortising and tenoning are completed.

First put the framing together dry, and mark all the parts so that they can be replaced correctly. When finally gluing, especially if the weather be cold, warm all the tenons, to prevent the glue from chilling before the framing is cramped together.

The back strut for supporting the easel in position is shown in Fig. 387, and in part elevation by Fig. 390. It is $\frac{7}{8}$ in. thick and 2 in. wide at the top, tapering to $1\frac{1}{2}$ in. at the bottom. The shaped head piece F is about 7 in. by 2 in., and mortised to receive the tenon on the top of the strut. Two brass butt hinges, about 2 in. long, are fixed to the head piece and to the back of the easel, and a length of brass chain as indicated in Fig. 387 should be attached. Holes as shown in Fig. 386, $\frac{1}{2}$ in. in diameter, are made in the outer stiles for the pegs, which should be about $3\frac{1}{2}$ in. long. For sketches, etc., less in length than the width of the easel, a lath about 3 in. wide by $\frac{5}{8}$ in. thick should be placed on the pegs, as indicated by the dotted lines in the same figure.

Another Easel, Figs. 391 to 395.—For the second design of easel (Fig. 391), the outer stiles G are $1\frac{1}{4}$ in. at the top, and taper to the bottom to $\frac{3}{4}$ in. on the face, and 1 in. tapering to $\frac{3}{4}$ in. on the side. The rails H, J, and K and the uprights L and M are 1 in. square. The fretwork pediment (Figs. 392 and 393), two arches as at N and one larger one at O can be $\frac{5}{8}$ in. or $\frac{3}{4}$ in. thick, and are not tenoned in position, but the central upright band of geometric fretwork can be very much thinner, and should be either grooved or rebated into the uprights L and M as in Figs. 394 and 395. The remainder of the measurements can be taken from the design. When making the framing, the horizontal rails should first be tenoned into the side stiles and put together without glue. The uprights are slightly tenoned at each end, the rails being mortised to receive them.

The cornice moulding is worked in one length with suitable hollow and round planes as in Fig. 393, and then mitred

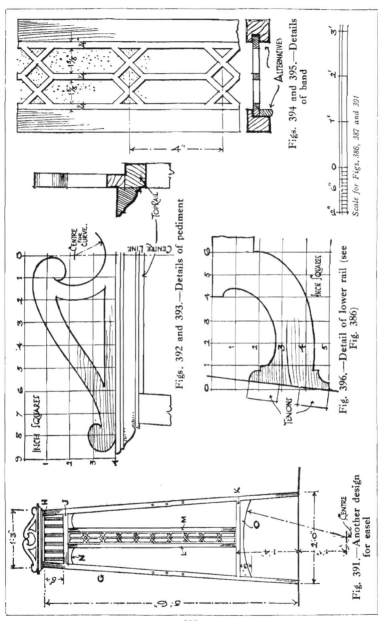

Figs. 394 and 395.—Details of band

Figs. 392 and 393.—Details of pediment

Fig. 396.—Detail of lower rail (see Fig. 386)

Fig. 391.—Another design for easel

Scale for Figs. 386, 387 and 391

and returned at the sides. The pediment is dowelled to the top rail, and the joint covered by the cornice. The balusters under the cornice are $\frac{1}{2}$ in. square, and set diagonally in position; or, if preferred, they could be quite suitably round or square-turned. Other details are the same as described for the first example.

CHAPTER XV

Hanging Cabinets or Cupboards

First Example, Figs. 397 to 406.—Probably no piece of furniture is more popular with craftsmen or more effective in appearance than the fairly small type of hanging cupboard variously described as " medicine cupboards," " smokers' cabinets," etc., although these terms are to a great extent interchangeable. The first cupboard or cabinet illustrated (*see* Figs. 397 to 406) is particularly suitable for production in oak, but pine would serve the purpose without any modification of the design; should, however, mahogany or walnut be decided on, it would be advisable to alter the design in order to bring it more into harmony with the wood used, as will be mentioned later.

Two sides pieces (as Fig. 398) are first prepared 2 ft. 8½ in. long and 7 in. wide, cut to the hollow curve shown at the bottom, and pieces 1⅛ in. deep and 1¼ in. wide cut out of the top front corners A. The levels of the shelves are then set out on the sides, shelf B (Fig. 397) being supported on fillets bradded to the sides, and ultimately hidden by the thin spandrel C, which will be fixed under this shelf about ⅛ in. back from the front edge. Shelf D is more elaborate, having its ends cut with projecting pieces in the centre as at E, F, G and H (Fig. 404), and arranged so that either end passes through a slot cut to receive it in the vertical side pieces. The joint is secured by means of wedges pushed through smaller slots in the projecting ends, this part of the work being explained by Figs. 403 and 404.

The sides are kept at their correct distance at the top by means of a piece J (Fig. 397) 1¼ in. by 1⅛ in. high and 1ft. 7 in. long, with shaped ends as in Fig. 402 fitting into the places cut out of the sides at A (Fig. 398). Above this is a flat shelf 1 ft. 10 in. by 9 in., with a moulded or chamfered edge on the three exposed sides as in Figs. 401 and 402, and under

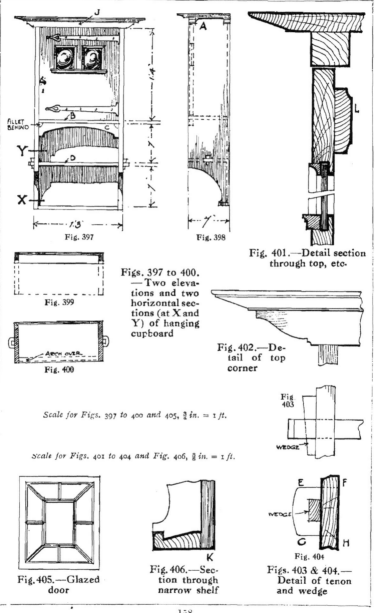

Fig. 397.

Fig. 398.

Fig. 401.—Detail section through top, etc.

Fig. 399.

Figs. 397 to 400.—Two elevations and two horizontal sections (at X and Y) of hanging cupboard

Fig. 400.

Fig. 402.—Detail of top corner

Scale for Figs. 397 to 400 and 405, ¾ in. = 1 ft.

Scale for Figs. 401 to 404 and Fig. 406, ⅜ in. = 1 ft.

Fig. 403.

Fig. 404.

Fig. 405.—Glazed door

Fig. 406.—Section through narrow shelf

Figs. 403 & 404.—Detail of tenon and wedge

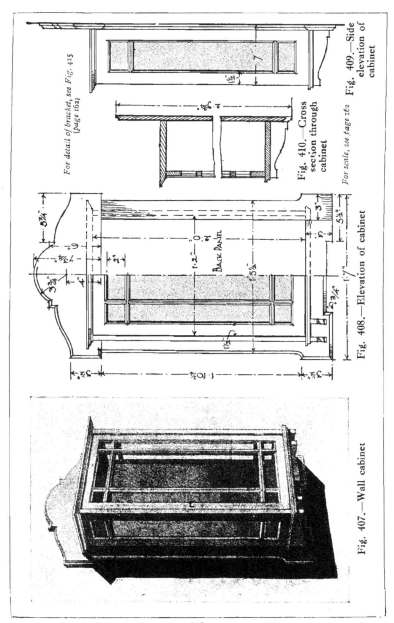

Fig. 409.—Side elevation of cabinet

Fig. 410.—Cross section through cabinet

Fig. 408.—Elevation of cabinet

Fig. 407.—Wall cabinet

this at the back next the wall is planted on a small bracket of the same projection, cut to an outline similar to the front bearer. The back might be filled in with thin tongued boarding or good three-ply, this being fitted into rebates cut in the sides. The back butts against the under-side of the top shelf, and it extends beyond the two lower shelves down to the bottom at K (Fig. 406), where a narrow shelf is fixed, this being grooved as shown in order to take photographs, etc.

The door is proposed to be made of boarding with flush joints (tongued for preference), and made to present a smooth external face. The boarding may be fixed on three small chamfered ledges as at L (Fig. 401), two "bull's-eyes" or plain squares of glass being inserted in the upper part by forming a rebated opening to take each small pane, and fixing it in position from the outside by means of very small beads arranged to project a little beyond the general surface. A rather wider rebate is employed at the bottom, in order to receive a horizontal moulding of the type shown and with returned ends.

When the door has been fitted and small stops provided for it on the inside, it can be hung with ornamental strap hinges or ordinary hinges with long sham fronts added.

In the event of mahogany or walnut being adopted for the cabinet, it would be appropriate to modify the design slightly, the customary polished surface of these woods calling for a correspondingly greater amount of detail and finish, whereas simplicity of style is eminently suited to oak. Accordingly it is thought to be more in keeping to omit the tenons and wedges to the bottom shelf, and to replace the first door with a proper framed and glazed one, with small wooden bars. The latter could be made rather decorative if desired, one simple way of doing this being shown in Fig. 405, in connection with which the reader is referred to page 26 for particulars of carrying out this kind of glazing. The interior can be fitted with pigeon-holes for letters, racks for pipes, etc., as required.

Second and Third Examples, Figs. 407 to 415.—These two examples could be effectively made without the labour usually expended on more elaborate cabinetwork.

Hanging Cabinets or Cupboards

They could be fitted with light shelving for the purpose of storing a few special volumes, or as wall cabinets. In both these designs the whole might be made out of ½-in. stuff. The back of the design shown by Fig. 408 could be framed together with mortise-and-tenon joints, and worked round cleanly cut, with a small ovolo or other moulding, and grooved on the inside edge to receive a light back panel.

The sides of the case should be tenon-framed, glued, and screwed to the back with clean-cut and worked bracket-shaped foot (see Fig. 415) and two similar brackets under the bottom of the case. If preferred, the work could be simplified by using a plain solid piece for the side instead of glazing as shown.

The top is either moulded as shown on the solid, or else finished with 1-in. cyma-recta moulding mitred at the angles.

Fig. 411.—Wall cabinet

The door to be ½-in. framed, moulded, and rebated to take glass with small moulded sash bars. The bottom has a small moulding either worked solid or planted on, and shelves can be fitted inside as required.

The foregoing would also apply to the design illustrated by Figs. 411 to 415, excepting that the glass door is shown with light leaded glazing. If this glazing is too difficult for the worker, a very simple and effective substitute could

L

be bought for a few pence, in the shape of reeded lead strips of a very light section. It can be obtained in small rolls of a few yards, and can be easily cut and curved and fixed in any pattern desired to a plain sheet of glass with any strong

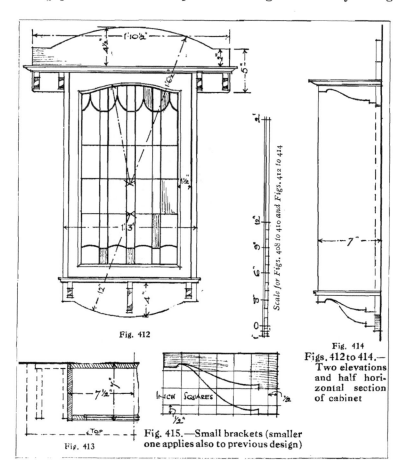

Fig. 412

Fig. 413

Fig. 414

Figs. 412 to 414.—Two elevations and half horizontal section of cabinet

Fig. 415.—Small brackets (smaller one applies also to previous design)

adhesive before the glass is fixed with wood beads to the frame, this giving a very light and airy effect to the work. This might also take the place of the wooden bars of design No. 1, the fitting of which is sometimes more than the amateur

Hanging Cabinets or Cupboards 163

can manage. In this case, it is less essential that the back be framed and it could, if preferred, be composed of several widths tongued or dowelled together.

Fourth Example: Smoker's Cabinet, Figs. 416 to 420.—In this hanging cabinet, the sides are stop-housed to receive the bottom, and the top ends are also left $\frac{3}{16}$ in. longer

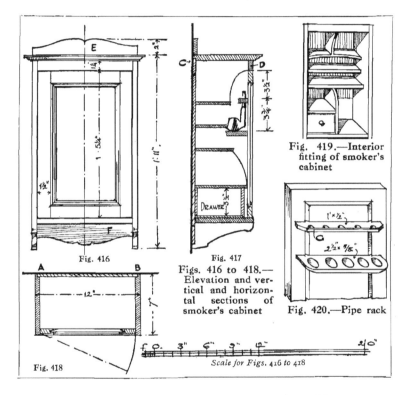

Fig. 419.—Interior fitting of smoker's cabinet

Figs. 416 to 418.—Elevation and vertical and horizontal sections of smoker's cabinet

Fig. 420.—Pipe rack

to house into the top. The back edges of the sides A and B (Fig. 418) and the inside edge of the top C (Fig. 417) should be rebated as shown to receive the back. The top is moulded along the under-side as shown in section in Fig. 417. The bottom ends of the sides should be cut to the shape shown in the same figure, or to any other suitable contour. The rail D (Fig. 417) is fitted in between the sides, and screwed

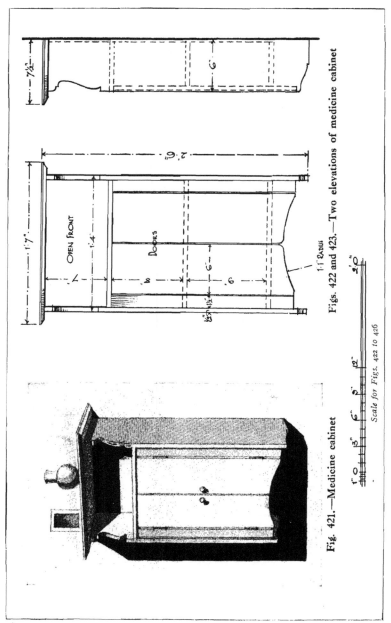

Fig. 421.—Medicine cabinet

Figs. 422 and 423.—Two elevations of medicine cabinet

Hanging Cabinets or Cupboards 165

into the top from the back. The top rail E and the bottom edge of the back F (Fig. 416) should be shaped as shown.

The door is of the ordinary construction and a plough groove is run along the inside edges to receive a corresponding tongue on the edge of the panel. The back of the panel should be flush with the inside of the framing. A moulding

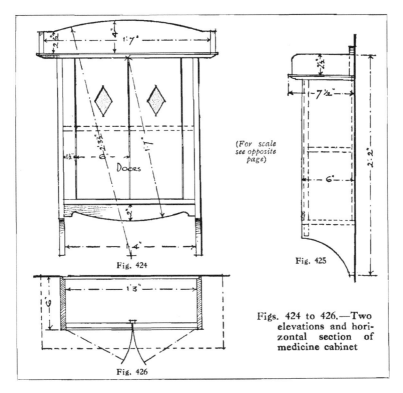

Figs. 424 to 426.—Two elevations and horizontal section of medicine cabinet

is mitred round the front of the panel as shown. The door is set back a little away from the face, and hung with ordinary hinges.

The interior arrangement of the cabinet will be understood from Fig. 419, and the spacing of the shelves can be obtained from Fig. 417, or they can be made to meet special requirements. The various pieces are just butted and nailed together, and a small drawer should be made for the bottom division.

Fig. 420 shows the arrangement for holding the pipes on the back of the door, and requires little explanation. A piece of leather G is nailed round the edge to hold the pipe-stems in position. The two pieces should be glued to the back of the door, and then screwed diagonally at the ends into the stiles.

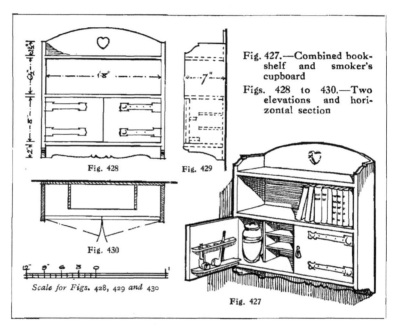

Fig. 427.—Combined book-shelf and smoker's cupboard

Figs. 428 to 430.—Two elevations and horizontal section

Two Medicine Cabinets, Figs. 421 to 426.—Two designs for inexpensive and easily-made bedroom hanging medicine cabinets are illustrated on pages 164 and 165.

Several lengths of 6-in. by ½-in. board being provided, they should be cut up into the required sizes, the curved portions being worked with a keyhole- or fret-saw, as convenient.

The doors are purposely arranged to be made with the same width of wood, so as to be easily constructed, obviating

Hanging Cabinets or Cupboards

any necessity for panels, dovetailing, etc. A pair of ornamental strap hinges on each door, such as those shown on pages 158 and 166 in this chapter, will add to the general effect. Full dimensions are given in the illustrations. White enamel would be very suitable as a finish.

Combined Bookshelf and Smoker's Cupboard, Figs. 427 to 430.—The final cupboard shown in this chapter needs but little description. It might be of $\frac{1}{2}$-in. oak or other wood, and the dimensions given must be taken as suggestions only, it not being essential to adhere to them. The shelves at the top will serve very well for a few popular reprints, and the inside can be fitted up for cigar boxes, etc., if desired, and pipe racks similar to that in Fig. 420 (page 163) attached to the insides of the doors. These latter are shown decorated with ornamental hinge-fronts, but can, of course, be plain, panelled or glazed if desired.

CHAPTER XVI

Corner Cupboards

The Reproduction of an Antique Corner Cupboard, Figs. 431 to 438.—For the antique cupboard shown on the opposite page, old wood should be used if possible. The top, bottom, and three shelves, also the two backs, are all of deal, finished $\frac{1}{2}$ in. thick. The dimensions are given in the figures. The front pilasters are of $3\frac{1}{4}$-in. by $\frac{3}{4}$-in. oak with a small bead run on the hinge edge. The front edge of the bottom is increased to $1\frac{1}{4}$ in. thickness by fixing on a piece of deal, A (Fig. 438), to be faced with the plinth moulding. A piece of deal $3\frac{1}{2}$ in. thick is fixed on the top in three sections, as B in Fig. 434, flush with the curved edge of the top piece; it is indicated at C in Fig. 438, and is intended to be faced with the cornice mould as shown. The small $\frac{3}{16}$-in. beading is fixed first on the lower edge with glue and needle points, then a cross-banding of mahogany veneer $1\frac{1}{2}$ in. wide and another beading $\frac{3}{8}$ in. wide.

The cornice mould is of mahogany, the grain running vertical. It is worked in a straight length, backed up with a batten of deal, D. To fit it to the curved front, it is sawn into $1\frac{1}{2}$-in. sections as at E in Fig. 434, and neatly fitted and glued piece by piece. When set it is trimmed and smoothed up. For the small blocks or "dentils" a length of stuff must be got out, $\frac{1}{2}$ in. by $\frac{3}{8}$ in. section, sawn up into $\frac{3}{8}$-in. blocks, and fixed with glue $\frac{1}{8}$ in. apart as in Fig. 437.

The doors should be of well-figured oak board 11 in. wide, ripped down into three lengths and jointed by means of oak cross-tongues at a suitable angle to form the curve (*see* Fig. 435). A slip of mahogany is fixed on the right-hand door; it is sunk on the face as in Fig. 436. It should finish nicely against the mouldings top and bottom as in Fig. 438.

If made in old wood it may be oiled over and french-polished

Corner Cupboards

until the mahogany grain is filled up; but a thick polish must be avoided for the oak. If made in new wood, it can be darkened to give the appearance of age by wiping over with a solution of bichromate of potash. The inside may be painted white, or stained and given a coat of thin varnish. As a matter of fact it will probably be preferred

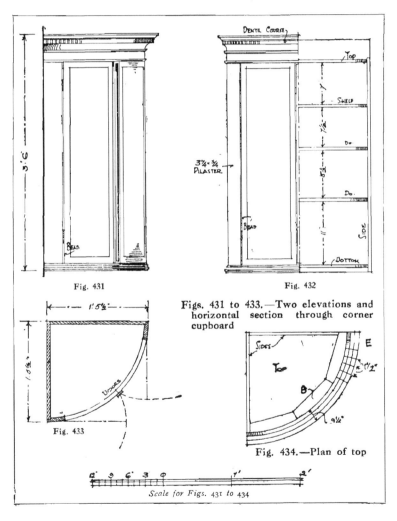

Figs. 431 to 433.—Two elevations and horizontal section through corner cupboard

Fig. 434.—Plan of top

Scale for Figs. 431 to 434

to make the exposed faces of the cupboard entirely in one variety of wood, but it will be understood that with old material this course was not adopted. A line of inlay on the doors as in Figs. 431 and 432 will be an effective finish.

Corner Cupboard to Hang or Stand, Figs. 439 to 446.—This cupboard is adaptable as a china-cabinet, as

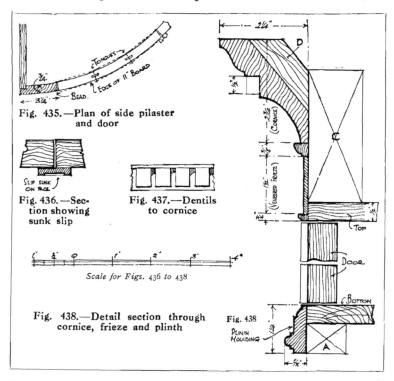

Fig. 435.—Plan of side pilaster and door

Fig. 436.—Section showing sunk slip

Fig. 437.—Dentils to cornice

Scale for Figs. 436 to 438

Fig. 438.—Detail section through cornice, frieze and plinth

Fig. 438

illustrated by Figs. 445 and 446. In making the cupboard, first set out a full-size plan of the front and sides as shown by Fig. 441; this will give the general size and construction. The return pieces at A and B should be set out at right-angles to the sides C and D.

To construct the sides of the cupboard, prepare three stiles and four rails 3 in. wide, and one stile 2 in. wide for the side C, all 1 in. thick, and of the necessary lengths. Mortise,

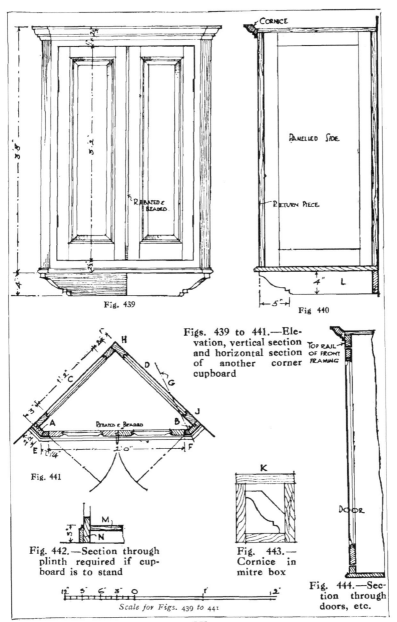

Fig. 439

Fig. 440

Fig. 441

Figs. 439 to 441.—Elevation, vertical section and horizontal section of another corner cupboard

Fig. 442.—Section through plinth required if cupboard is to stand

Fig. 443.—Cornice in mitre box

Fig. 444.—Section through doors, etc.

tenon, and plough for the panel, and rebate out to form the tongue on the two front stiles of the sides which fits into the pieces A and B as shown in Fig. 441. Frame the width of the front framing E F in a similar manner and perfectly square; then glue up and stand the work aside to dry. The panels of the side framing having been prepared to the required size, these also may be glued up, cleaned off, and shot to their proper widths, and tongued. The stiles of the front framing will require to be bevelled to form the angles at E and F; to do this, set a bevel, keeping the stock to the front horizontal line, and the blade to the extended line G (Fig. 441), and bevel the stiles accordingly. Next prepare the return pieces as at A and B, which should be $2\frac{1}{2}$ in. wide and ploughed to receive the tongue on the stiles of the side framing; these also must be bevelled and glued to the stiles of the front framing, and, when dry, cleaned up to form the angle as shown. The front and sides may now be put together, and secured with screws through the stiles at H and through the stiles as at J into the return pieces.

The shelves may be fixed on fillets cut in between the stiles and fixed to the panels. They should be $\frac{3}{4}$ in. thick. The top may be nailed on and cleaned off flush with the back of the framing as in Fig. 440.

An enlarged section of the cornice is shown in Figs. 443 and 444, while Fig. 443 is a section of the mitre box. This must be made in the clear of the sides—that is, the inside must be made equal to the projection of the cornice.

Thus in the present instance the width of the inside of the box must be about $2\frac{1}{4}$ in. Therefore prepare the bottom 1 in. thick, and nail on the sides wide enough to take the moulding, as shown in Fig. 443; the sides must be kept parallel by means of strips nailed on the top, as shown at K in Fig. 443. Now with the same bevel as used for the front framing and from the front side of the box, mark the top edges square down the lines; with a panel saw cut through the sides to the bottom, and put in the moulding as shown. Cut off the moulding, and when placed in position it will be perpendicular and of the required angle. Then cut the other piece off to the proper length and to the opposite angle, fix

Corner Cupboards

with blocks and glue as previously described, and when dry the return pieces can be fitted to the front cornice.

Fig. 440 at L shows the type of angle bracket proposed to be used to support the cupboard; the back end is dovetailed at the angle, and the whole should be 1 in. in thickness and 4 in. wide. This may be fixed with brass cups and screws to a well-plugged wall. The bottom should be glued up to the necessary width, and allowed to project $1\frac{1}{4}$

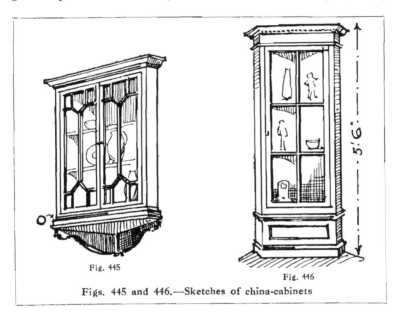

Figs. 445 and 446.—Sketches of china-cabinets

in. in front of the framing, as shown in Fig. 440, and a small moulding worked on. The moulding may be screwed through the bottom into the bottom rails of the front and side framing or, as indicated, worked on the solid bottom.

To make the doors, prepare the stiles and top rails 2 in. wide by 1 in. thick, and the bottom rails 3 in. wide. An ovolo is worked on the stiles and rails as shown in Fig. 439, therefore when setting out this must be allowed for on the rails to be scribed over the stiles. The panels should be $\frac{5}{8}$ in. thick, sunk and bevelled.

If the work is to be in polished hardwood, the doors should be rebated for the panels instead of being ploughed, as it will be necessary to polish the panels before they are put in. When fixing the cupboard, screw through the bottom into the bracket. Screw on brass plates for fixing to the wall at the top.

Should it be preferred to have such a cupboard standing upon the floor, the top can easily be finished off flush, projecting a little beyond the cornice, and the base can be arranged as in Fig. 442, where M represents the bottom and N the bottom rail of the flat framing, having a 3-in. skirting or plinth added as a suitable simple finish.

The cupboard can easily be developed into something more of the cabinet class : for instance, Fig. 445 shows it treated with a base moulding O, more elaborately shaped brackets and decorative glazing in the doors ; while Fig. 446 suggests an elongated form standing on the floor and rising to say 5 ft. 6 in. or so. In this case, the cornice is amplified by means of a frieze and necking, one glazed door is substituted for the others and the plain panelled base can be either fixed or made to open as a cupboard.

CHAPTER XVII

Stools

Old-fashioned Stool or Hall Seat, Figs. 447 to 452.—The illustrations on the next page show a small walnut stool of French sixteenth-century workmanship.

Its supports comprise two sloping ends 10 in. by 1 in. and 1 ft. 8½ in., long, which in the original are carved in low relief; but as most craftsmen will prefer a less ornate treatment, it has not been thought desirable to take up valuable space with particulars of this decoration. Between the supports are (a) two turned rails of about 1¾ in. greatest diameter and 1 ft. 5 in. long, with their centres 5 in. above the floor level and 6 in. apart horizontally; (b) two pieces as at x in Fig. 448, size 2¼ in. by ⅝ in., which are tenoned about 5¼ in. apart into the tops of supports, which should come to within 1 ft. 1 in. of each other at this level.

In setting out the joints allowance must be made for the fact that the supports are not at right angles to the horizontal pieces. On top of the whole framework is fixed a 1-in. seat 1 ft. 8½ in. by 11 in., having a simple moulded edge.

The modern variation shown by Figs. 449 and 450 should appeal to many who might not care for the original as it stands. The suggested shaping and piercing of the ends is set out in Fig. 449. The top and bearers below it remain unchanged, but in place of the turned rails flat square ones are employed, curved at their ends, holed for wedges, and fitted through slots in the end supports, all as at Y in Fig. 451. Fig. 452 shows it in side elevation, with a wedge in position.

If thought preferable, the turned rails might be retained, and they could be fixed in position by means of projecting pins turned on their ends and let into the supports.

Louis XIV. Stool, Figs. 453 to 457.—This walnut stool is a distinctive piece of work, quite free from the superabundance of ornament sometimes associated with French designs. It consists principally of four square-turned legs of striking contour, each built up of four different sections in the height, presumably dowelled together, united at the bottom by curved diagonal cross ties sunk on their upper

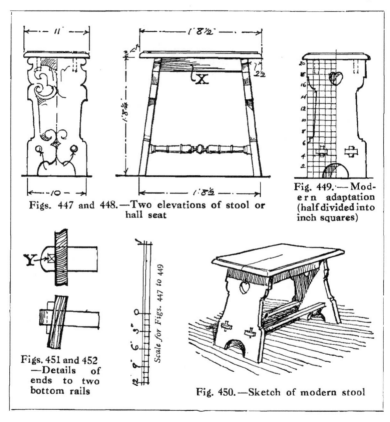

Figs. 447 and 448.—Two elevations of stool or hall seat

Fig. 449.—Modern adaptation (half divided into inch squares)

Figs. 451 and 452—Details of ends to two bottom rails

Fig. 450.—Sketch of modern stool

faces, and having a thin carved boss applied in the centre to conceal the joint between the two. The ends of the ties come rather awkwardly in relation to the square legs, at least when judged by modern standards, this being due to the fact that the curved tie had to start away from the leg (on plan, that is to say) neither parallel to any of its sides nor yet at an angle of 45°; this difficulty, however, has been circumvented in the suggestions for a modern version which follow later. Below the ends of the ties are circular-turned feet, very simply carved into flutings, while at the top there is an oblong seat rather scantily padded and covered with hide, secured by means of brass-headed nails at $\frac{3}{4}$ in. centre to centre. As the date officially given is late seven-

Fig. 453.—A Louis XIV. stool

teenth or early eighteenth century, there is very little likelihood of this upholstering being coeval with the frame.

The following deals with the making of a stool as near as possible to the original design, but avoiding various complications that might otherwise arise, and also deleting the carved portions. For the exposed work, walnut or mahogany with a dull polish finish are desirable, although almost any of the cheap woods could be employed and stained. The legs are square-turned between the seat and the tie, but circular below the latter, as shown in Fig. 454, from which the contour can easily be enlarged if the various dimensions are followed. In the original, the leg is built up of as many as four parts, but with a view to simplifying the work these are reduced to three, as in Fig. 454. At the top is a turned piece 5 in. long including a 1-in. stub-tenon at the top, and cut out of a piece say $3\frac{3}{4}$ in. square. The curves should be rather flat than convex, and a mortise must be formed on the under-side to take another stub-tenoned end, this time belonging to the top of the plain square tapered shaft A. In the original the sides of this are not quite straight but have a slight bulge or curve outwards in the middle. The lower end of this shaft is also stub-tenoned for $\frac{1}{2}$ in. or so, and fitted tightly into a mortise in the tie, the setting out of which is described later. At the bottom is the round-turned foot, from which it is suggested that the simpler carving might be omitted; it is fixed to the under-side of the tie by means of a long screw inserted through the bottom of the mortise last mentioned before it is filled by the tenon.

The general form of the ties as now proposed will be understood from Fig. 455; the central carved boss is purposely omitted. This work should be carefully set out on paper, full size, first of all drawing the centre lines B C and D E, and then marking off from them the centres of the various curves, as dimensioned in the figure and indicated by diagonal crosses, and also marking the centres of the legs in the same way. Then it will be simple to draw in with compasses the curved parts of the ties, making them $1\frac{3}{8}$ in. wide throughout, and to fill in the short straight portions. Fig. 455 shows them sunk on the top face as in the original (*see* Fig. 457), where the sinking terminates in a segment as at F; this, however, could be simplified to a square end as at the other corner, or deleted entirely, in order to avoid a rather tricky piece of work.

This curved work must really consist of two diagonal ties, halved together in the centre in order that they may cross each other. Fig. 457 shows the finished thickness to be $\frac{7}{8}$ in. As each tie may be cut out of a piece measuring 21 in. by 3 in., they really make the most of a comparatively small piece of wood. Fig. 456 shows one of the ties set out

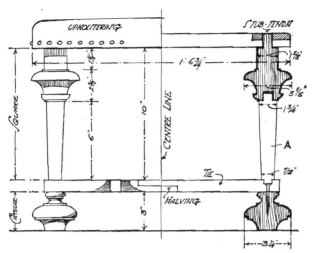

Fig. 454.—Part elevation and part vertical section of Louis XIV. stool

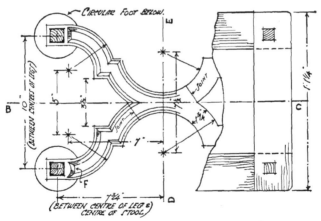

Fig. 455.—Part plan of ties and part plan of top framework

within the area just mentioned, and this should coincide exactly with the contour in Fig. 455, with the exception that the curve G meets the corresponding one H on the centre-line, forming an ogee curve broken by the projections J and K. The exact length and also the position of the mortices to secure the legs (indicated by the small square at either end) are obtained by the lines L and M, which of course represent the centre lines taken through the legs. The shaded portion of the tie should be cut away down to the middle of the thickness for the halved joint with the other

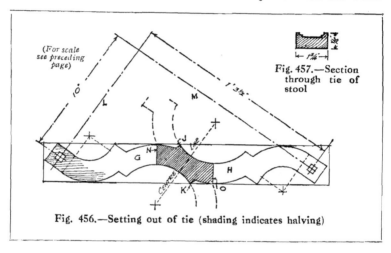

Fig. 457.—Section through tie of stool

Fig. 456.—Setting out of tie (shading indicates halving)

tie, and it is taken to the straight lines as at N and O as well as J and K rather than kept to the actual curve, in order to avoid any feather-edged portions, which would be difficult to finish accurately and would be liable to splinter afterwards; without the arrangement shown, these would be bound to occur, but as proposed it will be noticed that all the cut angles are comparatively obtuse, and consequently easier to fit against the parts they are intended to meet. This is especially helpful if the top surface is sunk as in Fig. 457, as it would be almost impossible to work across a raking joint, and any sinking decided upon should not be done until the two ties have been fixed together. The straight lines at

J, K, N and O should be set out radiating towards the centres of the various curves.

The framework for the flat seat is intended to be made simply of $2\frac{3}{4}$-in. by 1-in. stuff, halved together at the corners, which should be slightly rounded off, as should also the top outer angles. A stub-tenon is already provided at the head of each leg, and this should fit into a mortise going right through the halved corners and be finished off flat on the top. This should hold the entire framework in position without any trouble, and the stool will then be ready for the upholstery.

CHAPTER XVIII

Dining-room and Drawing-room Chairs

Dining Chair with Loose Seat, Figs. 458 to 463.—If strongly framed and simply designed, ordinary small hardwood chairs will not be found particularly difficult to construct. The first example here given (*see* Fig. 458) may be taken as a model capable of many alterations. It has a lift-out padded seat, covered with real or imitation leather, and its extreme simplicity makes it very suitable for execution in oak. The front legs are square at the top, 7 in. below which they taper as shown; the back legs are $1\frac{1}{4}$ in. on the face, cut out of a 3-in. width to the outline given in Fig. 463, or with care two legs could be obtained from a 5-in. width. They should be cut rather on the full side, and reduced to the exact curve when the whole is framed up, a template being useful for testing this work. The top rails of the seat are the full width of the legs (if the lift-out seat is desired) and rounded on the outer edges; the lower rails, however, need only be, say, 1 in. thick, and can be suitably fixed $\frac{1}{16}$ in. back from he face of the legs on all sides.

Fig. 458.—Dining chair with loose seat

The top and bottom rails of the back are $\frac{3}{4}$ in. and 1 in.

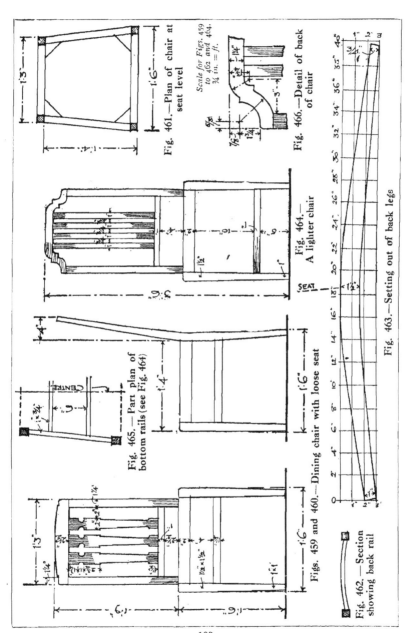

thick respectively, the former shaped as shown, and while these can both be straight if desired, it is distinctly preferable to work them to a slight curve on plan as in Fig. 462. The three shaped strips to the back could be $\frac{3}{8}$ in. or $\frac{1}{2}$ in. thick, cut to a variety of outlines and housed $\frac{1}{4}$ in. into the rails. Throughout the chair, all the joints of the framing should be neat mortise and tenons of the greatest length practicable in each position, due regard being given to the slight skew of the side rails, as in Fig. 461. The cushion would be contrived on a wood frame or plain board fitted to suit, and resting on four corner-blocks as in the last-mentioned figure; alternatively, of course, the upholstery can be arranged with webbing and springs, and the material brought over the top rails and tacked, as is often done, in which case the rail need not be as wide as the top of the leg. For setting out the work as in Fig. 460, it should be observed that the back leg in Fig. 463 will require tilting farther back until it suits the dimensions given in the figure previously mentioned.

Fig. 467.—Drawing-room chair

A Lighter Dining Chair, Figs. 464 to 466.—A somewhat lighter design has been adopted in the example in oak or mahogany shown by Figs. 464 to 466. The front legs and seat rails are as before, with the exception that the former taper downwards throughout all but the top 2 in. of their height. As an alternative applicable to practically all the designs in this chapter, the lower rails are arranged as in Fig. 465 about 5 in. above the floor level ; either one or two

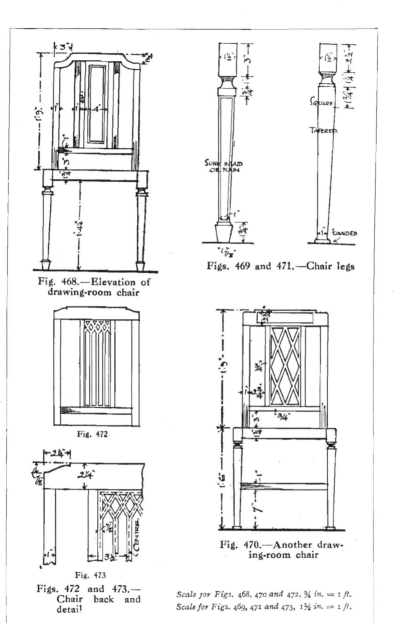

Fig. 468.—Elevation of drawing-room chair

Figs. 469 and 471.—Chair legs

Fig. 472

Fig. 473

Figs. 472 and 473.—Chair back and detail

Fig. 470.—Another drawing-room chair

Scale for Figs. 468, 470 *and* 472, ¾ *in.* = 1 *ft.*
Scale for Figs. 469, 471 *and* 473, 1½ *in.* = 1 *ft.*

cross rails can be used, and it will be found much better to set them back from the front when at so low a level, as they are otherwise rather a nuisance to the user of the chair. The back is made higher than before to suit the proportions of the design, and the back legs show only $1\frac{1}{4}$ in. on the face; they are tenoned into a shaped top rail of the same width, and with its top edges rounded off, set out in accordance with Fig. 466. This rail and the lower one can be straight or curved as in Fig. 462, and the plain upright rails to the back set closely together as shown will be found very effective in appearance, or, of course, they can be modified at the discretion of the craftsman. These chairs can easily be adapted for a padded back if preferred, this depending upon the use to which they are to be put.

Drawing-room Chair with Suggestions for Inlay, Figs. 467 to 469.—The third design is of quite an elegant type very appropriate for execution in mahogany, especially if a little inlay be introduced on the wide rail of the back (Fig. 468) and the outer faces of the front legs (Fig. 469); or these might be worked as slight sinkings below the general surface. The front legs are worked square to the design in Fig. 469, the small feet being made separately stub-tenoned and screwed from below, as in Fig. 618, page 241. The seat rails are made $1\frac{3}{4}$ in. deep, and the back legs reduced to 1 in. on the face, and made just a little thinner in contour than shown in Fig. 463. A straight or curved back can be used, and the front seat rail would look well if curved slightly forward, providing that a lift-out seat is not required. It will be noticed that it is proposed in this case to omit the rails below the seat entirely.

Drawing-room Chair with Bottom Rails, Figs. 470 and 471.—This is another chair approaching the regulation " drawing-room " type, and it can be used with or without the bottom rails according to the strength of the main tenons. Its legs are shown in detail in Fig. 471, and the top back rail is simply shaped and sunk or inlaid, its top being rounded off a little as shown. The lower rail of the back and the two uprights show a width of $\frac{3}{4}$ in. on the face, but had better be 1 in. from front to back; they are intended to be rebated

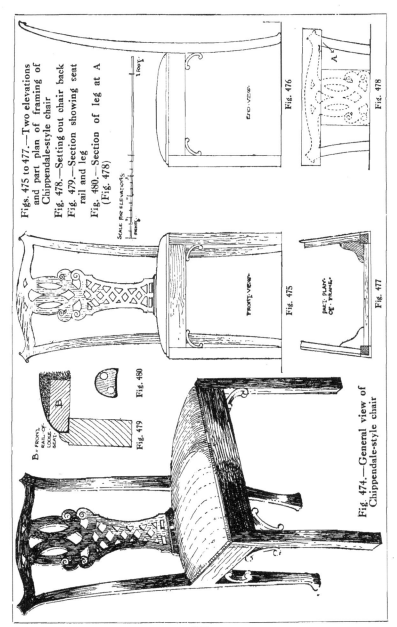

Figs. 475 to 477.—Two elevations and part plan of framing of Chippendale-style chair
Fig. 478.—Setting out chair back
Fig. 479.—Section showing seat rail and leg
Fig. 480.—Section of leg at A (Fig. 478)

Fig. 474.—General view of Chippendale-style chair

or ploughed for the trellis panel, which should be ½ in. thick and is fretted out to the simple arrangement given of lines at angles of 60° with the horizontal; each bar of the trellis should be about ⅜ in. finished on the face.

Alternative Design for Chair Back, Figs. 472 and 473.—The fifth example illustrated is really an alternative back, applicable equally to both the two preceding designs. It has a different fretted panel fitted as before described, and a simple top rail, both of which are detailed in Fig. 473.

Armchair.—For an armchair capable of being made *en suite* with the preceding small chairs, *see* page 201, where a design is given suitable for use at the head of a dining-table.

A Chippendale Chair, Figs. 474 to 480.—This is a copy of an authentic example of Chippendale's work, and its simple lines are such as to recommend it for easy production. Many of Chippendale's chairs were made with the square legs shown, and if suitably proportioned they present a solid and dignified appearance. A full size drawing is essential, in order that "templates" or patterns may be made for the various parts. The following templates should be prepared in three-ply wood or stiff cardboard. The first should give a true front shape of the back legs, the second the true side view of the back legs as in the drawing, and then templates should be made to coincide with the pierced part of the back and the top rail.

The construction of the back of the chair is the most difficult part, and should be proceeded with first. Both legs should be cut out and planed true all round, then the wood for the splat cut out curved slightly to fit the back. It is necessary to mark the lines on both splat and top, although the cutting is not done until all the joints have been made and fitted. The top rail it will be seen runs right through, and is secured to the legs with two dowels at each side as is indicated in the section (Fig. 478). The centre splat is also dowelled into the top rail and the seat rail, the dowels being arranged so as not to interfere with the pierced work. When fitted together the front part is levelled down and then separated and cut. Then the back parts of all the piercing is worked with rasps and files similarly to the

Dining and Drawing-room Chairs

section shown of the leg. After the back has been glued up the shaping and joints are finished off and the scrolls and ears carved. The seat part is straightforward; bevelled shoulders must be used on the side rails, and tenoning should be employed in preference to dowelling. The rails are rebated and, when glued up, angle brackets should be glued and screwed in the corners. The curved brackets can then be cut and fitted in the other angles of legs and rails. Fig. 479 indicates the sectional view of the front loose seat rail. This loose seat may be made dowelled together and rounded on the top edges, webbing being then stretched across either the top or underside and the seat made up with hair and calico. The morocco covering is then placed over the seat—with a layer of cotton wool between the calico and the morocco—and tacked on the underside. The usual full polish finish should be used, and if stained antique brown, the effect is much better than the reddish brown so much used in mahogany work.

A Fine Example of a Modern Chair, Figs. 481 to 487.—This chair was exhibited for some time in the Victoria and Albert Museum, and is described as being constructed of ash stained green, and having purple leather upholstering and ornaments, with brass nails where indicated. The details given in Figs. 482 to 487 are based on a study of the actual article.

The front legs are out of $1\frac{1}{4}$-in. square stuff, 1 ft. $5\frac{1}{2}$ in. long, with edges stop-chamfered and the upper part sunk and carved in low relief (or merely sunk) as in Fig. 486. The back legs are 3 ft. 3 in. long and out of $2\frac{1}{4}$-in. by $2\frac{1}{4}$-in. stuff, cut away in side elevation, as in Fig. 483, where the dotted line indicates the original piece, and cut out in front or back elevation, as in Fig. 484, either for the simpler or more elaborate version. The same figure gives the distance at the top and bottom at which these back legs are kept by means of four upper rails tenoned in position, as shown by the dotted lines, and ornamented with various chamfers on the front edges, and a plain rail at the seat level (not shown), also tenoned into the back legs in order to receive the upholstery. Similar bearers about 3 in. by $1\frac{1}{4}$ in. will be required on the

Fig. 481 - Modern (Hungarian) chair of ash ; designed by Edmund Farago

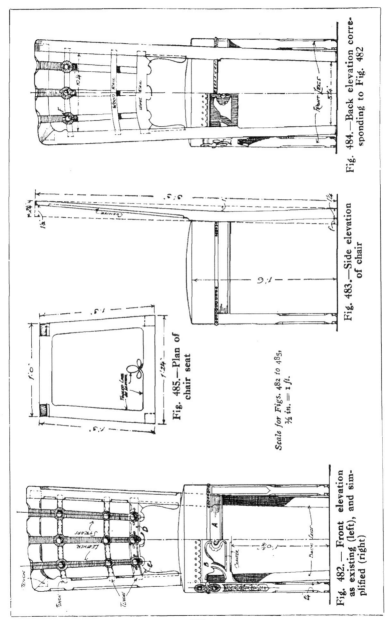

Fig. 484.—Back elevation corresponding to Fig. 482

Fig. 483.—Side elevation of chair

Fig. 485.—Plan of chair seat

Scale for Figs. 482 to 485, 3/8 in. = 1 ft.

Fig. 482.—Front elevation as existing (left), and simplified (right)

three other sides between the legs, in order to produce a seat as in the plan in Fig. 485. Under each of these bearers either a plain fascia with a bead as at A (Fig. 482), or a pierced and simply carved piece, as in the photograph, is fixed. This piece should be all in one about $\frac{7}{8}$ in. thick, and should repeat on three sides. The carved rosettes seen at the corresponding place in the photograph to B in Fig. 482 can be omitted, probably with advantage, and also those seen on the top rail of the back. A sunk line of a segmental section as at C in Fig. 486 will be noticed just above the pierced ornament.

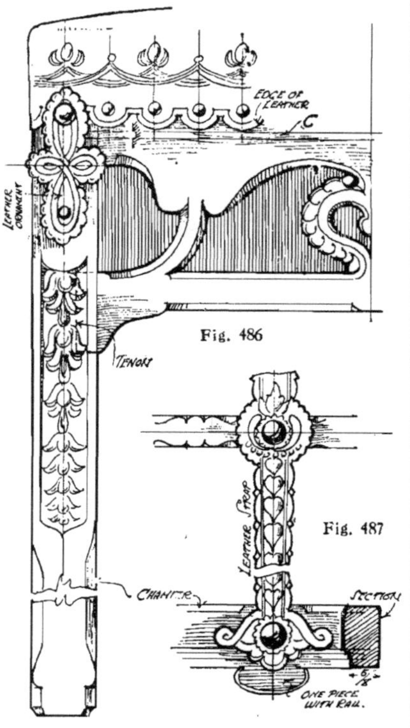

The back rail D (Fig. 482) is shown in section in Fig. 487, and is cut to a splay at E in order to mitre with the adjoining small piece, which is about $\frac{5}{8}$ in. thick, curved in outline and let into the side of the back leg, thereby improving the effect of the chair considerably. The outline of this rail will probably be most easily gathered from Fig. 484.

The pierced and carved part under the seat can be repeated at the back, or kept quite plain or omitted entirely as in Fig. 484, according to the uses of the chair. Or, of course,

Scale, one quarter full size

Figs. 486 and 487.—Details of ornament to legs and back

Dining and Drawing-room Chairs

the much simpler treatment given as an alternative (A, Fig. 482) can be adopted on all sides.

With regard to the leatherwork, the three decorated straps to the back (shaded in Fig. 482) are cut from soft leather to the contours in Fig. 487, and carefully tooled and embossed to the patterns there shown. They begin from about the level of D and E (Fig. 482), and are continued right up over the top rail and down to F (Fig. 484), each being secured with four large brass-headed nails where indicated, and tapering downwards both in width and spacing.

The seat should be upholstered in the usual manner with leather or other material, and either finished in a simple manner as on the right-hand side of Fig. 482, or with a tooled pattern and scalloped edges as in the original (*see* Fig. 486), which also has a sort of quatrefoil leather ornament fixed to each exposed face of the front legs.

Fig. 488.—Angle chair

These minor elaborations must be left to the discretion of the worker.

It should be clearly understood that Fig. 482 represents a front elevation showing the chair complete (left-hand side), and a simplified version (right-hand side). The latter has straight instead of curved rails to the back, plain underframing, and simple upholstery. Fig. 483 is a side view applicable to either version. The dotted line indicates piece from which back leg is cut.

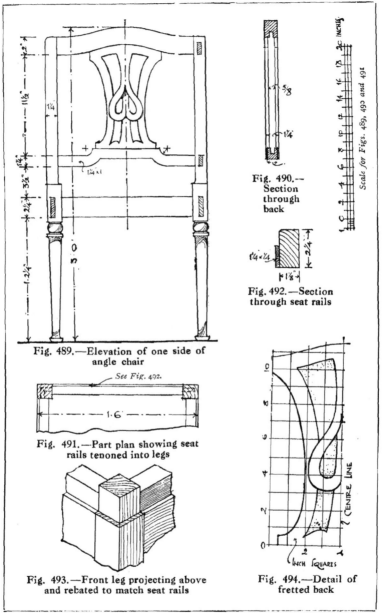

Fig. 489.—Elevation of one side of angle chair

Fig. 490.—Section through back

Fig. 491.—Part plan showing seat rails tenoned into legs

Fig. 492.—Section through seat rails

Fig. 493.—Front leg projecting above and rebated to match seat rails

Fig. 494.—Detail of fretted back

Dining and Drawing-room Chairs

Angle or Corner Chair, Figs. 488 to 494.—In this chair there are no involved angle joints or shaped work. First prepare the three back legs 2 ft. 11 in. long by $1\frac{5}{8}$ in. square. The top half of the legs is reduced to $1\frac{1}{4}$ in. square from a point $1\frac{1}{2}$ in. above the seat rail, but only on the two inner edges. Then mark the positions of the rails to the sizes given, and mortise the legs before turning. The top ends of the legs are mortised for the back rails. The seat rails are $2\frac{1}{4}$ in. wide by $1\frac{1}{8}$ in. thick, and may be of birch, with a clamp of wood $\frac{1}{4}$ in. thick glued on the face to form the rebate for the stuffing (*see* Fig. 492). The top of the front leg should not be kept flush with the top edges of the rails, but should stand $\frac{1}{2}$ in. above them. The rails are tenoned flush with the legs at a height of 1 ft. $4\frac{1}{2}$ in. from the floor to the top of the rail. The turning on the legs begins $\frac{1}{2}$ in. beneath the under edges of the seat rails.

The shaped top rail is 2 in. wide by $1\frac{1}{4}$ in. thick, and is flush with the face of the legs. Make the shaped rail under the fretted back $1\frac{1}{4}$ in. wide by 1 in. thick, and set it back $\frac{1}{8}$ in. from the front of the legs. All the rails, etc., are fixed with mortise and tenon joints. The fretted back (Fig. 494) is $\frac{5}{8}$ in. thick, and after being fretted the strapwork in the middle is cut with a chisel to make it overlap the surrounding straps. Fig. 490 shows the short tenons housed in the top and lower rails. To obtain the shoulders of the tenons, cramp up the legs and rails dry, then place the back in position, and mark the shoulders. A tenon $\frac{1}{2}$ in. long on each end will be sufficient. After cramping up the chair and allowing the glue to harden, cut the rebates across the exposed faces of the front leg (*see* Fig. 493).

A Small Bedroom Chair will be found illustrated on page 337.

CHAPTER XIX

Settees, Armchairs, and Window Seats

Simple Settee with Loose Spring-seat, Figs. 495 to 500.—The settee shown on this page is on very simple and commodious lines and would do duty on occasion as a temporary bed. It may be executed in oak or deal, all the parts being simply tenoned together. The seat is composed of three removable box spring cushions, or, of course, a solid bottom with loose down cushions might be substituted.

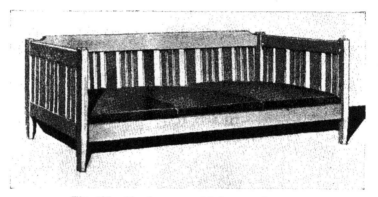

Fig. 495.—Simple settee with loose spring-seat

The framework consists of four legs each 2 in. square and 2 ft. $10\frac{1}{2}$ in. long, the lower 8 in. being tapered to $1\frac{1}{2}$ in., and the top angles slightly chamfered or rounded as shown; these legs are connected by lower rails as at A (Fig. 496) 4 in. by $1\frac{1}{2}$ in. central with the legs except at the back where the rail is brought right forward (B, Fig. 498) in order to obtain a slight slope as shown, which is an advantage although rather more difficult to construct. The top rail at back is 5 in. by 1 in. shaped at the ends as in Fig. 496, and thereby reduced to a width of

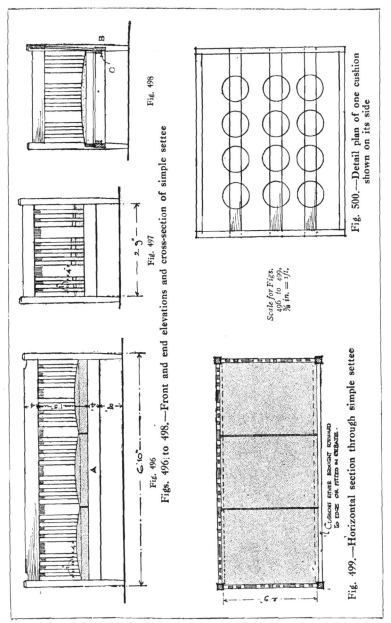

Fig. 498
Fig. 497
Fig. 496
Figs. 496 to 498.—Front and end elevations and cross-section of simple settee

Fig. 500.—Detail plan of one cushion shown on its side

Scale for Figs. 496 to 499, ⅜ in. = 1 ft.

Fig. 499.—Horizontal section through simple settee

4 in.; for the short side rails 4 in. by 1 in. will be sufficient as shown.

At the ends and back, the framework is filled in with rails 1 in. wide in groups of three alternating with pieces 4 in. wide as shown, all about $\frac{3}{4}$ in. or $\frac{5}{8}$ in. thick, and slightly tenoned top and bottom. Other designs could easily be adopted for this part of the work. Pieces as at c in Fig. 498

Fig. 501.—Armchair with adjustable back

should be attached to help support the loose cushions, which can either be arranged to drop into a slight rebate worked on the top of the front and back rails or merely kept in position by their own close fitting and weight.

The three cushions can be built up as shown on plan in Fig. 500 where the outer lines represent a sort of boxing, butted or framed at the angles and composed of say 3 in. by 1 in. wood, and crossed by three longitudinal strips notched into the sides: these take a series of strong springs of the

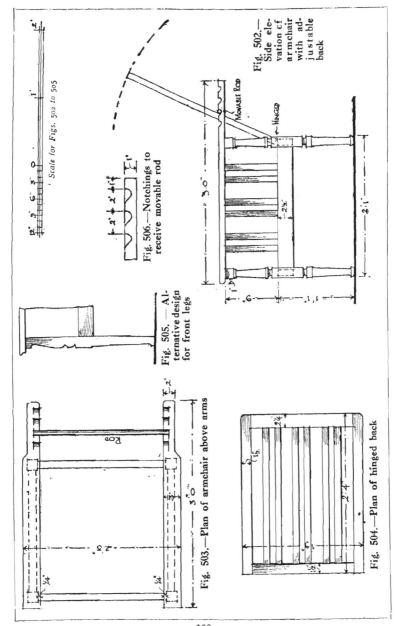

Fig. 502.—Side elevation of armchair with adjustable back

Fig. 506.—Notchings to receive movable rod

Fig. 505.—Alternative design for front legs

Fig. 503.—Plan of armchair above arms

Fig. 504.—Plan of hinged back

Scale for Figs. 502 to 505

usual type which should be corded together in the usual manner, and covered with padding and canvas ready to receive the final covering of cretonne, pegamoid, etc.

Armchair with Adjustable Back, Figs. 501 to 506.—The back of this chair can be adjusted to different angles by a simple arrangement, and is hinged to the seat rail. The arms are extended at the back, and notched on the top surface as shown, to support the $\frac{3}{4}$ in. rod which keeps the back at the angle required. Begin with the two sides (Fig. 502). The legs are $1\frac{3}{4}$ in. square, and square or round turned as shown, or merely tapered below the seat rail as preferred. (An alternative for a 2-in. by $1\frac{1}{4}$-in. leg shaped on the front is shown in Fig. 505.) Mark the position of the $2\frac{1}{2}$-in. by $1\frac{1}{4}$-in. rails, and mortise centrally into the legs.

The arms should be 3 ft. long by 3 in. wide by 1 in. thick. Fig. 503 gives a plan showing them shaped and reduced to 2 in. wide at the back. A series of notches 2 in. apart are cut on the surface to receive the rod which supports the back. The legs are mortised into the arms, and a series of small uprights, say $1\frac{1}{8}$ in. by $\frac{3}{8}$ in., are also lightly tenoned into position in three pairs as shown.

The back (Fig. 504) consists of a frame mortised and tenoned together, 1 in. thick, and of the widths indicated. Fig. 502 shows how it is hinged to the top end of the seat rail with a pair of brass butt hinges. It should be filled in with laths rather stouter than those specified for the sides, spaced as shown or at equal intervals. Its top corners should be rounded, as should also all the more exposed angles of the chair. If it is desired to have a chair folding into a small compass the back should be hinged on its front bottom edge instead of as Fig. 502, when it will fold easily down on to the front and back seat rails, which are, of course, exactly similar to the side ones.

With regard to upholstery, the seat can be either one of the ordinary types supported on webbing across the rails, or it can be filled in with several wood bearers to support a large square cushion made on the mattress model. The back as in Fig. 504 is intended to have a similar loose cushion,

Settees, Armchairs, Window Seats

but could easily be upholstered on the framework if desired, the wood filling shown being then omitted.

Dining-room Armchair, Figs. 507 to 509.—These illustrations give the setting-out for an armchair of the kind

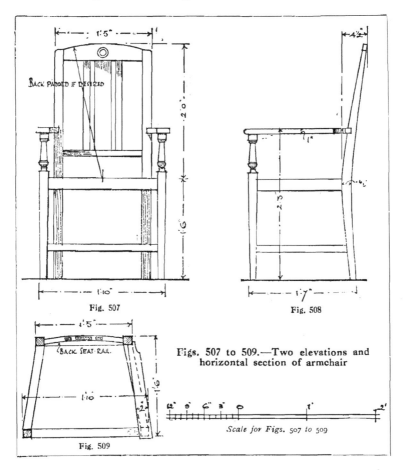

Figs. 507 to 509.—Two elevations and horizontal section of armchair

often provided for the head of the dining-room table. This, while constituting a new design as regards its details, can easily be adapted to match any of the smaller chairs in Chapter XVIII.; the pattern of legs and back and also the arrangement of the lower rails (if any) can readily be altered at will, without affecting in any way the general sizes of the armchair as illustrated. In some cases it might be preferred to pad the back.

In the particular design given the flat arm-rests will be found very useful, and the upper part of the front legs can be either round or square-turned as shown, or merely tapered upwards a little, leaving the thickest portions when the seat rails meet them. The bottom rails would be best arranged as in Fig. 465 (p. 183), and the shaped top rail can be relieved by a sunk beaded circle or other small ornament in the centre where indicated. It is desirable to curve the back a little as shown on the plan, but this is less essential than in the case of the smaller chairs shown in Chapter XVIII.

Fig. 510.—Upholstered seat

Upholstered Window Seat, Figs. 510 to 515.—In the museum at South Kensington is exhibited the window seat here illustrated. It is described as being English work dating from late in the eighteenth century. Its legs are in polished mahogany (the only mahogany in the whole example), the remainder being upholstered in horsehair cloth with rows of brass-headed nails along the angles. The effect would be very much more attractive if the covering were altered to cretonne, plain striped silk, etc., but, apart from this, the seat might suitably be copied as it stands.

The legs are 1 ft. $9\frac{1}{2}$ in. long, the lower 1 ft. $3\frac{3}{4}$ in. of each being intended to show, and accordingly tapered from $1\frac{1}{2}$ in. square at the top to $1\frac{1}{8}$ in. near the floor, where they have shaped square feet $2\frac{1}{2}$ in. high, measuring about $1\frac{3}{8}$ in. across their widest parts, and thence again tapering to $1\frac{1}{8}$ in. next the floor level. All faces of each leg are sunk slightly about $\frac{1}{16}$ in. deep, leaving $\frac{1}{8}$ in. margin along the angles, and ter-

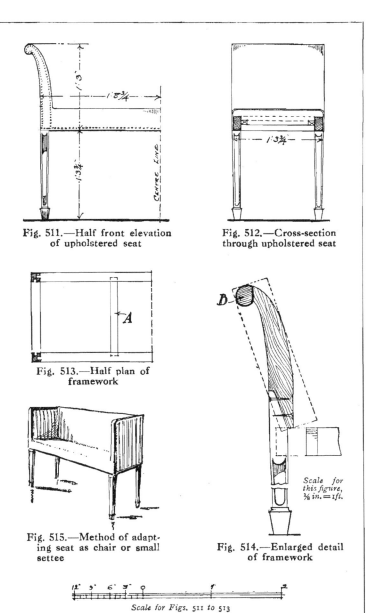

Fig. 511.—Half front elevation of upholstered seat

Fig. 512.—Cross-section through upholstered seat

Fig. 513.—Half plan of framework

Fig. 515.—Method of adapting seat as chair or small settee

Fig. 514.—Enlarged detail of framework

Scale for this figure, ⅛ in. = 1 ft.

Scale for Figs. 511 to 513

minating in semicircular curves at the top and bottom. The above work (which can be simplified if desired) is shown in Fig. 514, as is also the way in which the top of each leg is splayed off and connected by a lapped joint and long screws to a curved upright member, cut out of a piece of 1 ft. 1 in. by $3\frac{1}{2}$ in. and $1\frac{1}{2}$ in. thick, likewise one of the $2\frac{1}{2}$ in. by $1\frac{1}{2}$ in. bearers which have to be tenoned between all the legs to form the edges of the seat. These bearers are shown on plan in Fig. 513, which also serves to indicate at A the position of two transverse pieces.

The only remaining portions of the framework are two rounded top-rails to the ends, these being indicated in section by the dark top portion of the curved upright shown at B (Fig. 514), each of these being connected to the rolls by a stub-tenon or similar means. The two small pieces marked with diagonal crosses under the seat in Fig. 512 serve to secure the webbing for the upholstering work.

By its unusual form this seat would appear to have been especially designed for use in front of one of the low recessed windows of the period; but it could easily be made the model for a drawing-room chair or small settee, as shown by Fig. 515. The legs are continued up vertically and connected at the sides and back by horizontal top rails, the two top front angles being rounded off as indicated. Mahogany should be employed for the top and front edges of the upper part, the selected covering being fastened to the sides of the frame, and not taken over it.

CHAPTER XX

Cosy-Corner Fittings

Enclosed Corner Fitting with Shelves, Etc., Figs. 516 to 525.—A substantial piece of furniture in the style of Fig. 516 should, in the case of a small room, be placed against a wall or in a corner; but in a large apartment it can stand at right angles to a wall, preferably on one side of a fireplace, the result then being somewhat similar to that of an inglenook.

The structure, the minimum lengths and heights for which are shown, consists of a low, deep and high-backed seat of an L-shape on plan, partly enclosed with curtains, and made more of a feature by the addition of small shelves and a corner cupboard above. If desired, the seat could be of solid wood with loose cushions.

The total size of the work will need to be kept within the limits of size permitted by the approach to the room for which it is proposed (unless it can be built, and, at some future time, unbuilt in the apartment where it will be in use). If there is only an ordinary door available, the width shown on the plan as 3 ft. 2 in. will need reduction. It is seldom wise to have furniture put together in a room so as to be of such a size that removal intact is impossible.

Dealing with the wooden structure, this may be assumed to consist of good pine stained or painted, and the exact requirements as to size can readily be decided by actual trial.

Referring first of all to Fig. 519, this illustrates the position of seven uprights, each out of 2-in. by 2-in. stuff, and of lengths as follow : c, d, e and f, each 5 ft. 10½ in. ; g, 4 ft. 11¼ in., as this post, situated at the back angle, stops under the shelf and cupboard near the top ; h and j serve as minor supports and are 12 in. long each : in the bottom 9 in. of their lengths all these uprights are tapered off to 1⅜ in. square next the floor.

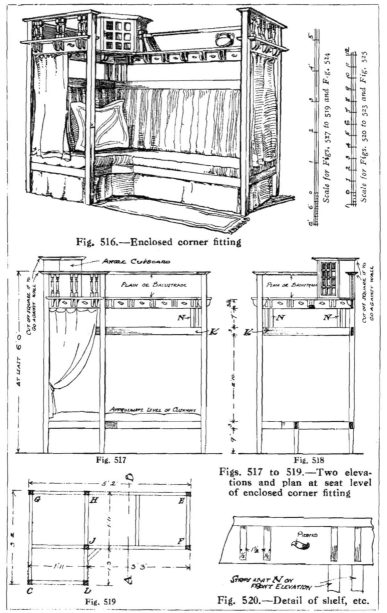

Fig. 516.—Enclosed corner fitting

Fig. 517

Fig. 518

Figs. 517 to 519.—Two elevations and plan at seat level of enclosed corner fitting

Fig. 519

Fig. 520.—Detail of shelf, etc.

Cosy-Corner Fittings

The uprights are connected by means of the horizontal bearers shown at a height of 9 in., with ordinary small tenon-joints, except in the case of the upright J, where the four bearers are dovetailed in position the better to resist any tensile strain. A piece about 7 in. long is tenoned across

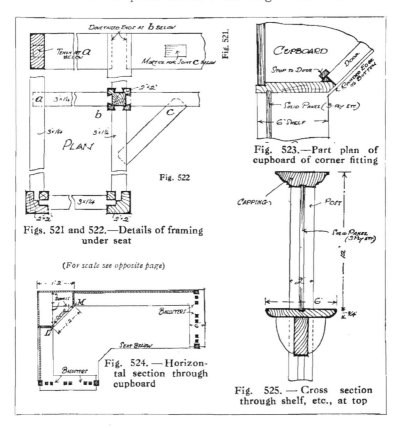

Figs. 521 and 522.—Details of framing under seat

Fig. 523.—Part plan of cupboard of corner fitting

Fig. 524.—Horizontal section through cupboard

Fig. 525.—Cross section through shelf, etc., at top

the angle at J, and the various joints are shown in Figs. 521 and 522.

At a height of 3 ft. 10 in. above the floor is fixed a 3-in. by 1½-in. bearer along the back of each part of the seat, that is, between C and G, and between G and E, and as shown at the level marked K in Figs. 517 and 518. This rail may be housed at the ends, and above it at a vertical distance of 7 in. is fitted a 3¼-in. or so by 1-in. piece; but in this case continued between posts D C, C G, G E, and E F. It is decorated with pierced leaf shapes and small cut brackets in pairs alternately (see Figs. 520 and 525) and serves to support a light shelf 6 in. wide, which in the case of the ends (C D and E F) projects equally on each side of the posts, as shown on the plan of the top. Where the sides are intended to come against a wall in the contemplated position of the fitting, the shelf should project on the inner side only, as is shown in the cases of the two longest sides of the example. Of course, in the event of the whole being exposed to view from both sides, the shelf would be fixed centrally with the posts all round. Figs. 525 serves to show a simple rounded edge to the shelf, which, however, should stop at the points L and M on the plan of the top, where a triangular piece is dowelled in the angle of the two lengths of shelving (secured together by the same means), to form the base of the cupboard.

The cupboard itself is boxed up of about ⅞-in. stuff, and has a glazed door of the usual type, with wood bars or leaded glass as preferred. A neat cornice is used to finish the top edges of the cupboard, a method for contriving the sides of which is shown in Fig. 523. A capping of similar character to the cornice is used along the sides on top of the posts, at a height of 6 ft. above the floor. The filling-in at the two ends should be a series of small plain or turned balusters, corresponding in spacing with the brackets below, while the long sides may either be treated in the same way, or filled in as shown with plain panels, fitting into grooves along the shelf, posts, and capping. As a small additional finish, thin upright strips, say 1 in. by ½ in., are fixed between the bearer K and the bearer to the shelf, as at N, on the front view and section A B; but they will not be wanted on the short outer ends, where either a curtain rod or a series of small hooks should be fixed.

Upholstered Corner Seat, Figs. 526 to 533.—The dimensions of the various parts can easily be obtained from the figures; but the different thicknesses of wood required are: Seat board A (Figs. 527 and 529), about ⅞ in.; legs

Cosy-Corner Fittings

about 2 in.; seat rails, 1½ in.; corner pieces B (Figs. 527 and 529), 1 in.; shelf G (Fig. 527), side pediments D, and corner shelf E, ¾ in.; and moulding F, about ⅞ in.

To allow the corner seat to be taken through doorways, it should be made in the following parts, namely: Wood seat and legs; backs between the seat and the moulding F (Fig. 527); the latter moulding and side frames below shelf C; and the latter and side pediments D.

The seat portion may be first taken in hand. One side of the seat board is got out the full length, and the other portion is dowelled into it; see plan (Fig. 528). As the legs are hidden by the drapery valances, their appearance and position is somewhat immaterial; but the legs next the wall must stand in sufficiently to clear the skirting board of the room, or the upper part of the seat will not fit against the wall. The front seat rail G (Fig. 528) is continued and connected to the back one H with morti e and tenon. Instead of being mortised, the front corner leg is fixed with glue, and screws driven from the inside faces of the seat rails. The remaining legs are mortised and tenoned. The back frames above A (Fig. 527) and below F extend the length of each side, and at J (Fig. 529) an upright stile is provided, so that the corner section of the stuffed back K, which is made in a separate frame, may be attached to it with screws; also the other side sections L (Fig. 529).

Before stuffing the backs, upholsterers' chair webbing should be tacked on the frames as in Fig. 531. The dotted lines in Figs. 527 and 529 show the outlines of the stuffed backs. For stuffing the latter, hair is the best, but most costly; but fibre or wool flocks will do very well. Under the outer covering there should be an inner one of calico or canvas, and to keep the flocks or hair from slipping downwards, stitches at intervals should be taken through from the front to the back, the outer cover, of course, hiding these. The valances are pleated and tacked on the top side of the seat board.

The seat cushion should be made loose, and all in one part, and to keep it from sliding off the wood seat, holes about ⅜ in. in diameter should be bored at wide intervals

O

near the front. Under the cushion are sewn tapes, which are passed through the holes, and then tied on the under side of the seat board.

The ledging F (Fig. 527) projects 1¼ in. over the stuffed backs, and follows the outline of the corner section, and thus forms a shelf as in Fig. 530.

In constructing the ledging, the sides are mortised and

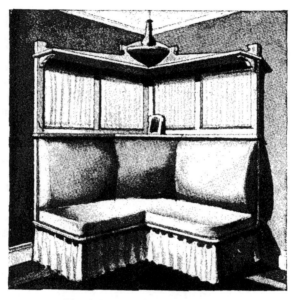

Fig. 526.—Upholstered corner seat

tenoned together, and grooved to receive the triangular corner piece, which is provided with tongues, the moulded edge being intersected as shown.

The open framings above F (Fig. 527) are made in two parts, one overlapping the other at the inside corner as show in Fig. 529. In each opening of the frames is a silk or muslin curtain, with an inch hem on the top and the bottom. Through the latter is passed a ⅜-in. diameter rod, which fits in holes bored in the inside edges of the frames. To enable the rods to be taken out, one hole is double the depth

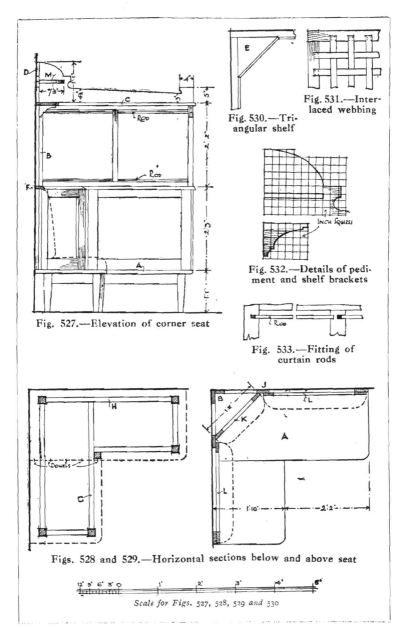

Fig. 527.—Elevation of corner seat

Fig. 530.—Triangular shelf

Fig. 531.—Interlaced webbing

Fig. 532.—Details of pediment and shelf brackets

Fig. 533.—Fitting of curtain rods

Figs. 528 and 529.—Horizontal sections below and above seat

Scale for Figs. 527, 528, 529 and 530

of the other (*see* Fig. 533); the rods are $\frac{1}{2}$ in. longer than the size of the opening. In putting a rod in it is pushed in the deepest hole, and then inserted in the shallower one. To allow for an effective fullness, the curtains should be made double the width of the openings of the frame.

The shelf c (Fig. 527) is constructed in the same manner as the seat board, and the side pediments D are dovetailed at the corner, and connected to the shelf with screws driven from the under side.

The corner quarter circular shelf M is connected with screws driven from the wall faces of the pediments, likewise the two brackets which support the shelf c. To connect the shelf and the pediments with the frame below, drive screws from the under side of the top rails of the open frames.

CHAPTER XXI

Urn and Plant Stands and Pedestals

Small Mahogany Stand, Figs. 534 to 540.—The graceful little stand here shown is in South Kensington Museum, where it is designated as being of English workmanship dating from the middle of the eighteenth century. Work on such an article as this may be begun with four legs out of stuff 1 in. square, each 1 ft. 10 in. long, which will extend from the floor to the level marked A (Fig. 535). The inner angle of each of these is chamfered off as shown on the plan (Fig. 536) until it measures about $\frac{5}{8}$ in. across the splay, which stops, however, 1 ft. 8 in. above the floor. This splay is obviously introduced to lighten the appearance of the legs. Small bearers (as B, Fig. 535) 2 in. by $\frac{1}{2}$ in. and $9\frac{1}{2}$ in. long are then tenoned $\frac{3}{8}$ in. into the square tops of the legs, and screwed as indicated by the dotted lines.

In Fig. 539 is a bearer in section, with a leg behind showing the chamfered part stopped as previously mentioned. The bearer has a slight rebate $\frac{1}{4}$ in. wide, to take a flat top C, $10\frac{1}{4}$ in. square and of, say, $\frac{3}{8}$-in. thickness, secured by means of a slip D below, while along the bottom edge at E is a small " cock bead " mitred all round the stand. It should be noted that, before the work is glued up, a small moulded plinth as in Fig. 540 is mitred firmly round the bottom of each leg, and splayed off as shown in Fig. 536; or this could be left out.

The remaining parts comprise the fretwork, which is very delicately cut out of $\frac{1}{4}$-in. stuff, and is quite as thin on the face as shown by Fig. 537. The eight brackets would be secured by means of fine wire brads. The four sides of the gallery have rounded top edges and are exactly mitred and fitted in the rebate formed as in Fig. 539, by the projection of the top C above the bearer. They require more brads, to cover the ends of which a small bead F is finally planted all round

The slide seen in Fig. 535 occurs also in the small Hepplewhite table forming the next example, and was possibly introduced to support a tea-cup under the outlet of the urn.

Hepplewhite Urn Stand, Figs. 541 to 546.—This is another example at South Kensington, where it is officially described as "an urn stand, satinwood, mahogany, and tulip-wood. Hepplewhite, late eighteenth century." It is an extremely graceful little article, and when its oval top has been altered to a circle, and the veneering and inlay omitted, it becomes quite a straightforward piece of work, more especially for execution in mahogany. Of course, a certain proportion of the inlay might be retained with advantage, more especially the lines down the faces of the legs.

Fig. 534.—Small mahogany stand

Each leg is square, and tapers from 1 in. at the top down to ½ in., excepting for a short piece 1½ in. long and 1¾ in. up from the floor, where it is very slightly larger all round. The legs are arranged to converge upwards from the distance apart marked in Fig. 543, until their inner faces touch the circumference of a circle of 11⅝-in. diameter, as in Fig. 544. Here they are connected together by means of four pieces as at A, curved on plan in such a way as to form part of the complete circle

Urn and Plant Stands and Pedestals

shown, and 1⅞ in. deep and about 1·15/16 in., or 1/16 in. less than the top of the legs in thickness. They need projecting tenons ¼ in. wide, fitting into mortises in the legs, and had better be put together round a temporary circular piece of wood of 11⅝-in. diameter, in order to secure accuracy of outline.

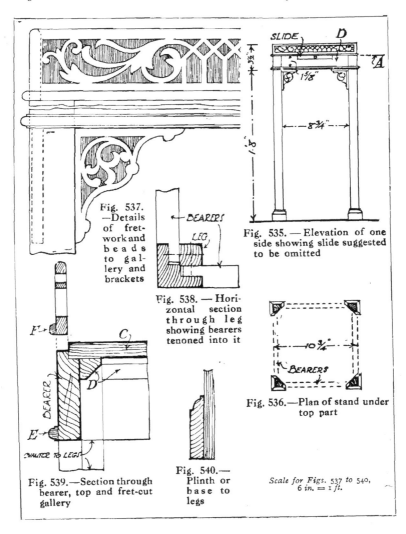

Fig. 537.—Details of fretwork and beads to gallery and brackets

Fig. 538.—Horizontal section through leg showing bearers tenoned into it

Fig. 535.—Elevation of one side showing slide suggested to be omitted

Fig. 536.—Plan of stand under top part

Fig. 539.—Section through bearer, top and fret-cut gallery

Fig. 540.—Plinth or base to legs

Scale for Figs. 537 to 540, 6 in. = 1 ft.

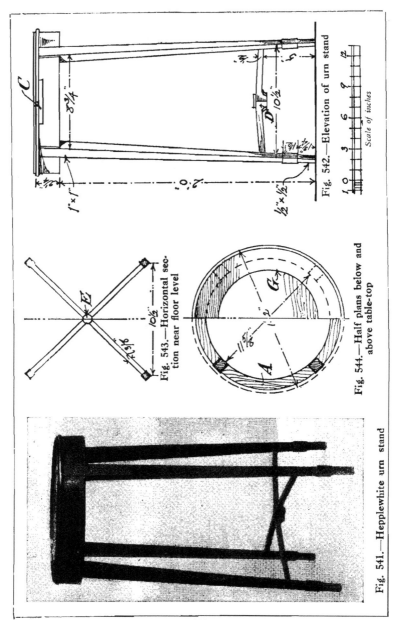

Fig. 542.—Elevation of urn stand
Fig. 543.—Horizontal section near floor level
Fig. 544.—Half plans below and above table-top
Fig. 541.—Hepplewhite urn stand

Urn and Plant Stands and Pedestals

A top piece projecting ¼ in. all round can then be prepared, with rounded angles and ¼ in. thick, fixed by means of small angle blocks B (Fig. 546). In the original, a tiny slide 4¼ in. by 3/16 in. has been arranged as at C (Fig. 542) to pull out. This is similar to one found in the square stand of earlier date already described. It may be preferred to omit this slide as immaterial; but the cross-ties shown 5 in. above the floor should on no account be omitted, as the effect depends largely upon them. Generally speaking, they measure ⅜ in. by ½ in.; but in the centre they curve out to ⅞ in. (D, Fig. 542), and it will be noticed also that they rise towards the intersection, where the two diagonal pieces will have to be halved together. They will require very neatly tenoning into the legs, and in the centre a tiny piece as at E (Fig. 543) 3/16 in. thick is fixed on the top. In the original this

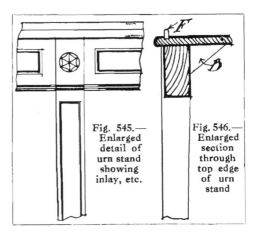

Fig. 545.—Enlarged detail of urn stand showing inlay, etc.

Fig. 546.—Enlarged section through top edge of urn stand

is oval to correspond with the table top, which has here been modified to a circular form on account of a difficulty involved in the setting out of the legs, which start from the corners of a square at the floor, but narrow in to an oblong at the top, and consequently cannot be set out with their sides at right angles to one another.

Round the top edge is fixed a small bead F (Fig. 546) which could be omitted. Fig. 545 shows the inlay. Line G (Fig. 544) shows the inner edge of a band of mahogany veneer, the centre being satinwood.

Modern-style Plant Stand, Figs. 547 to 552.—This plant stand is designed to support a pot containing a large plant, at a sufficient height to benefit by the light from an ordinary window without blocking the outlook. A note of interest is struck by the introduction of a line of inlay on the sides where shown ; or a well-designed finger plate of the bronze or oxidised types would show to advantage in such a position. Having prepared the various pieces, the next step would be to cut the corners of each shelf as at A (Fig. 550), and to form corresponding notches in the legs as at B, at the correct levels indicated in Fig. 551, so that when the work is fixed the edges of the shelves will finish flush.

The shaping of the feet is shown at C (Fig. 551), and it will be advisable to mortise them $\frac{1}{4}$ in. deep as shown dotted, to receive the legs before the small hollow is worked round them. Fixing is best ensured with a long screw from the under-side. The set of three $\frac{3}{8}$-in. strips shown on two sides should be housed $\frac{1}{4}$ in. at the top and bottom, and set about $\frac{3}{8}$ in. back from the edges of the shelves, so that the inside faces line with the legs. The curved gallery pieces are set out with a radius of $10\frac{1}{2}$ in. They should, however, be housed about $\frac{3}{16}$ in. into the legs as at D (Fig. 549), and with a slight rounded finish to the top of the legs as shown in Fig. 551 the work will be complete.

Square Pedestal, Figs. 553 to 555.—Fig. 553 shows a simple but effective pedestal for a vase or a bust. It is composed of $\frac{3}{4}$-in. sides fitted, glued, and nailed together, and either decorated with a small bead mitred and planted on in two panels on each face where indicated, or else built up with small moulded strips as A and B in Fig. 554, to simulate panelled framing. A plain flat top and suitably moulded capping and skirting are required, the two latter being made out at the back to the extent of $\frac{1}{2}$ in. with plain stuff if Fig. 554 is followed. A rough bottom as at C in Fig. 553 will be found very useful to fix both the sides and the bottom edge of the skirting.

Octagonal Pedestal, Figs. 556 to 559.—For this pedestal, sides as at D (Fig. 559) are cut from 1-in. stuff, and the edges bevelled to the required angle as shown. Two sides should be first glued together, and when set, nails may be driven as at E in the skirting. Next add two sections which are already glued together ; then the remaining two joints.

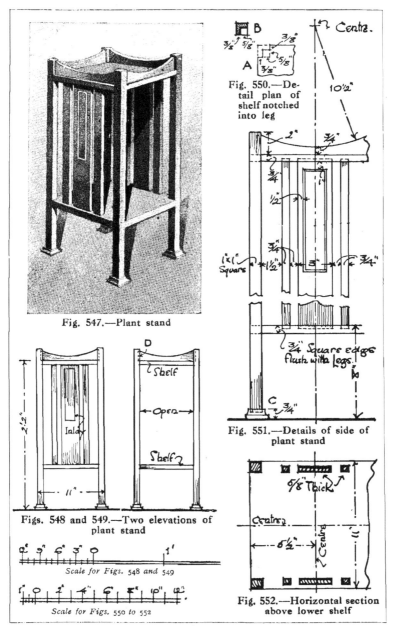

Fig. 547.—Plant stand

Fig. 550.—Detail plan of shelf notched into leg

Fig. 551.—Details of side of plant stand

Figs. 548 and 549.—Two elevations of plant stand

Scale for Figs. 548 and 549

Scale for Figs. 550 to 552

Fig. 552.—Horizontal section above lower shelf

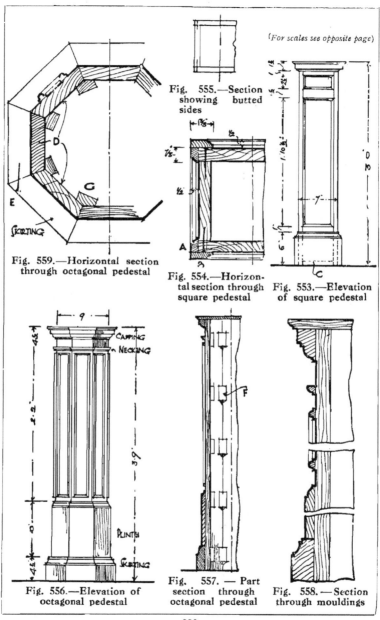

Fig. 555.—Section showing butted sides

Fig. 559.—Horizontal section through octagonal pedestal

Fig. 554.—Horizontal section through square pedestal

Fig. 553.—Elevation of square pedestal

Fig. 556.—Elevation of octagonal pedestal

Fig. 557.—Part section through octagonal pedestal

Fig. 558.—Section through mouldings

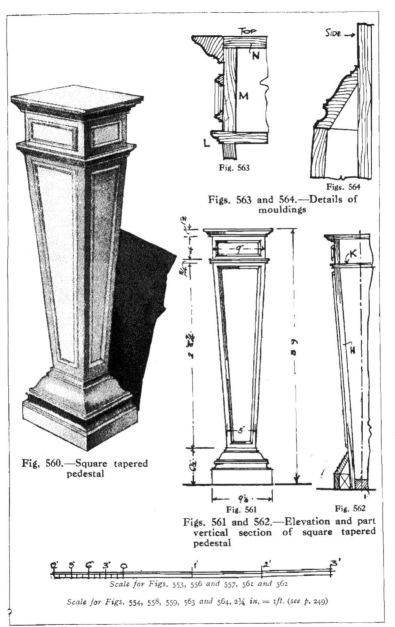

Fig. 563

Figs. 564

Figs. 563 and 564.—Details of mouldings

Fig. 560.—Square tapered pedestal

Fig. 561

Fig. 562

Figs. 561 and 562.—Elevation and part vertical section of square tapered pedestal

Scale for Figs. 553, 556 and 557, 561 and 562

Scale for Figs. 554, 558, 559, 563 and 564, 2¾ in. = 1ft. (see p. 249)

The capping and necking mouldings are planted round the column and mitred at the corners. The plinth and skirting are moulded. If it is inconvenient to use so thick a piece of wood for the latter, joint and glue 1-in. or $\frac{3}{4}$-in. stuff together. The top of the pedestal is of $\frac{3}{4}$-in. stuff with moulded edges. To strengthen the column, blocks should be glued inside at intervals (*see* F, Fig. 557, and G, Fig. 559). The long narrow panels are formed with small fillets or beads, as mentioned for the first example.

Tapered Pedestal, Figs. 560 to 564.—A tall tapered pedestal is capable of varied treatment and can be built up as shown in Fig. 562. Here the sides H are fitted together as in Fig. 555 (p. 220) to the required slope, secured at the bottom to a block J, and at the top to a flat piece K having a projecting moulded edge as at L in Fig. 563. Above this is shown an upright portion M, which can be built up and fixed on L, a top N being afterwards added and finished with a capping mould as given in the detail; or the top could be arranged to come right over if preferred. The sides are finished with applied beads, unless the built-up principle in Fig. 554 (p. 220) is adopted.

A heavily moulded base and plain skirting are essential to the stability of the whole. The bottom must be made out with blocks as marked with a cross near J (Fig. 562) to take the skirting, above which the moulded work can readily be fixed.

CHAPTER XXII

Small Tables

The small tables illustrated and described in this chapter are only some of those dealt with in this book, for in the chapters on urn and plant stands and pedestals, showcase or curio tables, and writing-tables and desks will be found descriptions of other tables most of which are adaptable to a number of different purposes.

Modern French Table, Figs. 565 to 575.—This example is of a singularly graceful and pleasing outline, and while essentially modern in style is free from the eccentricities often complained of in this type of design. Its main charm consists in the lines of its framing rather than the low-relief carving, etc., with which it is decorated, quite good though this may be, and accordingly, in order that this article may appeal to a wider circle of readers, this carving (together with one or two rather embarrassing little details) has been omitted in the working drawings. The latter apply in the main to the version shown by Fig. 566, but a further modification is also suggested later on the slightly simpler basis of Fig. 567. For material, mahogany or Italian walnut would be the most suitable.

Taking the suggestion in Fig. 566 as a basis, the parts required would be as follow: (*a*) A top finished size 3 ft. 1 in. by 1 ft. 11 in., with edges rounded or moulded as at A or B (Figs. 571 or 572). This can be several widths tongued together, or framed up as a flush panel. (*b*) Four legs $2\frac{1}{2}$ in. square, each 2 ft. 6 in. long. (*c*) Two straight rails $1\frac{1}{4}$ in. by $1\frac{1}{2}$ in., each 2 ft. 7 in. long (as C, Fig. 566). (*d*) Two similar rails 1 ft. 6 in. long (as D, Fig. 567). (*e*) One piece $4\frac{1}{2}$ in. by $1\frac{1}{4}$ in. and 2 ft. 9 in. long (for two curved rails as E, Fig. 566). (*f*) One piece $4\frac{1}{2}$ in. by $1\frac{1}{4}$ in. and 1 ft. 9 in. long (for two curved rails as F, Fig. 567). (*g*) Two thin panels 5 in. by 2 ft. 7 in. (long sides). (*h*) Two thin panels 5 in.

by 1 ft. 5 in. Also sundry small odd pieces for the concealed portions.

For the simpler version the variations on this list would be as follows : (*b*) Legs out of 2 in. by 2 in. instead of $2\frac{1}{2}$ in. (*g*) and (*h*) All panels 2 in. shorter. There would also be a small extra item of eight pieces as G (Fig. 566), $1\frac{1}{4}$ in. by $1\frac{1}{4}$ in. and about 6 in. long.

Fig. 565.—Modern French table

First of all the shape of one of the legs should be set out full size from the detail in Fig. 571, where each square represents a half inch division. Note particularly that the floor line H makes an angle of 85° with the run of the wood before the latter is cut to shape at all, also that the top outer face (*a*) is at right angles with the floor, that is, vertical, this being necessary in order to simplify the later stages of the work, and giving a purpose for the slight hollow curve of the outer line. It will be best to cut two templates in wood, cardboard

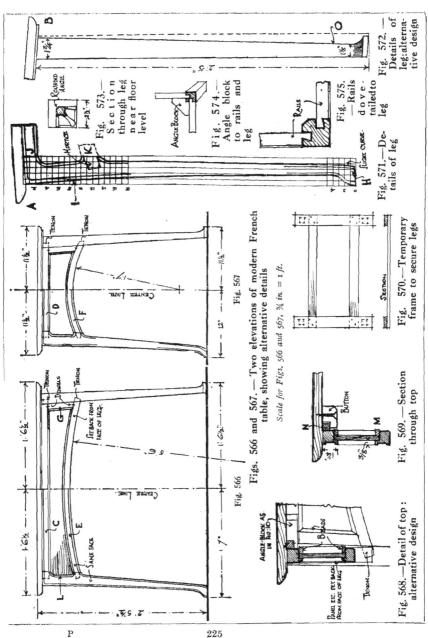

Figs. 566 and 567.—Two elevations of modern French table, showing alternative details

Fig. 568.—Detail of top: alternative design
Fig. 569.—Section through top
Fig. 570.—Temporary frame to secure legs
Fig. 571.—Details of leg
Fig. 572.—Details of leg: alternative design
Fig. 573.—Section through leg near floor level
Fig. 574.—Angle block to rails and leg
Fig. 575.—Rails dovetailed to leg

225

or zinc, to the exact outline cut to fit against the two edges from the outsides, the right-hand one to include the projections at J and K. With these in hand the work can be gradually continued without fear of deviation, and each leg made to match its fellows. A leg should first of all be cut away to the right hand contour in Fig. 571 on both its inner faces, the finishing touches being left till later on, when the inner corner should be well rounded off as in Fig. 573. At this stage, the outer faces will still be square, and one of them can be set out with the curve and cut away *nearly* to its outline (allowing a certain amount for the final shaping and smoothing up), and the remaining side gradually brought to the same state with the constant aid of the template. The finishing process includes the slight sinking of the two outer faces leaving a flat bead or fillet on all the three exposed angles, as shown on the left in Figs. 571 and 573, the whole being carried to completion with spokeshave, chisel, and fine glasspaper when the framing has been entirely put together. The rails c (Fig. 566) and D (Fig. 567) are next required and should be dovetailed into the extreme tops of the legs as in Fig. 575; their inside edges should have a rebate $\frac{1}{4}$ in. wide and extend to about $\frac{3}{8}$ in. from the front, as in Fig. 569. The curved rails E and F (Figs. 566 and 567) should then be set out in accordance with the curves of which the centres are indicated, rebated as before and also slightly sunk to match the legs (this applies also to the straight top rails). The curved rails are slightly tenoned at their ends to fit mortises in the legs as at K (Fig. 571), great care being taken to make these joints meet accurately, especially on the outer faces.

Having prepared the twelve parts which comprise the main framework and ascertaining that all the joints and lengths are right, the procedure suggested is as follows: Glue and clamp together the two legs and rails seen to the left in Fig. 566, also the corresponding parts at the back. When this is done, glue in the short rails at ends, inverting the table (which now begins to take shape) on a suitable flat bench-top, etc., and firmly secure to same with blocks. Then screw on the ends of the legs a temporary piece of

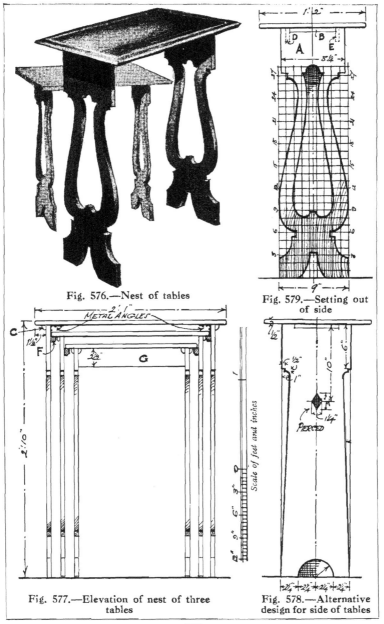

Fig. 576.—Nest of tables

Fig. 579.—Setting out of side

Fig. 577.—Elevation of nest of three tables

Fig. 578.—Alternative design for side of tables

framework as in Fig. 570 sufficiently strong and accurately set out to keep them in their correct positions; this should keep the whole rigid for the finishing work and shaping of the legs, and can be kept on until completion. The top angles should be strengthened with stout blocks strongly screwed in position (*see* Fig. 574), and the rebates on the rails continued on the backs of the legs as at L (Fig. 566). The panels can then be shaped and fitted in on all sides, fixed with beads at the back as M (Fig. 569). To attach the flat top and yet allow for the probably slight shrinkage usually taking place in a wide surface, a stout fillet as at N should be fixed to the top rail, and a series of " buttons " as also indicated roughly cut to fit over it when screwed to the wide side of the table-top and yet to allow a slight play on occasion.

The simpler version (the right-hand halves of Figs. 566 and 567) will be found quite easy to produce. Its legs are set out on two sides as O in Fig. 572, and the inside angle of each should be boldly rounded off in order to lighten the appearance. The piece G (Fig. 566) is merely fitted between the rails and fixed with dowels as indicated. Otherwise the construction is exactly the same.

An even simpler alternative would be to make the whole spandrel on each side of the table in one piece only, about 1 in. thick, grooved into the legs and secured at the back similarly to the method in Fig. 574.

Nest of Three Tables, Figs. 576 to 579.—A series of three occasional tables in which each of the two smaller units fits into the table a size larger is very useful for drawing-rooms and similar positions; they can be stowed into a very small space, and can also be easily moved as a whole. Half inch or $\frac{5}{8}$-in. oak or mahogany would serve, as it is advisable to keep the work on the light side. A very simple alternative is shown in Fig. 578.

Dealing first with the largest of the tables, the dimensions in the set illustrated are 2 ft. 1 in. by 1 ft. 2 in. with a height of 2 ft. 10 in. The edges of the table-top are rounded off slightly, and a band of simple inlay mitred round the top about $1\frac{1}{4}$ in. from the edges would be a great improvement, this being confined perhaps to the largest table.

Small Tables

For this table the uprights will be 2 ft. 9½ in. long, and in all three cases they are cut out of 9 in. widths to the desired outline in Fig. 579. For the supports of the smaller tables, the only difference will be a decrease in the height of the plain top part as at A in Fig. 579. The connection between support and top is partly effected by means of a small strip planted along the junction (B, Fig. 579, and C, Fig. 577) and carefully bradded to both; this it will be necessary to reinforce with two small angles screwed on the inside as D and E (Fig. 579).

Fig. 580.—Gothic side table

At a distance of 1½ in. below the underside on each support, should be fixed a chamfered fillet 1 in. by 6 in. long as at F in Fig. 577, which illustrates the way in which this fillet will keep the middle table in place. This table will be made on precisely similar lines to the one just described, but with its top 20¾ in. in length instead of 25 in. and the total height 2 ft. 8½ in. instead of 2 ft. 10 in.

Table No. 3 again will be shortened in length and height, but instead of the angles previously mentioned, a bearer as at G (Fig. 577) is fixed centrally between the two supports as a stiffener.

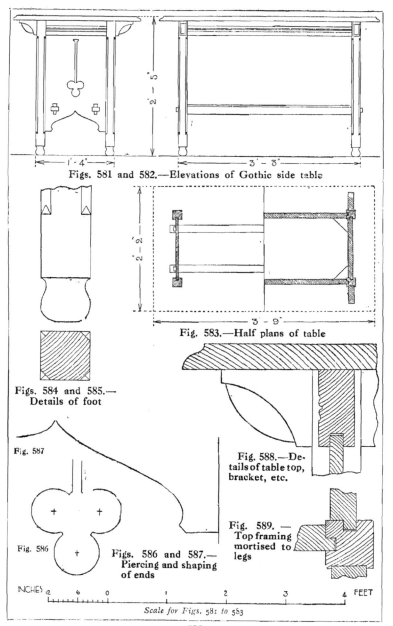

Figs. 581 and 582.—Elevations of Gothic side table

Fig. 583.—Half plans of table

Figs. 584 and 585.—Details of foot

Fig. 588.—Details of table top, bracket, etc.

Fig. 589.—Top framing mortised to legs

Figs. 586 and 587.—Piercing and shaping of ends

Scale for Figs. 581 to 583

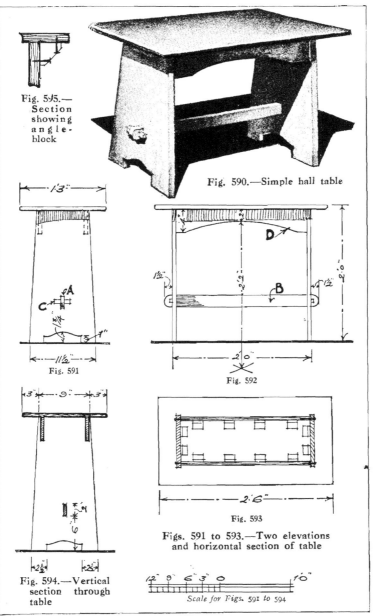

Fig. 595.—Section showing angle-block

Fig. 590.—Simple hall table

Fig. 591

Fig. 592

Fig. 593

Figs. 591 to 593.—Two elevations and horizontal section of table

Fig. 594.—Vertical section through table

Scale for Figs. 591 to 594

Gothic Side Table, Figs. 580 to 589.—The top framing of the little table here illustrated is formed of 1-in. stuff mortised to the legs, the bracket continuations of the bearers being slightly housed. Blocks are glued to the inner angles of the framed bearers. A mould is shown round the bearers and stopped against the legs. The last-mentioned are out of $1\frac{7}{8}$-in. square stuff, with chamfers on all four angles. The small spurs shown are a variation on the usual method of stop-chamfer, and are in keeping with the general Gothic character. The table-top is 1 in. thick, constructed of two pieces, with the joint running longitudinally. The end pieces, with cut trefoil and stem ornament, are $\frac{1}{2}$ in. thick, and should be let into grooves in the bearer and legs. These end pieces are pierced to receive the reduced extremities of the two lower bearers, which are secured in position by wedge-shaped dowels. The bearers are 2 in. deep and $1\frac{1}{2}$ in. wide. As it is probable that these bearers will be used as a foot-rest, they should be rounded on the upper faces.

Simple Hall Table, Figs. 590 to 595.—This little table can be made and put together very quickly. It is of stuff about $\frac{1}{2}$ in. thick, and comprises two uprights 1 ft. $11\frac{1}{2}$ in. long, tapering from $11\frac{1}{2}$ in. to 9 in., shaped as in Fig. 591, and having a slot 2 in. by $\frac{1}{2}$ in. as at A in the same figure; this slot allows a 2-in. by $\frac{1}{2}$-in. rail as B (Fig. 592) to project $1\frac{1}{2}$ in. beyond the upright, where it is finished with a rounded outline and a $\frac{1}{2}$-in. square oak peg (c, Fig. 591). At the top the uprights are connected by two horizontal pieces as at D in Fig. 592, 4 in. wide curved in the centre to a radius of 2 ft. 2 in., as indicated. The horizontal pieces should be connected to the extreme tops of the uprights by means of brads or screws through the latter into the end grain of the others. The table top measures 2 ft. 6 in. by 1 ft. 3 in., has its edges slightly rounded, and is attached by means of a series of angle-blocks, as shown in Fig. 595.

Coffee Table, Figs. 596 to 602.—This small table offers itself as an easy undertaking. A general thickness of $\frac{3}{8}$ in. or $\frac{1}{2}$ in. would be found quite sufficient, and as a commencement a top 18 in. by 12 in. should be prepared, and its four edges chamfered as in Fig. 600. Two plain uprights 1 ft. 10¾ in. long and 9 in. wide will be needed, each having a pierced diamond ornament, as in Fig. 597 at A, divided into four by means of bands ⅜ in. wide.

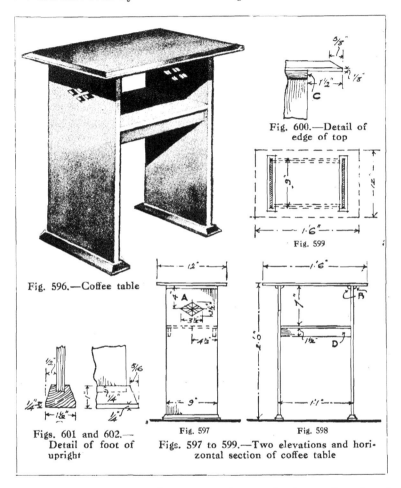

Fig. 600.—Detail of edge of top

Fig. 599

Fig. 596.—Coffee table

Figs. 601 and 602.—Detail of foot of upright

Fig. 597

Fig. 598

Figs. 597 to 599.—Two elevations and horizontal section of coffee table

The foot of each upright has a piece 10 in. long, chamfered as shown in Figs. 601 and 602. Each of these should be housed 9 in. by ½ in. and ¼ in. deep for the foot of one of the uprights screwed from below. Each upright is fixed to the top by means of small fillets of a quadrant section, one on each side as at B (Fig. 598).

The work will be braced considerably by a lower shelf 12 in. long and 9 in. wide, fixed 7 in. below the top by screws, and having under each edge a piece as at D (Fig. 598) 12 in. long and $1\frac{1}{2}$ in. deep.

Work Table, Figs. 603 to 607.—There are more elaborate types of work table, but the present example will be found simple and unobtrusive, and apart from the pleated silk bag which slides out from one of the longer sides it would pass as an ordinary small table. The four legs are 2 ft. $5\frac{1}{4}$ in. long, $1\frac{1}{8}$ in. square at the tops tapering down to $\frac{3}{4}$ in. at the bottom, where they are merely finished off square; should a more elaborate termination be preferred, the feet can be worked as in Fig. 618, p. 241, and elsewhere.

The legs are connected by three rails as in Fig. 605, out of 4 in. by $\frac{3}{4}$ in. stuff curved along its under edges as at A in Fig. 604, which shows a segment of a circle of 2 ft. 2 in. radius, that for the shorter sides being proportionately less. At the points B and C in Fig. 605 the rails should be tenoned into the legs with the adjoining mortises and tenons at different levels in order to avoid cutting away the leg too much at any one point. The joints at the other two angles are ordinary tenons. Four rails $1\frac{1}{4}$ in. by $\frac{3}{8}$ in. are introduced 6 in. above the floor, tenoned slightly into each leg in order to tie the four together.

A top, 1 ft. $10\frac{1}{4}$ in. by 1 ft. $5\frac{1}{4}$ in. and $\frac{3}{4}$ in. thick, out of one piece of well seasoned and nicely marked wood will be required; it is intended to have square edges with their angles just taken off, and can be fixed with small oak dowels let into the top of each leg. Alternatively it can be easily secured by screwing in a slanting direction through the top inner edges of the rails.

For the sliding top from which the workbag is intended to swing, a front similar in thickness and outline to A in Fig. 604 (but without any tenons) will be needed; this, it is intended to fix to the other pieces in the manner shown in Fig. 607; these are pieces of 3-in. by $\frac{1}{2}$-in. stuff put together in the simplest manner, and arranged so that the length at D will

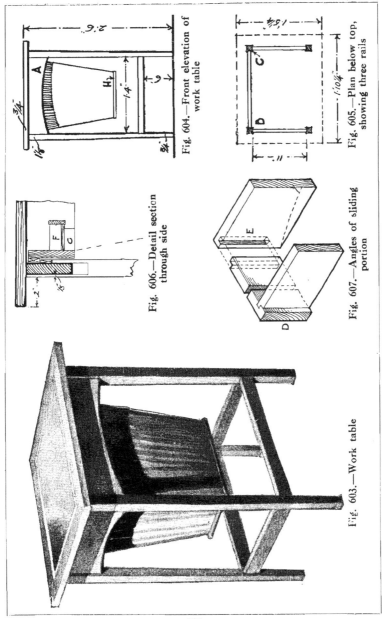

Fig. 604.—Front elevation of work table

Fig. 605.—Plan below top, showing three rails

Fig. 606.—Detail section through side

Fig. 607.—Angles of sliding portion

Fig. 603.—Work table

235

stop the whole from sliding inwards beyond the right point. The joint at E is really little more than a makeshift, although if secured properly it is quite a serviceable one; strictly the joint should be dovetailed, but considering the lightness and loose working of the whole, it has been thought sufficient. Along the top edges at each end of this sliding portion should be fixed oak strips about $\frac{3}{4}$ in. by $\frac{1}{4}$ in., as runners to work upon similar strips on the side rails, marked with diagonal crosses in Fig. 606. Along either end of the sliding part also it will be useful to fit a ledge for pins, scissors, cotton, etc. As shown in section in Fig. 606, this can be done with $\frac{1}{4}$-in. stuff throughout, first planting a piece as at F $1\frac{3}{4}$ in. by $\frac{3}{4}$ in. on the inside of the front and back portions, this serving as fixing for a bottom and side piece, the top angle of the latter being rounded as shown: these ledges would be fitted along the two short sides, while under them at all four angles it will probably be advisable to fix a triangular block to stiffen them and preserve the rectangular outline. These triangles will be concealed by the ledges over, and should be fixed flush on the underside; they help to ease the pleated silk of the bag round the corners. This silk can be of any desired length and degree of fullness, and should be carefully tacked round where indicated by a dotted line in Fig. 606, and similarly attached to a thin wooden bottom (H, Fig. 604) measuring about 10 in. by 5 in.

Folding Card Table, Figs. 608 to 613.—A handy card table that can be easily taken down and put away, yet will stand firmly when put together, is here shown.

The top is 2 ft. 1 in. square by $\frac{5}{8}$ in. thick, glue-jointed and dowelled if necessary to make up the width, and clamped across the ends with pieces $1\frac{1}{4}$ in. wide, tongued on and mitred at the corners, all as shown in Fig. 608. Four pieces of wood, each 1 ft. 11 in. by 2 in. by $\frac{3}{4}$ in., mitred at the ends to form a flat square, must next be made and bevelled off to $\frac{1}{4}$ in. thick on the outside edges, as shown at A (Fig. 612). Then firmly screw them to the under side of the table top, leaving a margin round the edge 1 in. wide, as shown at B and C (Fig. 611). The legs should be 2 ft. $1\frac{1}{2}$ in. long by $1\frac{1}{4}$ in. square at the top, tapering to $\frac{7}{8}$ in. square at the bottom; or they can be turned.

Small Tables

If turned, a piece 3½ in. long must be left square at the top of each leg. Two framing pieces are next prepared, each 1 ft. 7 in. by 3 in. by ½ in., and these are tenoned into the tops of the legs to form two pairs as shown in Fig. 608. The framing pieces are shouldered on the outside only, and the leg mortises are

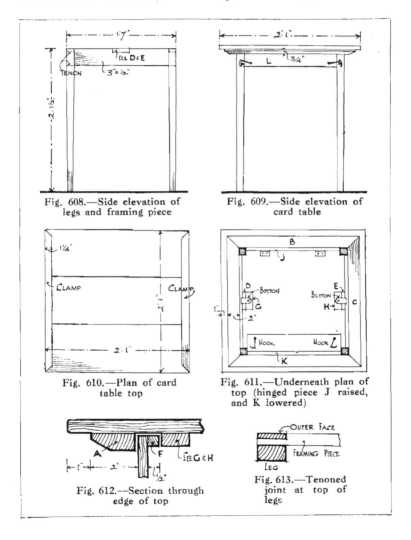

Fig. 608.—Side elevation of legs and framing piece

Fig. 609.—Side elevation of card table

Fig. 610.—Plan of card table top

Fig. 611.—Underneath plan of top (hinged piece J raised, and K lowered)

Fig. 612.—Section through edge of top

Fig. 613.—Tenoned joint at top of legs

gauged to bring the outer faces of the legs and frame flush as in Fig. 613. They must be strongly glued and screwed together.

Each pair of legs when finished should fit neatly and fairly tightly into the inside square of the frame on the under side of the table top, as shown on the right- and left-hand sides of Fig. 611, the framing pieces pressing against the corresponding inside edges of the square part marked B and C. Two pieces of wood 3 in. by ½ in. square are then fixed, one on each of the framing pieces connecting the pairs of legs in the centre, flush with the top edge of the inside, as shown at D and E (Fig. 611) and F (Fig. 612), and also shown in Fig. 608. The top of the table is then placed upside down on the bench, the legs fitted in position, and two pieces of wood 3 in. by 1¼ in. by ½ in. screwed to the under side of the top level with the two last pieces and touching them as shown at G and H (Fig. 611). A button is then screwed to the centre of each of these two pieces, so that when turned they prevent the pairs of legs being moved. Two more pieces of wood, 1 ft. 4½ in. by 3 in. by ½ in. each, can now be fitted into position, as shown at J and K (Fig. 611) and L (Fig. 609), and kept in place by two hinges screwed to each piece on the inside about 3 in. from the ends, and to the under side of the table top, as at F (Fig. 608). These pieces can next be fitted with a brass hook at each end on the outside near the lower edge, to fasten over round-head brass screws fixed in the legs, as shown in Fig. 609. The table is then ready for polishing, etc.

To take the table apart, unfasten the four hooks, and lay back the two hinged side-boards, as shown in the case of K in Fig. 611. Turn back the two buttons, and take out the two pairs of legs, thus completing the operation.

CHAPTER XXIII

Showcase or Curio Tables

First Example, Figs. 614 to 623.—A showcase table, suitable for holding curios or small articles of value, is shown completed on page 240. It may be made of mahogany and french-polished. Four legs are required, each $1\frac{1}{4}$ in. square at the top, tapering from the rail down to the foot, where it measures $\frac{7}{8}$ in. The top rails A (Fig. 619) are $\frac{7}{8}$ in. wide by $\frac{3}{4}$ in. thick. The legs are mortised to receive the tenons, which are rebated on the top edges as at B (Fig. 623). The bottom rails C (Fig. 619) should be $\frac{7}{8}$ in. by $\frac{3}{4}$ in., and have their inside edges rebated for the bottom of pine $\frac{3}{8}$ in. thick D (Fig. 619). The inside corners of the legs are rebated at E (Fig. 623) flush with the inside of the rails as shown also in Fig. 620. The small moulding F in the same figure is glued and sprigged to the edges of the rails, and mitred at the corners. The glass is laid on the rebate thus formed, and beaded in from the inside. The legs can be simply square throughout their length, or a shaped foot as at G in Figs. 615 and 616 could be adopted, worked stub-tenoned and firmly screwed as in Fig. 618.

After the table has been framed up, the bottom, $\frac{3}{8}$ in. thick, should be carefully fitted in the rebates on the bottom rails, and sprigged in. The lid is framed up like a door, the mortices being in the front and back rails, and the tenons on the short rails. Fig. 619 shows a section of the rail which could be moulded in a variety of other ways, the moulding being run on the outside edges after the lid is framed up. The moulding H is glued and mitred to the inside edge of the lid and the glass beaded in from the inside.

The diagonal ties between the legs can be straight as arranged in Figs. 615 to 617, neatly tenoned at their ends and halved obliquely at the centre as in Fig. 622, the small shelf being about $\frac{3}{8}$ in. thick, and of rectangular, oval or circular shape, and with rounded or moulded edges; alternatively the ties would look very effective arranged as in the table illustrated below: here they are cut out of ⅜-in. by 2½-in. stuff to the contour in Fig. 621.

A pair of 1½-in. brass butt hinges is required to hinge the lid to the top rail. The bottom could be covered with plush or velvet of a suitable colour.

Second Example, Figs. 624 to 629.—This table was

Fig. 614.—Showcase or curio table

designed to hold a small part of the collection of a world-wide traveller, and it was required to be not so much a museum case as an occasional table for the drawing-room. It consists of a top compartment of the shape shown by the half plans in Fig. 626, under a bevelled plate-glass top in a moulded frame. This is hinged at the back to open when required; but is purposely prevented from opening, unless moved away from the wall, by the shaped and pierced " pediment," which is fixed to the back of the lid. Below the top compartment there are six shallow drawers, a small cupboard with glass door at each side, and at the corners two triangular

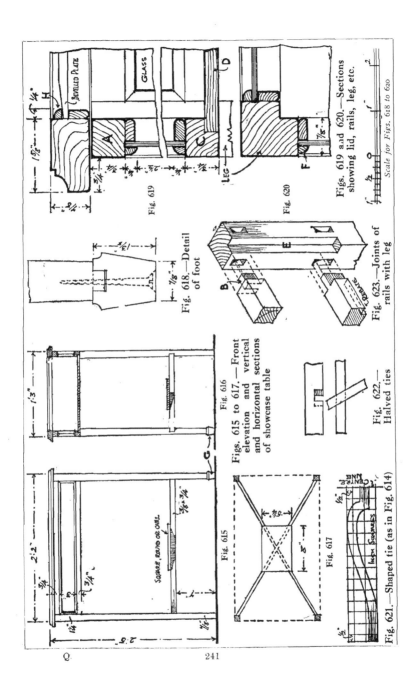

recesses for vases. These different parts are shown by Fig. 627.

The first step will be to prepare six legs similar to those described for the previous example, and these should be

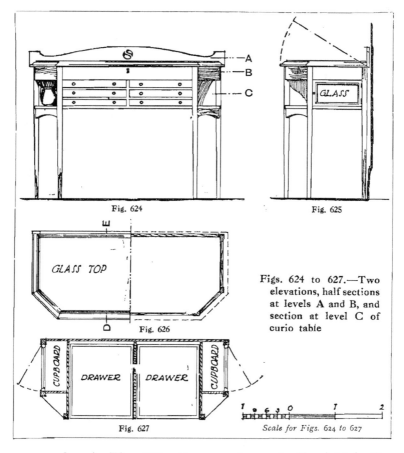

Fig. 624

Fig. 625

Fig. 626

Fig. 627

Figs. 624 to 627.—Two elevations, half sections at levels A and B, and section at level C of curio table

Scale for Figs. 624 to 627

arranged as in Fig. 627; there are two actually right in the front and two pairs at the sides. The back legs are connected by a $3\frac{1}{2}$-in. by $\frac{3}{4}$-in. rail (G, Fig. 628) which is continued down to the extent of the drawers as at H. This takes another rail as at J (Fig. 629), $11\frac{3}{4}$ in. deep, tenoned into

Showcase or Curio Tables

one of the two front legs, and at its bottom flat edge is dovetailed to a 4-in. by ¾-in. rail fixed flat under the bottom drawers as noted. The main purpose of this is to support the ¾-in. solid division between the two sets of drawers seen in Fig. 627, which is 7½ in. deep and comes to the front to receive the small ¾-in. by ¾-in. rails between the drawers as at K in Fig. 628, and is tenoned at the back

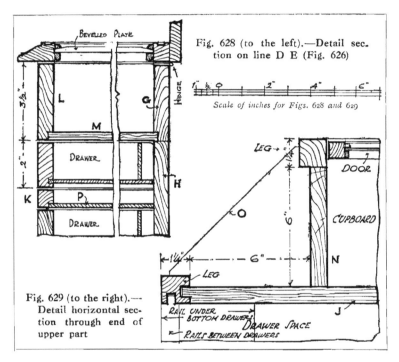

Fig. 628 (to the left).—Detail section on line D E (Fig. 626)

Fig. 629 (to the right).—Detail horizontal section through end of upper part

into the rails G and H; it also supports the necessary drawer runners in the centre. The front legs are connected by a tenoned 3½-in. by ¾-in. rail as at L, which is repeated at the sides and across the splay as in Fig. 625, all the rails being rebated for the bottom of the glazed case (M, Fig. 628) which extends over the whole area as in Fig. 626. Under it comes the rail J in Fig. 629 already mentioned, and also a shorter one N forming the angle recess. The bottom to this and the side cupboard adjoining it can be in one piece, fitted into position level with the rail under the bottom drawer and following the outline at o. The recess is finished with a small arched spandrel under o as in Fig. 624, and the side cupboard with a glazed door. Drawers of a very light nature but framed on the usual lines should be prepared; they are, of course, only for butterflies, coins, etc., and should not be increased very much in depth, or the proportions of the table will suffer. The thin filling between the drawers seen at P in Fig. 628 is an improvement, although not absolutely essential.

The moulding of the top might be mitred and dowelled at the angles; it is cut square at the back to take the shaped pediment shown in Fig. 624.

CHAPTER XXIV

WRITING-TABLES AND DESKS

Small Table, Figs. 630 to 634.—The illustrations herewith show a simple table for use in writing-room or office. Fig. 633 explains the construction of the framing underneath the table top and, together with the enlarged section (Fig. 632) describes the setting out for the curved legs and the carcase

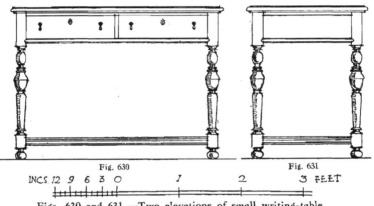

Figs. 630 and 631.—Two elevations of small writing-table

work. The framing follows the general character for the execution of a table of this kind. The top, front and side rails of the framing are stopped dovetailed into the legs, and the bottom rails pinned and the back rail grooved into the legs. The front vertical rail of the drawer division is pinned to the top rail and the horizontal rail, grooved into the vertical rail one end and housed dovetailed to the back rail the other. The vertical rail is made thicker than the horizontal rail to allow the drawer fillets fixed to the latter to finish flush with it on each face. The drawers are supported on the bottom cross rails as shown. Angle blocks are fixed where shown on

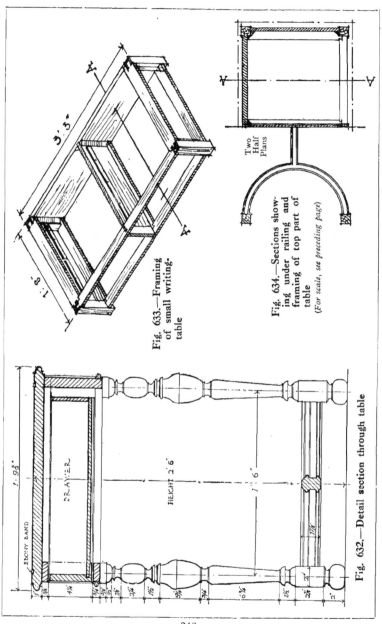

Fig. 633.—Framing of small writing-table

Fig. 634.—Sections showing under railing and framing of top part of table
(For scale, see preceding page)

Fig. 632.—Detail section through table

Writing-tables and Desks

the half plan. The moulded table top is screwed on from underneath.

Converting Plain Table to Writing-table, Figs. 635 to 640.—These illustrations show an addition suitable for almost any small oblong table, transforming it into a writing-table. It will be much less cumbersome and office-like than a desk of the conventional type.

The wood used should match the table under treatment, and the sizes can be modified to meet requirements. It will be understood that the construction here described may not be the one likely to be adopted in expert cabinetwork; but care has been bestowed on the matter with a view to simplifying the work as much as possible.

The completed work comprises a drawer sliding in a box on each side, connected by a shaped back having a simple pierced ornament in the centre. The box containing the drawer shown consists of two 8-in. by $4\frac{1}{4}$-in. sides $\frac{5}{8}$ in. thick (*see* E) slightly rebated along their back edges (at F, Fig. 637) to take a thin back-piece 4 in. high, and also rebated along their inside bottom edges (G, in Fig. 639) to take a $\frac{3}{8}$-in. bottom-piece, which shows in both sections, and has a length of 8 in. minus whatever the exact thickness of the back is made. A top about $\frac{3}{4}$ in. thick is then prepared, $\frac{3}{4}$ in. wider all round than the box now formed, the back edge being left square (*see side elevation*). The three others have a sunk chamfer, or some simple moulding, worked along them as a finish. Grooves $\frac{5}{8}$ in. wide, $\frac{1}{4}$ in. deep, and 8 in. long are made in the under-side of the top to receive the upper edges of the two sides, which, it will be observed project $\frac{1}{4}$ in. above the back-piece, which is not housed; but the sides will eventually be tightly wedged in and glued up to the top. The drawer has a $\frac{5}{8}$-in. front; the other parts are of $\frac{1}{4}$-in. or $\frac{3}{8}$-in. stuff. A good fit for this part of the job is rendered easier by the fact that the front of the drawer is larger than the opening, and so conceals the actual fitting parts when closed. This is explained by the plan and section (Figs. 637 and 640) which show the front $\frac{1}{4}$ in. wider than the opening of the box on each side and along the bottom, and also a chamfer which is taken off along these three edges on the front. Fig. 637 shows that the front has a rebate worked along both the upright edges wide enough to take the sides of the drawer (either $\frac{1}{4}$ in. or $\frac{3}{8}$ in. as selected), in addition to the $\frac{1}{4}$ in. to which extent it overlaps the side piece (*see* J). It has a similar rebate along the bottom inside edge, only a little wider to allow for the space necessary between the bottom of the drawer and the box, which will be about $\frac{3}{16}$ in. The two sides fit into the rebated front, and at the back are slightly rebated in their turn to take the back, as at F on the plan, and all of these parts are grooved about $\frac{1}{4}$ in. up from their lower edges on the inside, to take the bottom piece of the drawer (*see* K *on the sections*).

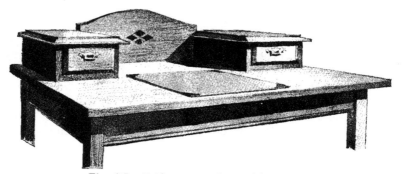

Fig. 635.—Table converted to writing-table

The curved back-piece, which is 7 in. or so high in the centre, is then prepared of the required width, and if possible cut out of one piece. It is fitted to a rebate down the back corner of the box on each side, and will necessitate a small piece being cut out of the edge of the top piece to fit. Four small diamonds are pierced in the centre.

The work should be fixed on the table with screws from below, or through the base of the drawer-box, in which case the top should be left off until last.

Pedestal Kneehole Desk, Figs. 641 to 650.—This desk has four drawers on one side and a cupboard on the other, with a drawer over the knee-hole. The principal points in the making are as follow: Having cut the various pieces for the framing and the doors to size, plane them true to

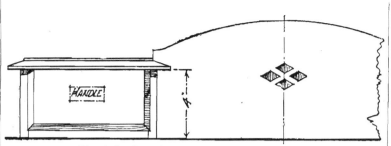

Fig. 636.—Part front elevation of writing-table

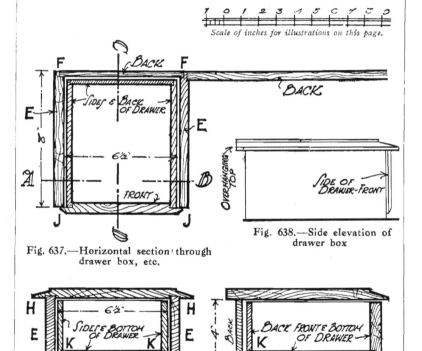

Fig. 637.—Horizontal section through drawer box, etc.

Fig. 638.—Side elevation of drawer box

Figs. 639 and 640.—Cross sections through drawers and boxes on lines A B and C D (Fig. 637)

breadth and thickness, and set out the stiles and rails for mortises and tenons. The tenons are inserted two-thirds the depth. A joint between a stile and rail is shown by Fig. 647, and that between a muntin and rail by Fig. 649. Make the mortise and tenon joints, then plough the stiles and rails to receive the panels, which finish flush with the inside, and therefore require rebating all round (*see* A, Fig. 646). The several parts should now be fitted together. The different joints may be numbered and each frame taken apart and the moulding, etc., done. Then the frames should be put together, the joints being kept far enough apart to be glued and cramped up. It will be necessary to glue the joints properly, and, whilst they are held together with the cramp, two screws should be inserted into the back of the stiles through each joint.

The framing of the top is similar, excepting that the panel is made almost flush with the stiles, as shown in Fig. 644, and the edge can be rounded, moulded or chamfered. For the panel it will be necessary to joint up two or three widths of the best seasoned material,.

The horizontal divisions between the drawers consist of the two side rails and one front rail, held together by mortise and tenon joints, and ploughed to receive thin panel boards as shown in Fig. 646. Next smooth off the inner sides of the two pieces of framing on each of the drawers, put them together, and set out and make the housings to receive these divisions. The same method of procedure applies to the housings receiving the divisions under the drawer over the knee-hole.

The bottom of the cupboard is of boarding, housed into the vertical divisions. The top rail B (Fig. 641) should be prepared and fitted into the vertical end framing, dovetailed as in Fig. 648.

All the framing should now be smoothed off, and the stiles at the back angles should be mitred together as in Fig. 645. These joints, as well as those at C, may be glued in and blocked. Next glue in the divisions under the drawers, the front rails being additionally secured at each end by a screw inserted obliquely from the under side. The top should then be

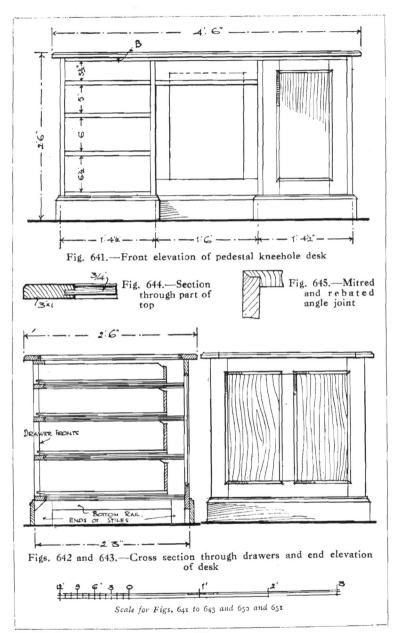

Fig. 641.—Front elevation of pedestal kneehole desk

Fig. 644.—Section through part of top

Fig. 645.—Mitred and rebated angle joint

Figs. 642 and 643.—Cross section through drawers and end elevation of desk

Scale for Figs. 641 to 643 and 650 and 651

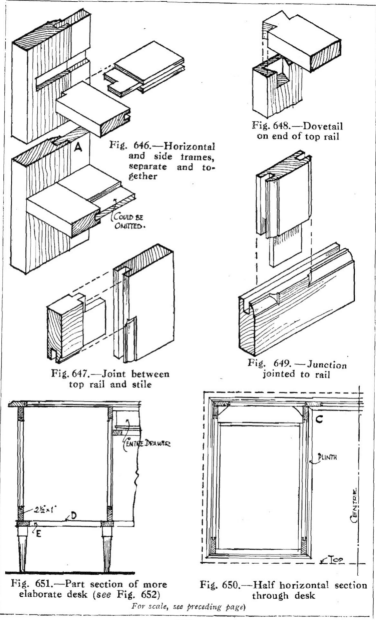

Fig. 646.—Horizontal and side frames, separate and together

Fig. 648.—Dovetail on end of top rail

Fig. 647.—Joint between top rail and stile

Fig. 649.—Junction jointed to rail

Fig. 651.—Part section of more elaborate desk (see Fig. 652)

Fig. 650.—Half horizontal section through desk

For scale, see preceding page

Writing-tables and Desks

turned face downwards, and the carcase properly adjusted and secured with a few screws inserted obliquely and a number of blocks. The chamfered or moulded plinth should next be prepared, and fixed round, to hide nail holes. The drawers are of the usual type and shelves may be fitted on fillets inside the cupboard.

Leather or American cloth should be procured for the top. The thickness of this should be carefully noted, and

Fig. 652.—Pedestal kneehole desk on legs

the stiles and rails of the top planed down if necessary, so as to leave the recess equal to the thickness of the leather, which should be stretched on a flat surface, sized on the back, and allowed to dry, the panel being treated in the same way, this preventing absorption taking place too quickly. The material may then be cut to the exact size. Then, in a warm room, with hot glue of a moderate consistency, the panel should be quickly fastened, without allowing any glue to get on the framing. The leather should next be placed in position and pressed with a roller having brown paper under it. A tooled and gilded design may be worked on the leather top of the desk before it is pasted down. For ease in moving about, castors may be fixed; these would raise the desk, and therefore the height of the pedestals might require slight adjustment.

Suggestion for more Elaborate Desk, Figs. 651 and 652.—The completed desk shown on page 253 is of a rather more decorative character, being better adapted for home use than the very businesslike example just described. The portion above the line D (Fig. 651) is constructed in precisely the same manner as before, although the framing might be reduced to $2\frac{1}{2}$ in. in width; it is carried on a horizontal framework of, say, 2 in. by $1\frac{1}{4}$ in. (E), mitred and rebated as in Fig. 645 at the corners (or alternatively mitred and tenoned), and supported by tapered or turned legs 8 in. high stump-tenoned into it. Castors or " domes of silence " might be fitted, and for a really good finish mahogany, etc., inlaid as in the example, and with planted panel mouldings and a skirting with moulded capping along the back edge of the top, would all be quite suitable.

CHAPTER XXV

LARGE TABLES

Pembroke Dining-table, Figs. 653 to 662.—The table illustrated on this page is an adaptation of the well-known " gateleg " type, which although extremely picturesque is hardly suited for ordinary dining purposes because of the large number of legs it requires (*see* the next example).

Fig. 653.—Pembroke table

In the case of the " Pembroke " table there is very much less material used, and the result is correspondingly lighter in appearance, while in practice the table is remarkably rigid. The drawers introduced will be found very convenient.

To draw the outlined oval of the top for the full-size drawing, make a horizontal line 5 ft. 0¾ in. long, and a central vertical line 3 ft. 6 in. long (*see* dotted lines in Fig. 656). With a radius of half the length, A to B, draw an arc, taking C as the centre, and where it cuts the horizontal line at E and F drive two nails through the paper and into the floor, and another nail at c. Stretch and tie a length of string extending round c, E, and F, forming a triangle. Remove the nail at c only, and draw the outline of the oval by keeping a pencil upright, pressing against the inside of the string. The above rule applies to an oval when the length and width are first decided on. The two vertical lines G and H, 1 ft. $8\frac{1}{4}$ in. apart, represent the hinged joints of the leaves.

The legs and framing can then be set out in accordance with Fig. 656. Here it will be seen that legs I and J are fixed, while the other two swing on a hinged wing-piece as at E and F to support the flaps when raised. All four are 2 in. by 2 in. square for the top $5\frac{1}{2}$ in., below which they taper to $1\frac{1}{8}$ in. The central framework which serves to connect the legs should be constructed as in Fig. 662; it consists of two rails K and L, $5\frac{1}{2}$ in. by 1 in., connected by 2-in. by 1-in. dovetailed and screwed bearers each end as M and N, and small continuous runners should be fixed for the drawers as partially indicated. The latter are of the ordinary type (Figs. 659 and 660) but with their fronts (o) overlapping 1 in. all round in order to conceal the rails K L M and N, and to suit this their sides should be tenoned into the fronts as dotted at o. In order to facilitate opening, the front and rail should be cut away a little as at P in the same figure.

Returning to the main framing, the fixed legs should be attached by screwing in the positions shown, this construction being strengthened by a fillet $\frac{7}{8}$ in. wide as at Q and R, similar fillets being also fixed at s and T to take the shorter rails $5\frac{1}{2}$ in. by 1 in. (U and V) to which the wing-pieces (also of this size) should be attached, each with either one large or two smaller hinges. They are tenoned into the movable legs $\frac{1}{8}$ in. from one face as at F in Fig. 656, and their exact length can best be determined from the full-size plan already advocated, which will serve to make the whole work much clearer than any description.

The table top should be of 1-in. stuff ($\frac{3}{4}$-in. for smaller tables), the centre part and the leaves being made up of widths jointed together and dowelled. If the hinged joints of the table are to be of the rule-joint kind, as in Fig. 661.

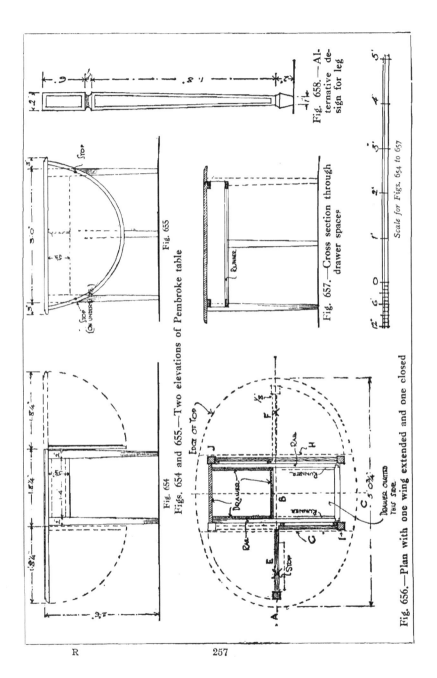

Fig. 654

Figs. 654 and 655.—Two elevations of Pembroke table

Fig. 655

Fig. 657.—Cross section through drawer spaces

Fig. 658.—Alternative design for leg

Scale for Figs. 654 to 657

Fig. 656.—Plan with one wing extended and one closed

R 257

then the central fixed leaf must be widened accordingly. This joint is made with special planes; it has a neat appearance, forming an ovolo moulding when the leaves are down. If the table is used mainly with the leaves raised, then the ordinary joint, as at Fig. 654, is sufficient.

Brass hinges on the underside should be used, one pair to each flap and two wood stops, as in Fig. 656 at E, will serve to adjust the leg in its correct position, and also to stiffen the flap if necessary. A bullet-catch is also rather good to clip the leg in its open position, while to prevent the flaps

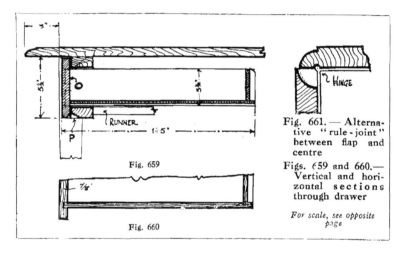

Fig. 661. — Alternative "rule-joint" between flap and centre

Figs. 659 and 660.— Vertical and horizontal sections through drawer

For scale, see opposite page

when down from swinging small pegs or stops can be inserted in their under-sides (as indicated in Fig. 655) projecting against the legs.

The table-edge can be moulded, or as was often done in the case of old mahogany furniture, left square in section. Should a more elaborate form of leg be desired Fig. 658 might be followed; it shows a square design, and the inner lines can be either inlaid or the edges of slight sinkings. It will be observed that the drawer-fronts in the finished table illustrated have a line of inlaid banding.

Gateleg Table, Figs. 663 to 668.—The accompanying illustrations show a table 4 ft. 6 in. by 3 ft. 6 in., which when

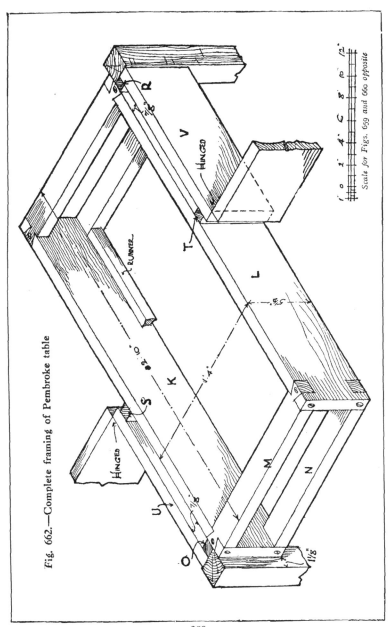

Fig. 662.—Complete framing of Pembroke table

both leaves are down measures 3 ft. 6 in. by about 1 ft. 6 in., and placed against a wall makes a convenient side table. The oval top can be set out as described for the " Pembroke " table (p. 255) or a top of the type shown in Fig. 668 might be substituted, and the legs may be about 2 in. square ; for a 3 ft. 6 in. table about $1\frac{3}{4}$ in. ; for a 2 ft. 6 in. table about $1\frac{1}{2}$ in. The lower cross-rails can be about 2 in. by 1 in. and the upper ones 5 in. by 1 in.

The rails are all tenoned into the legs, and the " gates " each consist of the two rails and leg A B and C (Fig. 663), the top one being hinged to the long rail D-D, and the bottom pivoted on a very thick screw passing through it into the bottom rail E-E. To allow for the gate-legs closing against the lower side rails, the latter must be notched for nearly half their thickness, and the gate-legs to correspond (see Fig. 667). But this is obviated in the top case by arranging the top rail on the inner face of the legs as F in Fig. 666, and the top gate-rail on the outer face as at G, which allows the whole to fold away within the joint on the top indicated by the line H. Note that the centre or pin of the hinge on the top rail should come exactly over the screw or pivot in the lower rail, or the gate will not swing level.

Modern-style Dining-table, Figs. 669 to 674.—This table is comparatively easy to produce, and is an effective piece of furniture.

The elevations show the general proportions and design of the table, from which it will be seen that octagonal legs inlaid on four faces are the main feature. Enlarged details of one of the legs are shown in Fig. 674, and to execute the work it should be chamfered as indicated, each end of the chamfer being finished or " stopped " with an ogee curve. Inlaying the chamfers can then be proceeded with, which necessitates the use of a box without ends, such as is illustrated at C, Fig. 672. The leg is fixed inside the box so that one chamfer is level with the top edges, and a scratch stock can be operated from one edge to cut the groove shown, which receives the inlaying or stringing.

To obtain the grooves for inlaying the octagonal type with a spindle machine, a box is necessary in order that the

Large Tables

chamfer can be retained in a perfectly level plane. The leg should be fixed in the box with the chamfer to be grooved lining up with the box sides. The box is then laid on its side and the spindle cutter adjusted to the required height. When

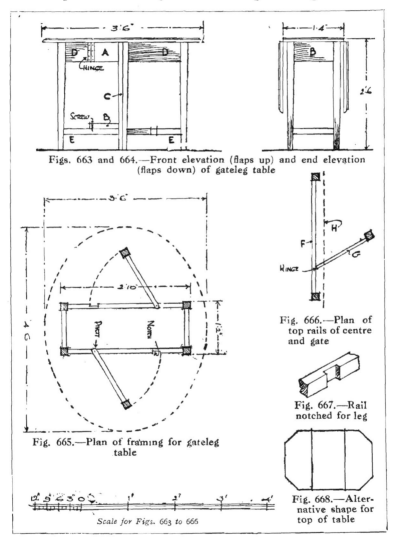

Figs. 663 and 664.—Front elevation (flaps up) and end elevation (flaps down) of gateleg table

Fig. 665.—Plan of framing for gateleg table

Fig. 666.—Plan of top rails of centre and gate

Fig. 667.—Rail notched for leg

Fig. 668.—Alternative shape for top of table

Scale for Figs. 663 to 666

one side of the leg has been grooved, the leg must be taken out of the box and turned one quarter, and so on until all are worked.

The framework should be tenoned together after the legs have been inlaid and the chamfers cleaned up. A good plan is to put the four legs together side by side on the bench and then secure them with a handscrew at the centre. Lines can then be squared across the legs to indicate the shoulder lines at the bottom, finished length at the top, and other lines for the mortices.

Similarly, the rails should be secured in pairs in the bench vice, and the shoulder lines are then marked across the top edges; when separated the shoulders should be returned upon the front and back faces. Fig. 673 shows the connection between the rail and the leg; twin tenons are employed with a haunch between them and at the top. At the bottom of the leg the joint takes the form of a through tenon, which should be wedged from the underside for greater security.

Shaping the rails should be proceeded with prior to gluing up the frame, the small centre parts being cut from $\frac{1}{2}$-in. material, and cut into the centre of the rails until they project $\frac{1}{4}$ in. beyond the face side. The curved bottom parts may then be "bow" or "bandsawed," the four pieces being fixed together with the edges level, which economises labour in cutting. Before being separated, the curves should be filed and glasspapered. When the tablets have been glued in, beads are mitred and glued round as shown, which effects a neat finish.

The part requiring most attention in a table of this type is undoubtedly the top. With a large surface of this character, the wood must be most carefully selected in order to obtain suitable figuring and colour. Small splash figure in oak is that most sought after for the purpose, and the boards should be carefully tried in various positions before the joints are decided on.

Oak, particularly, is a wood that shades according to position, and joints made without reference to this will often show one light and one dark piece, which cannot afterwards

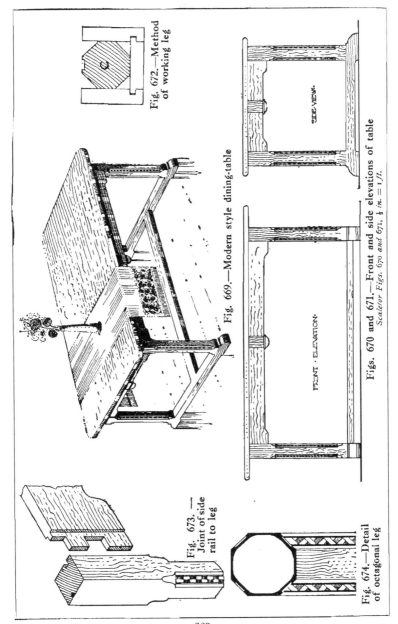

Fig. 672.—Method of working leg

Fig. 669.—Modern style dining-table

Figs. 670 and 671.—Front and side elevations of table
Scale for Figs. 670 and 671, ⅜ in. = 1 ft.

Fig. 673.—Joint of side rail to leg

Fig. 674.—Detail of octagonal leg

be satisfactorily dealt with. The joints should be either dowelled or cross-tongued.

After the joints are dry and squaring is completed, cleaning up should be proceeded with. In this connection it may be well to mention that scraping should be entirely dispensed with in the case of oak. A well-sharpened metal plane, taking off very fine shavings, will provide a fine, level and smooth surface which will need only a moderate amount of glasspapering to bring to a perfect finish. The action of a scraper is such as to remove the soft parts of the timber, leaving the hard silver grain projecting slightly

Fig. 675.—Extension dining-table

above the surface. This slight projection is increased when glasspapering is proceeded with, the paper also cutting away the soft wood. When polished or waxed, the projecting silver grain is quite obvious and unpleasant.

To fix a large top of this character, buttoning down is recommended as mentioned for the hall seat in Chapter X p. 116.

Extension Dining-table, Figs. 675 to 687. — This table can be simply and rapidly extended without having separate leaves for insertion, or the use of long screws and keys.

The table shown is 3 ft. 3 in. square on plan when closed and 2 ft. 7 in. high, and extends to 5 ft. 8 in. by 3 ft. 3 in.

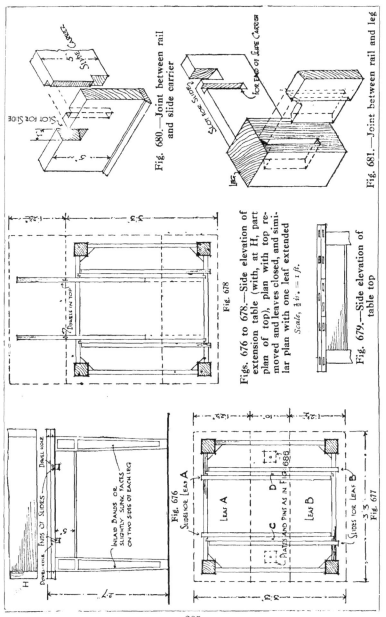

Fig. 680.—Joint between rail and slide carrier

Fig. 681.—Joint between rail and leg

Figs. 676 to 678.—Side elevation of extension table (with, at H, part plan of top), plan with top removed and leaves closed, and similar plan with one leaf extended. *Scale, $\tfrac{3}{4}$ in. = 1 ft.*

Fig. 679.—Side elevation of table top

265

Larger sizes than this can easily be prepared on exactly similar lines. The legs are $3\frac{1}{2}$ in. square, tapering to $2\frac{1}{2}$ in., or various types of turned legs can be procured; they are first framed together with 5-in. by 1-in. rails, these having mortice-and-tenon joints, mitred at their intersection (*see* Fig. 681), and the shoulders drawn close with a single draw-bore pin to each joint. These joints, if preferred, may be made with three 3-in. by $\frac{3}{8}$-in. birch dowels. In each case, the inner angles should be strengthened with 2-in. by 2-in. diagonal blocks (*see* plan, Fig. 678), and the appearance of the rails can be enhanced by thickening pieces on the bottom as in Fig. 680.

The extension top is double, each section being 1 in. thick, and although the under section is afterwards subdivided into three parts, the two should be framed together of the same size with $2\frac{1}{4}$-in. mortice-and-tenon clamps across their ends (*see* Figs. 679 and 687). The middle portion of the divided top is less in width than the outer parts, and the tenons must be arranged accordingly (*see* Fig. 679), so that a tenon is near the end (from $1\frac{1}{2}$ in. to 2 in.) on each piece. Two pieces of 5-in. by 1-in. stuff are framed across between the outer rails, jointed at the ends (*see* C and D, Fig. 677), *and also* Figs. 678, 680 and 684; these carry the slides, which support the extended leaves. In this way the two outer sections or leaves of the under thickness of the top can be drawn out so as to form one continuous surface, thus adding 2 ft. 5 in. to the length of the table. The table is shown with one side extended on plan in Fig. 678, and in section by Fig. 683. The hardwood slides (Figs. 682 to 684), 2 in. by 1 in., are arranged in pairs, one pair working inside the carriers and the other pair outside, as noted in Fig. 677. To obtain the angle at which the slide is to be set, it must be understood that in drawing out the slides the leaf attached to them must rise a distance equal to its own thickness, so as to bring it level with the upper surface. In this case, the leaves being 1 ft. $2\frac{1}{2}$ in. wide, the slope requires to be 1 in. in $14\frac{1}{2}$ in.; the top edge of the slides can be bevelled accordingly, and fixed to the top with screws, as shown in Fig. 682. The groove in which the slides work is formed by screwing $\frac{3}{4}$-in.

Large Tables

by 1-in. guides to the sides of the carriers as in Figs. 683 and 685, allowing only sufficient play to work freely. It will be seen, by reference to Fig. 683, that the upper guide, when fixed, is tapered off to a feather edge, and that the extended slide rests on this. The guide, however, does little or no

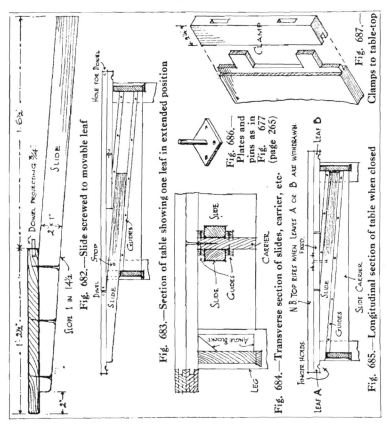

work, as the middle portion of the lower top is screwed down to the frame and carriers (*see* Fig. 684), and the leverage is consequently resisted by the fixed portion, the guide at this point serving as a packing.

In order to allow the sliding leaves to be drawn out, the top (upper portion) should lift easily, and this is provided for by fixing two plates and pins on the under-side of the top (*see* Figs. 677 and 686), the plates being housed flush with the surface as in Fig. 685 and screwed, and the pins passing through holes bored in the central fixed portion. The leaf can thus be drawn out, the top rising with it until they are clear of each other, when the top drops back again to its original level, and the leaf is pushed close to the edge of the top. A connection between the two is required in the form of two dowels, which are fixed in the edge of the leaf, projecting ¾ in. and rounded at the point (*see* Figs. 676 and 682). Corresponding holes are bored in the edge of the upper top to receive the dowels, and the middle fixed portion of the lower top should be cut to accommodate them loosely, and on the under-side of the leaves, sinkings are formed as finger-holds in drawing out (*see* Figs. 683 and 685). To prevent the leaves drawing out too far, a pin or stop is fixed in each slide at the required position, as shown in Fig. 683.

CHAPTER XXVI

SIDEBOARDS

THE sideboard affords the craftsman great scope for decorative work, and at the same time has a sound utilitarian value. Some fine examples of elaborate finish are included in this chapter, but if the reader hesitates to tackle so extensive an undertaking he should be able to retain the same forms and arrangements divested of some of their surface decoration and enrichments.

Small Modern Sideboard, Decorated with Veneer, Figs. 688 to 701.—The first design given in this chapter is for a sideboard, 4 ft. 6 in. on carcase; it could easily be extended by lengthening the centre drawers. Decorated with figured veneers, this piece looks exceptionally well when polished, and the breaking up of the doors in the design is such as to generally improve the general proportion. Mahogany furniture of this character should be well finished with french polish in the usual way preparatory to a " dulling down " process, effected by means of a brush and finely ground pumice-powder. Metalwork, such as handles and rails for curtains, should be oxidised silver.

The constructional part of the sideboard is shown in the sectional views representing the carcase with all drawers, trays, and doors removed. A framed-up division is employed immediately below the top drawers, and the inside carcase ends are pinned or tenoned into the cross rails of this part. Drawer rails of this and similar work may either be stub-mortised and tenoned into the inside carcase ends, or they may be secured by slip or diminished dovetailing. The latter method is to be preferred, as by this construction, open shoulders in the front are avoided. It will be noticed that the drawer divisions are framed together; drawer runners are stub-tenoned into the drawer rails at the front, and trenches

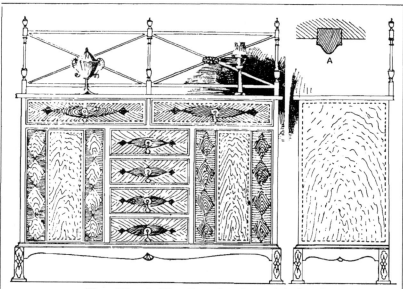

Figs. 688 and 689.—Two elevations of sideboard

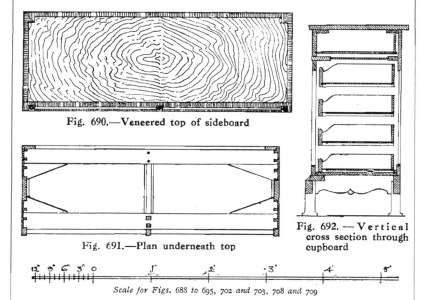

Fig. 690.—Veneered top of sideboard

Fig. 691.—Plan underneath top

Fig. 692.—Vertical cross section through cupboard

Scale for Figs. 688 to 695, 702 and 703, 708 and 709

Sideboards

or grooves are made to receive the runners as shown in the front sectional view. Dust boards are inserted in the grooved runners, and the frames are then completed by adding a grooved back rail stub-tenoned to fit the grooves in the

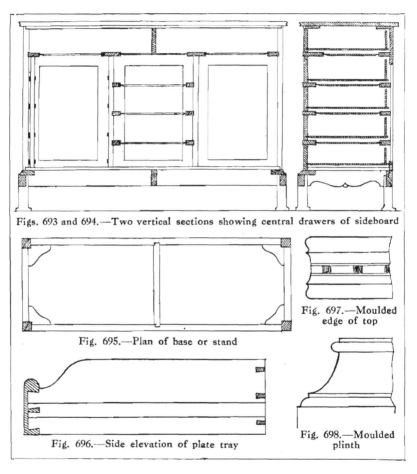

Figs. 693 and 694.—Two vertical sections showing central drawers of sideboard

Fig. 695.—Plan of base or stand

Fig. 696.—Side elevation of plate tray

Fig. 697.—Moulded edge of top

Fig. 698.—Moulded plinth

drawer runners. This feature should also be noted in the end sectional view.

A plan of the stand or base is shown (*see* Fig. 695), and it will be seen that $2\frac{1}{2}$-in. material is used for the legs with

$1\frac{1}{2}$-in. rails mortised and tenoned between. A centre cross or stretcher rail is also employed as a strengthening factor,

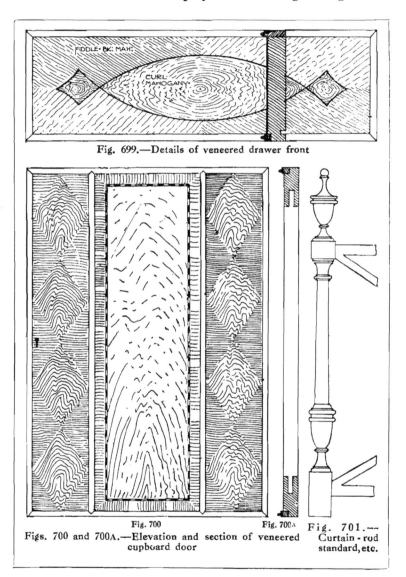

Fig. 699.—Details of veneered drawer front

Figs. 700 and 700A.—Elevation and section of veneered cupboard door

Fig. 701.—Curtain-rod standard, etc.

Sideboards

and brackets should be screwed in the corners as shown. Recessing is employed as a decorative feature for the legs, and is usually done by carving. It should be outlined with gouges and cut away or " grounded out " to a depth of about

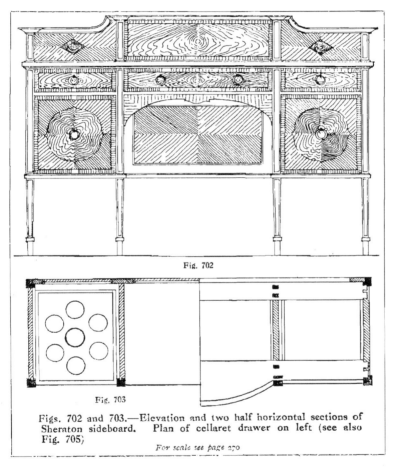

Figs. 702 and 703.—Elevation and two half horizontal sections of Sheraton sideboard. Plan of cellaret drawer on left (see also Fig. 705)

For scale see page 270

$\frac{1}{8}$ in. In small parts such as the legs shown, carving is satisfactory; but where large quantities have to be produced a different practice is followed. This consists of cutting separate frets or traceries from $\frac{1}{8}$-in. material, and gluing them to the groundwork. Eight, and in some cases twelve, frets can be cut at one machining by temporarily gluing them all together with paper between the pieces, which permits of easy separation. When gluing down frets of this type, care must be exercised in applying the glue, the difficulty of which will be appreciated when it is considered that in parts the tracery does not exceed $\frac{1}{8}$ in. in width. If a board of pine or soft timber is prepared and covered with a thin coating of glue, a fret can be pressed down on same, and carefully removed with a thin layer of glue adhering. This is slightly warmed, and then laid on a groundwork, securing the same with a board and hand screws until dry.

Plate trays are a necessary adjunct to the modern sideboard, and should be lined with baize; one of these is shown in Fig. 696. The front is narrower than the sides and back, and should be obtained from 1 in. stuff. A groove is made in each side to a depth of $\frac{1}{4}$ in., which receives slips or fillets screwed inside the carcase ends. The right-hand side should be fitted up with trays, whilst the left-hand side cupboard is utilised for a cellaret drawer, as in Fig. 703 (p. 273) and Fig. 705 (p. 275). It should be remembered when constructing the sideboard that a false end is necessary in the cupboards in order that the trays, or cellaret, may clear the doors. One false end in each cupboard is sufficient. It should be made from $\frac{3}{4}$-in. mahogany, with a piece of $1\frac{1}{4}$-in. stuff tongued into the front edge. The space occurring between the false end and the carcase end should have an occasional fillet fixed inside immediately underneath the tray fillets. The false end should be not less than $\frac{1}{8}$ in. thicker than the finished door.

The decoration of the doors is shown in Fig. 700. Finely-figured curl mahogany should be utilised for the veneered diamonds, and fiddle-back veneer for the cross-banding and groundwork of the side panels. The centre panel would be most effective executed with curl veneer. A sectional view, Fig. 700A, shows the construction of the door with mortised and tenoned cramps.

To execute the latter part, a drawing should be made of the door design on a stiff sheet of cartridge paper glued to a board.

Sideboards

The sideboard rail is constructed in parts in order to facilitate fixing. A square plate is riveted to a long rod, and the former is screwed down to the top with the rod vertical. The various parts are then dropped over the rod, and the whole secured by screwing down the terminals

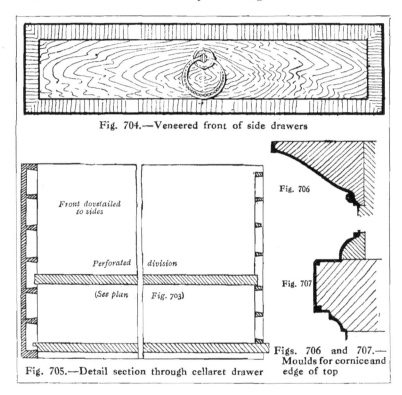

Fig. 704.—Veneered front of side drawers

Fig. 705.—Detail section through cellaret drawer

Figs. 706 and 707.—Moulds for cornice and edge of top

(*see* Fig. 701). Curtains of silk are frequently attached to the rail, falling behind it.

When veneering is completed, the doors should be grooved and rebated round the edges, to receive the mouldings. These project beyond the surface, and a section of them is given in Fig. 689A. A moulded and inlaid top is introduced. Inlaying the edge would be proceeded with after the moulding had been worked.

Fig. 691 (p. 270) shows an economical and rigid method for arranging the carcase top. Two rails are introduced with a bracket of triangular shape glued at each end; the rails are dovetailed into the ends.

Sheraton Sideboard, Figs. 702 to 707.—The Sheraton-style sideboard here shown introduces similar decorative features to the preceding example. It would also look well fitted with curtain rails as before in lieu of the solid back shown. Cellaret drawers are substituted for the cupboards, and a kneehole cupboard space is also provided. The half plan shows a curved centre drawer, and a method of dovetailing the rails into the ends, with pinned or tenoned joints in the divisions passing through the rails. A plan of the cellaret drawer is given in Fig. 703. It should be strongly constructed, and a pierced board introduced about $4\frac{1}{2}$ in. from the bottom in order to receive the bottles.

The drawer front is of simple design, and moulded details for the top and back are illustrated in Figs. 706 and 707. The edge of the top should be cross-banded with $\frac{1}{8}$-in. square ebony lines inlaid on the corners; an effective finish is given to this part of the work by rounding off the upper corner.

Another Sheraton Sideboard, Figs. 708 and 709.—Another design for a sideboard based on Sheraton lines, but reminiscent of Chippendale in the treatment of its legs, is given in Figs. 708 and 709. It relies on good proportion, veneering and inlaying for decorative effect, and is fitted with three cupboards and drawers. The former could be fitted. as follows: On the left-hand side: cellaret drawer and shelf, centre cupboard, fitted with shelves for general accommodation. On the right-hand side: trays for plate and cutlery.

Simple Pedestal Sideboard, Figs. 710 to 715.—The sideboard shown complete on page 278 is intended to be produced in mahogany, and the construction will be found fairly simple. It is made with end pedestals, each of which is fitted with a drawer and cupboard. The central space is filled with a drawer and shelf. The legs, drawer fronts, door panels, and the top of the sideboard are inlaid with satinwood bandings, and the door panels are quartered.

In making the sideboard, first begin on the pedestals,

Sideboards

which are framed up in the manner shown in Fig. 715. There are eight legs A, which are 3 ft. 1 in. long by 1½ in. square, and four sides B, which are 2 ft. 4 in. long by 1 ft. 5 in. wide by 1 in. thick. The legs and sides are dowelled or tongued

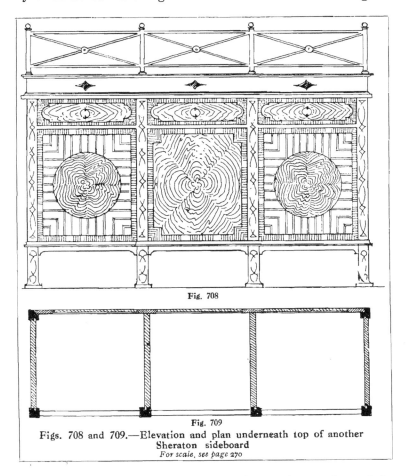

Figs. 708 and 709.—Elevation and plan underneath top of another Sheraton sideboard
For scale, see page 270

together, the sides being kept flush with the inner edges of the legs as in Fig. 713. The top and bottom drawer rails, C and D, are 1½ in. wide by 1 in. thick. The top drawer rails are dovetailed into the top ends of the legs, and the bottom rails are tenoned as shown. The top drawer bearers E are 1 in. square, simply screwed in position. The bottom drawer bearers F are 1½ in. by 1 in.; they are grooved ⅛ in. into the sides, and may also be tenoned into the drawer rails. The edges of the bottom drawer rails and bearers are grooved to receive ¼-in. dust-boards, which are pushed home from the back. The bottom shelves G are 1 in. thick, and are mortised and tenoned into the legs and sides as shown, the mortices being cut to a depth of ¾ in.

Fig. 710.—Simple pedestal sideboard

The framework of the centre portion of the sideboard is clearly shown in Fig. 715, to the right. The top and bottom drawer rails, H and I, are 1½ in. wide by 1 in. thick. The top rail is dovetailed and the bottom rail is tenoned into the sides in the positions indicated in Fig. 713. The top drawer bearers J are 1½ in. by 1 in. and screwed to the sides. The bottom drawer bearers K are 2 in. by 1 in., grooved into the sides and can be tenoned into the drawer rail in a similar manner to those in the pedestals. The bottom drawer rail and bearers are grooved to receive a dust-board as before. The legs overhang the sides by ½ in., and it will be necessary

Sideboards

to fill up the drawer opening with pieces L to allow the drawer to open. The filling-up pieces should be ¾ in. thick, and are screwed in position. The bottom shelf M is 1 in. thick, mortised and tenoned into the sides and back legs as shown,

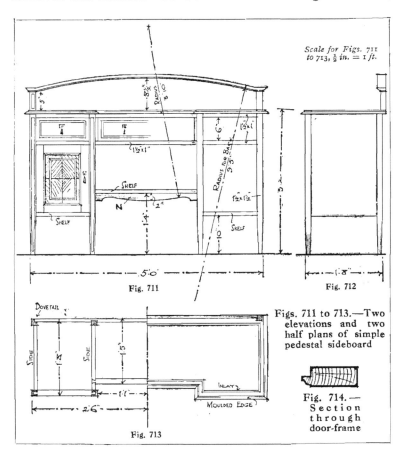

Figs. 711 to 713.—Two elevations and two half plans of simple pedestal sideboard

Fig. 714.—Section through door-frame

the mortises being cut to a depth of ¾ in. A shaped span rail (N, Fig. 711) 2 in. deep by ¾ in. thick is fitted underneath the bottom shelf, and housed about 3/16 in. into the sides.

The bottom ends of the legs are tapered to 1⅛ in. square in section, and the back edges of the back legs and bottom boards are rebated ½ in. deep by ⅜ in. wide to receive the back boards. The front legs are inlaid, the stringings used being about 1/16 in. wide. In fixing the parts together, first deal with the pedestals. The legs and sides are glued up. The drawer rails, bearers, and bottom shelves are then fixed; but it will be found best if the fixing of the dust-boards is left until after the top of the sideboard is in position.

A top rail o (Fig. 715), the whole length of the carcase, is fitted at the back. It is 3 in. deep by 1 in. thick, dovetailed

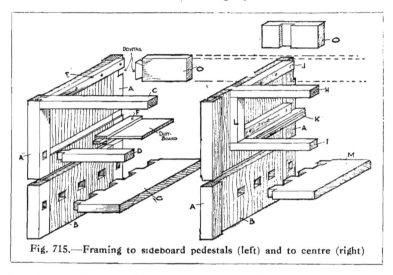

Fig. 715.—Framing to sideboard pedestals (left) and to centre (right)

into the end legs, and lapped to the middle legs, as shown also in Fig. 713. The bottom edge of the rail is rebated to receive the back boards, and it is screwed in position. The back is of boards ½ in. thick, screwed in position.

The top of the sideboard is 1 in. thick, and is shaped as shown in Fig. 713. The front and end edges overhang 1 in., and they are moulded. The top is inlaid with a ¼-in. banding, which is set about ½ in. in from the moulded edges and 1 in. in from the back edge. The top is fixed in position with screws through the drawer rails, bearers, and back rail.

The back of the sideboard is 1 in. thick, cut to the shape shown in Fig. 711. The ends of the back are finished with

Sideboards

two uprights, which are $1\frac{1}{2}$ in. square, mortised and tenoned to the ends or rebated as in Fig. 713. The face of the uprights should be inlaid with bandings as shown. The top edges of the back are finished with a moulding $1\frac{3}{4}$ in. deep, which, with careful fitting, can be bent to the required curve and may be either screwed to the back or tongued to its top edges.

The drawers are made up in the usual manner, their fronts

Fig. 716.—Cottage sideboard

being $\frac{3}{4}$ in. thick, and inlaid with bandings, and the sides, back and bottom can be about $\frac{3}{8}$ in. thick.

The framework of the doors is $2\frac{1}{4}$ in. by 1 in., moulded and rebated as shown by Fig. 714. The panels should be $\frac{1}{4}$ in. thick, with veneer quartering and bandings.

Cottage Sideboard, Figs. 716 to 727.—This sideboard is of a very simple type. Oak or American walnut is very suitable for its construction, and a finish obtained by slightly wax-polishing.

The lower part is separate from the upper, and its main

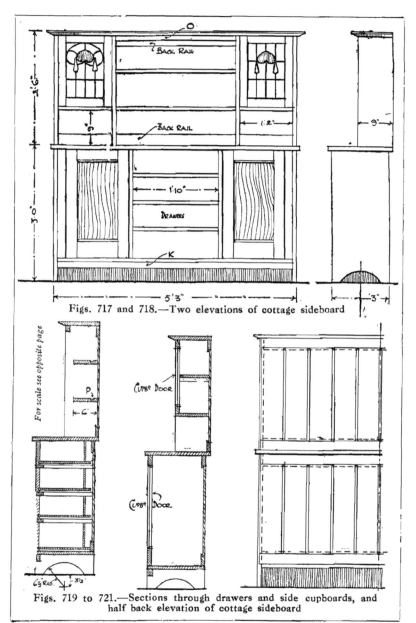

Figs. 717 and 718.—Two elevations of cottage sideboard

Figs. 719 to 721.—Sections through drawers and side cupboards, and half back elevation of cottage sideboard

Sideboards

construction will be gathered from Fig. 723, which shows an upright end A not less than ¾ in. thick, 1 ft. 3 in. wide, 2 ft. 11¼ in. long, plus two 2 in. by ⅜ in. projections at the top; a bottom B 5 ft. 11½ in. long, plus ⅜ in. projecting ends for housing into stopped grooves (as at C, Fig. 724); and an

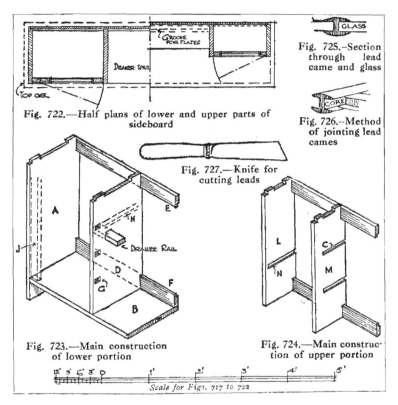

Fig. 722.—Half plans of lower and upper parts of sideboard

Fig. 725.—Section through lead came and glass

Fig. 726.—Method of jointing lead cames

Fig. 727.—Knife for cutting leads

Fig. 723.—Main construction of lower portion

Fig. 724.—Main construction of upper portion

Scale for Figs. 717 to 722

upright division D with two housing projections to fit into grooves in the top and bottom shelves. The top shelf (not shown in Fig. 723) is 5 ft. 5 in. by 1 ft. 5 in., with square or moulded edges, and overhanging 1 in. at the back as in Figs. 718 to 720. The work is stiffened by the rails E and F, 3 in. by ¾ in., rebated into A and continuous through D which is cut to suit them; they are rebated to receive a thin back filling of tongued and V-jointed boarding as in Fig. 721. The end A should be rebated along its inner back edge ⅜ in. by ⅜ in. to take this boarding. Near the front of D should be formed sinkings to receive the stop-housed 2 in. by ¾ in. drawer-rails as at G, the bottom drawer being a little deeper than the others. Oak runners should also be screwed on as at H, an upright style as dotted at J 2 in. by ¾ in., and a piece 1½ in. deep as at K (Fig. 717) to conceal angle-blocks fixed to strengthen the joint between the bottom shelf and ends. The doors are quite plain, single-panelled, with top and bottom rails splayed or moulded as indicated; the framing of them can be tenoned in the ordinary way, or simply effected by the use of dovetailed halving on the back; the panels should be chamfered as necessary and beaded into rebates from behind. The drawers can be made in accordance with the instructions given on p. 34.

Fig. 728.—Sideboard dresser

The upper portion of the sideboard is explained by Fig. 724, the uprights L and M being 9 in. by ¾ in. and 8⅝ in. by ¾ in. respectively, and both 2 ft. 5 in. long, plus 2 in. by ⅜ in. housings at the top. For the bottom of the end cupboard a shelf 8⅝ in. wide (allowing for a ⅜ in. back-filling) is required, stop-housed 3/16 in. deep as at N, while the two central shelves are only 6 in. wide and housed as shown,

Sideboards

or they might be fixed with dowels only. A pair of rebated back rails as before are fitted at the top and bottom, and the top shelf (5 ft. 7 in. by 11 in. by ¾ in. with a wide chamfered or moulded edge on three sides) requires fitting to the housed

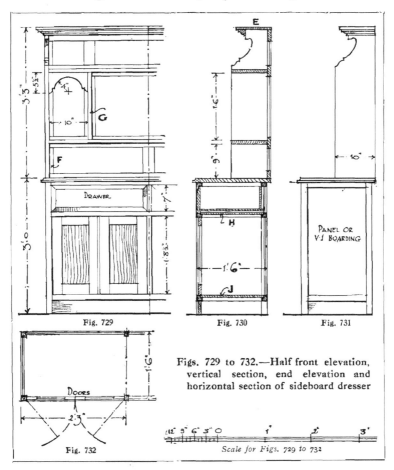

Figs. 729 to 732.—Half front elevation, vertical section, end elevation and horizontal section of sideboard dresser

ends; it is finished underneath by a 1¼ in. fillet as at o in Fig. 717. It might be as well to have two couples of oak dowels in the top of the lower portion, fitting into sockets in the bottom of the end uprights of the upper part. The glazed doors can be tenoned in the regular manner, or being small merely halved (not dovetailed) together, and it is usually desirable to have a groove or bead to support plates on the shelves as at P (Fig. 719).

The leaded panels.—The process of lead glazing is not difficult. The materials necessary consist of some "leading," in section as shown in Fig. 725, a variety of glass of different colours, a glass-cutter, and soldering appliances. First make a full-size sketch of the design, and cut out the various shapes with scissors, leaving about $\frac{1}{16}$ in. waste between each shape, as the " core " of the lead is about this in thickness. These are employed as patterns to guide the progress of the tool in cutting the glass, the colouring of which should be judiciously planned in the above-mentioned design.

When all the glasses are cut to the correct shape and pieced together, but with a space between the leads, the glazing can be begun. First straighten the lead, then cut lengths for the outside border, and afterwards the design, working all the long lines first, and finishing, wherever possible, close and true against the " core " of another lead (see Fig. 726). An old table-knife ground down to the shape shown in Fig. 727 serves admirably for cutting. The loose glasses may be held in position while measuring and cutting off the leads, with brads driven into the table. True up with a straight-edge, and solder up the joints on both sides. To avoid the glass rattling in the leads, fill up the cavities with putty and lampblack, when the panel is completed.

The leaded panels are held in place by strips of beading, fixed with wire nails or brads. If the beading does not fit quite tightly, thin strips of wood should be wedged between it and the rebate; or strips of wash-leather can be placed in it for the glass to rest on to prevent rattling, taking care that both are covered by the beading, which should be neatly fitted and mitred at the corners.

Sideboard Dresser, Figs. 728 to 738.—The kitchen sideboard is an indispensable but at the same time unlovely fitting, which can, however, be much improved in general design and style of finish, or relegated to the scullery and replaced by a compromise between sideboard and dresser on

Sideboards

the general lines of that illustrated on p. 284. This has small cupboards at the top having plain doors with small fillets planted on them, a curved spandril-piece in front of a mirror

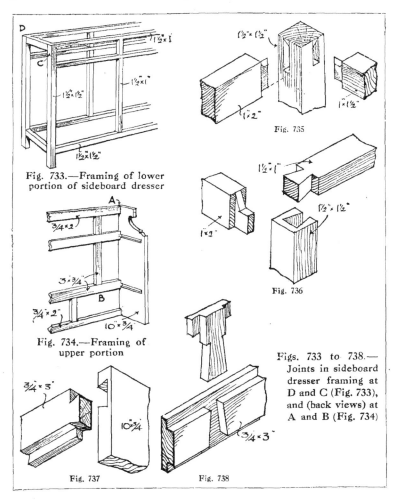

Fig. 733.—Framing of lower portion of sideboard dresser

Fig. 734.—Framing of upper portion

Figs. 733 to 738.—Joints in sideboard dresser framing at D and C (Fig. 733), and (back views) at A and B (Fig. 734)

enclosed by a small moulding, and shaped heads to the four lower doors, all of which can readily be arranged; or the working drawings, which give a slightly simpler version of the same design, can be followed. Fig. 734 shows the framing-up of the essential parts of the upper half, and Figs. 737 and 738 the joints advised to be employed. The shelves are stop-housed into the rebates in the upright sides, which last are cut back and shaped, finished with a flat top, 8 in. or 9 in. wide, and a mitred cornice moulding E (Fig. 730).

Three small pieces at each end, as at F, etc., in Fig. 729, can be filled in without special jointing, and the whole of the back should be rebated for the necessary thin panels. When fitted together the uprights G and the shaped arches can be added unless the small cupboards are adopted, and at completion the whole can be fitted by means of dowels (or screws inserted from below) to the top of the lower section. The main framing of the latter is as shown in Figs. 733, 735, and 736, and should be rebated for flat boarding as at H and J in Fig. 730, and the back filled in. The drawers are of the ordinary type, but with bevelled fronts and drop-handles, and the doors can be varied as desired.

The ends should be grooved for the panel shown in Fig. 731, and a skirting can be filled in next to the floor at front and sides. The top has a moulded edge.

CHAPTER XXVII

A BEDROOM SUITE

Wardrobe, Figs. 739 to 757.—To discuss the practical features of the wardrobe shown on page 291 the best plan will be to take each part separately, dealing with particular points as they would occur in the making.

The plinth frame should be the first part constructed. A basswood frame is through dovetailed at the front corners, with a back rail slip dovetailed in position as in Figs. 747, 748, etc. Fig. 748 shows the back rail made wider than the front and sides, this being necessary in order to save fitting in a filling piece after the plinth mouldings are glued in position. Fig 749 shows this part more clearly, with part notched away in order to receive the mouldings.

There are various methods of finishing the plinth after the groundwork has been dovetailed together, the best being to " face up " the dovetailed groundwork with $\frac{1}{4}$-in. mahogany, this being mitred on to the groundwork as shown in Figs. 749 and 750. After the groundwork has been levelled down and toothed, one side is placed in the mitre block and planed until a correct mitre is obtained. Then the piece should be thoroughly warmed and glued and hand-screwed in position. The end piece should be followed by the front, carefully testing the mitre before gluing. Blocks may be introduced to strengthen the whole frame.

When the frame is dry, it should be planed true, taking care to test it for winding, which would prevent the top carcase from standing vertical and would cause trouble with the door frame.

The next item in the construction is the " surbase," this part of the work being shown by Figs. 741, 742, etc. It is really a small carcase containing one drawer, and is usually made separate from the main carcase.

Fig. 741 shows the top rails bracketed in order to economise the material. By this means 3-in. rails can be used, the brackets being obtained from odd material. Fig. 741 shows also the general spacing and arrangement of the dovetails, and it will be seen that a small dovetail is introduced at the front and back of the work. A full carcase bottom would be introduced, with a small dovetail back and front, as is the case with the top rails. The back for this part would be solid and fixed into a bevelled rebate as shown.

It is well to remember that framings and carcases for drawer work should be made slightly larger at the back, in order that the drawer may act properly.

The surbase is completed by mitreing and gluing round the moulded pieces to the position indicated in Fig. 746.

The hanging carcase is proceeded with very similarly to the surbase. The dovetails should be cut differently from the drawers because of the unwieldy size. The best plan is to cut the pins first, and then to mark the dovetails from them by supporting the ends in a vertical position whilst the bottom and top lie flat on the bench. The back is made with a wide rail at the top (*see* Fig. 753), and the framing is tenoned together; an enlarged sectional view (Fig. 752) shows the size of the groove and rebated panel. If a fixed shelf, as shown, is desired, slip dovetails are employed as in Fig. 752A. The hooks are of the swivel pattern for fixing underneath the shelf, with the ordinary kind screwed to the sides and back.

Wide-panelled pilasters are simply dowelled and glued to the front of the carcase, then veneered as described for the drawer front, completing them by inlaying the elliptical pieces of well-figured satinwood in the following manner: The door is made by first planing up all pieces to width and thickness, then it is set out and mortised and tenoned together, after which the rails are cut to the outline shown, moulded, and rebated. When the mouldings have been cleaned up they should be mitred, finishing the tenons at the same time, and then glued up. Figs. 754 and 757 show the arrangement of the glass, this being fixed by means of small blocks glued and pinned at intervals in the rebate. Fig. 756 illustrates the construction of the back glass frame. One vertical

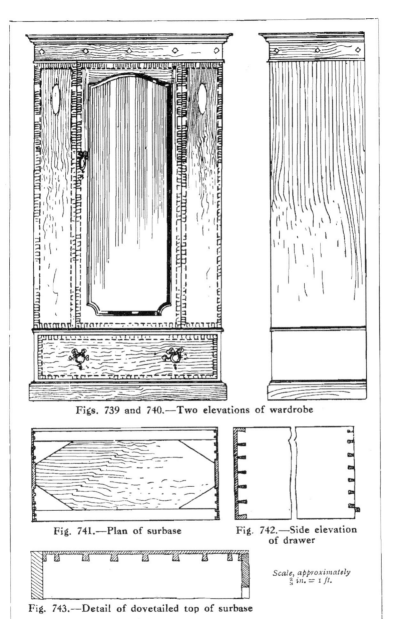

Figs. 739 and 740.—Two elevations of wardrobe

Fig. 741.—Plan of surbase

Fig. 742.—Side elevation of drawer

Fig. 743.—Detail of dovetailed top of surbase

Scale, approximately $\tfrac{2}{3}$ in. = 1 ft.

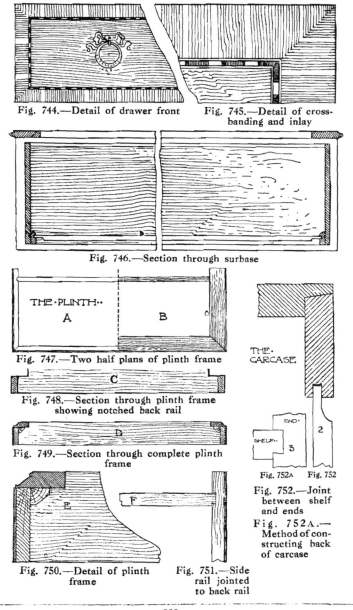

Fig. 744.—Detail of drawer front

Fig. 745.—Detail of crossbanding and inlay

Fig. 746.—Section through surbase

Fig. 747.—Two half plans of plinth frame

Fig. 748.—Section through plinth frame showing notched back rail

Fig. 749.—Section through complete plinth frame

Fig. 750.—Detail of plinth frame

Fig. 751.—Side rail jointed to back rail

Fig. 752.—Joint between shelf and ends

Fig. 752A.—Method of constructing back of carcase

A Bedroom Suite

bar runs through with two cross rails mortised and tenoned into it; ¼-in. or ⁵⁄₁₆-in. panels are used, fitting into a groove as shown. The bars must, of course, be notched over the door frame to allow the panels to be screwed down, this being effected with four ⅜-in. brass round heads.

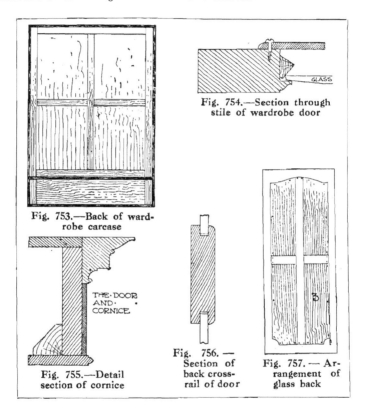

Fig. 753.—Back of wardrobe carcase

Fig. 754.—Section through stile of wardrobe door

Fig. 755.—Detail section of cornice

Fig. 756.—Section of back cross-rail of door

Fig. 757.—Arrangement of glass back

The construction of the cornice is similar to the plinth frame. A groundwork is first dovetailed together, and then faced up as shown in Fig. 755, leaving a rebate, which receives the cornice. It will be noticed that the cornice projects above the frame in order to form a rebate for the reception of the dust-board. A frieze moulding mitred and glued on the under-side completes this part of the work.

When fitting the whole job together, blocks should be used on top of the carcase fitting the corners of the cornice frame. The pine parts, such as the shelf back, etc., should be treated with a mixture of size, umber, and burnt sienna, well mixed and applied hot. After it is thoroughly dry the surfaces can be smoothed with very fine glasspaper and slightly polished.

Dressing-chests, Figs. 758 to 776.—Elevations and part plan of the dressing-chest are presented by Figs. 758 to 760. They show a swing mirror of shield shape which is supported by two side pieces with inlaid satinwood decoration. Two jewel drawers are provided. Where good drawer space is provided elsewhere in a chest of drawers, wardrobe, etc., a good plan would be to make a legged table with two drawers only underneath the top.

After the legs have been planed square and tapered, the ends are planed to length and width, with the bottom end shaped. Dowels are employed as a connection between the ends and legs (*see* Fig. 766). These are marked for position by pricking five small holes through the veneer, which is then placed on the edges of the ends and again pricked through. Lines are marked across the legs indicating their finished lengths, and the veneer may then be transferred to their inside surfaces and again pricked to correspond with the ends. The preliminary work of marking is then completed by gauging a line in the centre of the end, then the gauge is knocked out $\frac{3}{16}$ in. before gauging the insides of the legs. This has the effect, when bored and dowelled, of setting the carcase ends back from the legs, a necessary feature in this type of work. To ensure all dowel holes being made of equal depth, a wooden gauge should be fitted to the twist- or dowel-bit, so that it automatically ceases boring when 1 in. or so deep.

Before cleaning up the ends and gluing them between the legs, grooves must be provided on the insides to accommodate the drawer runners, as is indicated in Fig. 766.

When the ends have been glued up the legs should be levelled down to the ends, and then the rails and bottom can be set out with mortise and tenon joints, as is shown in

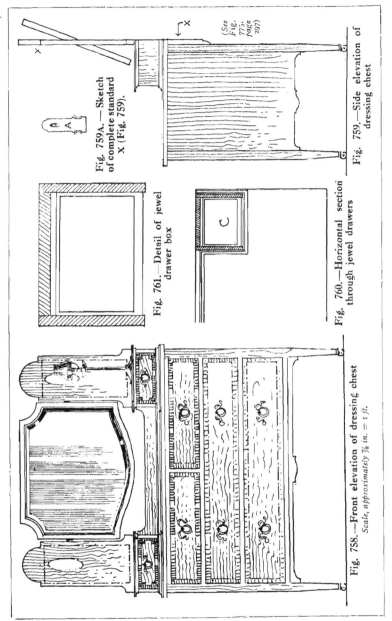

Fig. 759A.—Sketch of complete standard X (Fig. 759).

Fig. 759.—Side elevation of dressing chest

Fig. 761.—Detail of jewel drawer box

Fig. 760.—Horizontal section through jewel drawers

Fig. 758.—Front elevation of dressing chest
Scale, approximately ⅛ in. = 1 ft.

Figs. 766 and 774, which show the rebates in the back legs which are intended to receive the panelled back; this is framed up as is shown in Figs. 762 and 763. The carcase when jointed up should have the drawer runners fitted into the rails and grooved, and afterwards finished by fitting in dust-boards. The carcase back can then be screwed in position, and the whole piece levelled down and glass-papered. A span rail should be shaped and fitted between the legs.

Dovetailing, slipping, and screwing in the drawer bottoms being completed, the next thing to consider is the fitting of the drawers. They should first be planed out of winding on the bottom edges, taking care not to touch the drawer front, and then each side should be carefully planed down to the end grain of the front and back. Next, the ends should be gauged and planed down to the same width of the front, after which one drawer should be tried in; if too tight, a few fine shavings should be removed from the shiny part until all fit fairly easily.

Where a number of drawers fit into one piece of work it is a good plan to "flush" them off with the carcase. This is effected in the following manner: Unscrew the carcase back, and nail small wooden blocks to the legs, just allowing the blocks to touch the drawer backs. The carcase is then turned over, and the drawer fronts, rails, and legs all levelled off together; this ensures the drawer fronts lying in exactly the same plane when completed, which has a most pleasing effect. It will next be necessary to withdraw the drawers and to glasspaper the rails and legs.

The drawer fronts are toothed previous to veneering, the latter being proceeded with as follows: First glue together two pieces of well-figured veneer, connecting them by means of a slip of paper glued on the face side. Next glue the veneers down to the drawer fronts, preferably by means of cauls. The latter consist of pieces of $\frac{3}{4}$-in. pine or whitewood planed true and heated. The veneer should be placed on the glued groundwork; then paper is placed on the veneer in order to prevent it sticking to the caul should any glue exude. The caul being heated is placed on the

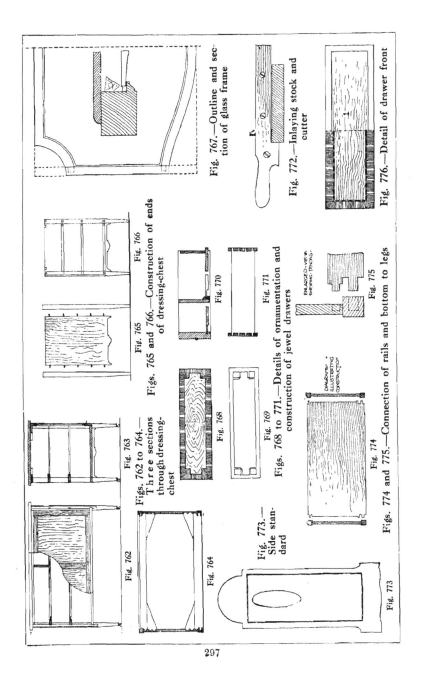

paper, which causes the glue to run freely, and the whole firmly hand-screwed together.

It will be necessary to gauge a margin round the drawer fronts. A cutting gauge is usually employed for this purpose; but a proper inlaying stock and cutter (*see* Fig. 772) is shown in action, with the butt end pressed against the edge of the front; at the same time a slight downward pressure is exerted, which cuts a small channel as shown. The superfluous veneer is then removed, and the mosaic stringing can then be mitred and glued round previous to fitting and gluing down the cross-banding.

When all the drawer fronts are veneered they should be scraped and glasspapered; then the drawers are finally glasspapered up all round, and stopped back slightly with the aid of small drawer stops.

This completes the chest part of the piece, after which the top can be taken in hand. Well-figured Cuba mahogany is best for this part, and the joints should be well dowelled and glued. An ovolo moulding worked on three edges of the top surface helps the design, and, in addition, mosaic stringing can be inlaid about $\frac{7}{8}$ in. distant from the three edges. To fix this part, screw through the front and back top rails, with screws pocketed into the ends at intervals.

The main top part really consists of three distinct units. The glass frame is the most important feature, this being executed as described later by reference to Fig. 767. Dotted lines show the stiles and rails during the process of mortising and tenoning. Full lines indicate the finished shape and also the position of the tenons. First carefully set out the shapes of the top and bottom rails on to the material, and then proceed with mortising and tenoning. When this is completed the top and bottom rails are sawn out and carefully filed to outline; then the mouldings and rebates are worked on all pieces. A moulding plane can be used for the stiles; but the rails are best executed by scratching the mouldings, this process being effected by means of a scratch stock and curved cutter set close to the butt part. The mouldings should be mitred at the corners, testing the frame for accuracy—and adjusting if necessary—before gluing up.

A Bedroom Suite

When quite dry the spare parts of the stiles are sawn off, and the outline completed.

The bevelled mirror only overlaps the moulding about $\frac{1}{8}$ in. (*see* Fig. 767). This is the usual amount for even large doors or frames, and the glass is kept in position by the insertion of small wooden blocks as shown. The glass should be fixed after the movements or pivoted centres have been fitted to the glass frame, and just previous to the general fitting up of the piece. The two side supports are shown also in Figs. 759A and 773. A dotted line indicates the planed-up material, and full lines the shape to which these pieces are cut with a bow saw.

A mosaic string is inlaid as shown, and then the elliptical satinwood pieces are cut in.

The jewel boxes are made by dowelling the ends between moulded tops and bottoms, this being almost as good as making small separate dovetailed boxes of each. The inset diagram A in Fig. 773 shows how the jewel boxes are notched over the standards, bringing the ends flush with the latter. The standards project some 6 in. or so beyond the bottoms of the jewel boxes, these parts in turn notching into the tops. They act as horns for fixing the whole top part of the piece to the bottom part.

The best movements for swinging the glass frame between the standards are those which act with a cup-and-ball action. They should be cut into the glass frame before the table is fitted up. Thumbscrews at the back of the movements enable the mirror to be fixed in any desired position. An important point to note in connection with the mirror is that the rebate which receives it and the edge of the glass should be coloured black, otherwise a very unsightly edge will show. The best way to effect this blacking is by means of a mixture of lampblack and french polish mixed together and applied with a small camel-hair brush.

The top of the dressing chest should be of selected mahogany. It should have an inlaid stringing and cross-banding. The top should be squared up, and then rebated to receive the veneer cross-banding. A shoulder plane will be found the best tool for this purpose, as the rebate only requires to be a veneer thickness in depth. The stringing is glued against the edge, and then the cross-banding is glued round piece by piece until the whole is completed. An ovolo moulding is worked round three edges of the top.

To fix the latter, it should be screwed through the front rail, with screws also pocketed through the carcase ends. The top part is fixed by means of the horns, and to complete this part a rail should be fitted between the jewel boxes, as is shown in the front elevation (Fig. 758). This piece prevents small objects from being pushed off the table part. A piece of base moulding is fixed to this, and the other pieces are, of course, worked about $1\frac{1}{2}$ in. wide and mitred round the under-sides of the jewel drawer boxes.

Washstand, Figs. 777 to 785.—A standard height of washstand, from top side of the marble to the floor line, is 2 ft. $4\frac{1}{2}$ in. It should be remembered that the finished height of a washstand or dressing-table includes the castors, if used, in which case an allowance of $1\frac{1}{4}$ in. should be made. The depth from the back to the front of the marble washstand-top is usually 20 in.

The construction of the ends closely resembles the ends of the dressing-table already described. The end pieces should run vertically and be dowelled between the ends. The carcase bottom should also be grooved into the ends, or "trenched," as it is frequently termed. Fig. 779 shows a sectional plan, and Fig. 782 shows the working detail for the front and back corners of the carcase bottom. The top rails should be made 3 in. wide, with brackets glued at each end, as with the dressing-table and the surbase carcase of the wardrobe. When fixing the top back rail it should be set back $\frac{3}{8}$ in. to allow for the carcase back. The bottom also sets back a similar amount, as is indicated in Fig. 782. A two-panelled back should be employed.

Framing this part of the washstand together is desirable, as otherwise the same amount of rigidity is unobtainable. When an ordinary solid back is employed, it is made from $\frac{1}{2}$-in. material.

The most important parts of this piece are the doors and centre pilaster, as shown in the illustrations. The pilaster

A Bedroom Suite

must line up level with the legs, top rail, and bottom. A good plan is to set the ellipse in position, routing the space away from the groundwork. Then shoulder lines are set out all round the piece at both ends, after which the pilaster

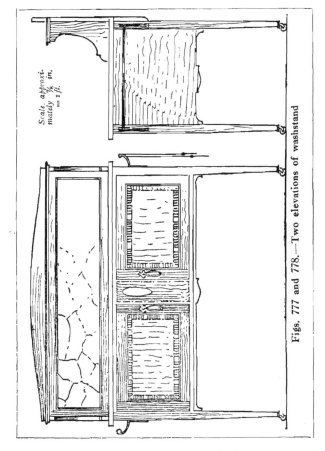

Figs. 777 and 778.—Two elevations of washstand

is tenoned into both the top rail and the bottom. When perfectly dry, the front can be toned and cleaned up ready for the reception of the door frames.

An enlarged detail of the door frame is shown by Fig. 780. This should be tenoned together similarly to the glass frame of the dressing-table. An ogee moulding worked on the front and a rebate worked ¼ in. on the back edge provide the necessary accommodation for the veneered panel. When working a moulding of this type an ordinary moulding plane should be utilised. As an alternative, however, they can be scratched with an inlaying stock, with the cutter shaped reversely to the section required, and fixed close to the butt part of the stock. It will be found advantageous to slightly chamfer away the sharp corners of the stuff on the face side, which allows the cutter to come into action soon after cutting is commenced.

Rebating would, of course, follow the mouldings, which should be well damped in order to raise the grain. When thoroughly dry, glasspapering the mouldings should be proceeded with. This process should be effected by means of glasspaper and a "rubber," the latter term meaning a piece of wood shaped reversely to the moulding on one edge. Four inches will be found the most convenient size for papering up rubbers.

It is usual to polish mouldings before mitreing up the various pieces. In the particular example being described, polishing should be proceeded with before the doors and back frames are mitred up. Muddy corners, such as seen when mouldings are polished in angles, are thus obviated, to the advantage of the work.

The door panels follow on similar lines to the wardrobe pilasters and drawer fronts of the dressing-table.

The doors are simply fitted between the legs and the pilaster, and secured by means of bullet catches. A doorstop should be glued behind the edges of the pilaster.

The marble top of a washstand is not actually fixed in position, but is best keyed so that it cannot move. For this purpose, four square blocks of ¾-in. pine or whitewood, about 4 in. square, are prepared, and after the marble has been carefully adjusted, they are glued to the underside, fitting into the angles between the carcase ends and the rails. When the blocks are dry the top can be removed and replaced without difficulty.

Figs. 783 to 785 show the upper part of the washstand,

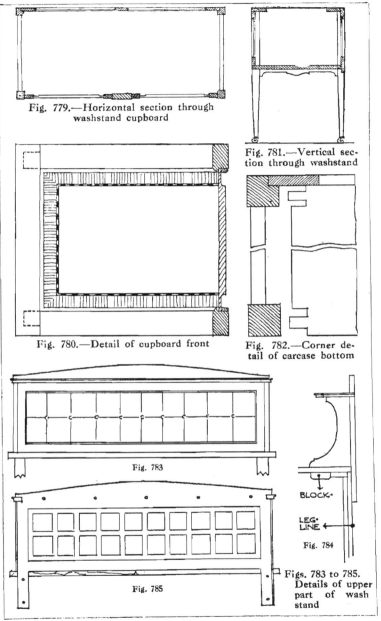

Fig. 779.—Horizontal section through washstand cupboard

Fig. 781.—Vertical section through washstand

Fig. 780.—Detail of cupboard front

Fig. 782.—Corner detail of carcase bottom

Fig. 783

Fig. 784

Fig. 785

Figs. 783 to 785. Details of upper part of wash stand

the construction of which is, with the exception of the back, similar for a tiled or marble panel. The main features are two stiles, with a wide rail at the top tenoned between the stiles, a narrower rail being introduced in the same manner at the bottom. Moulded edges, similar to the doors of the bottom part, provide the necessary rebated part to receive a panel. A half plan of the shelf is shown in Fig. 785. This should be slip-dovetailed over the side brackets, and screwed also from behind, as in Fig. 782. If tiles are employed for the panel part, a rough $\frac{1}{2}$-in. skeleton framing (see Figs. 783 to 785) acts as a groundwork for the tiles. The latter are usually secured to this with plaster-of-Paris, taking care to make good joints between the tiles. If marble is employed, a thin $\frac{1}{2}$-in. slab, polished on one side, is the usual thing. In each case, brads should be driven into the framing to secure the panels, or blocks can be glued on at intervals. These, when dry, are levelled off, and then a $\frac{1}{4}$-in. back is made rather larger than the panel size, so that it overlaps the framing, this being screwed down. The horns of the stiles are necessary in order to fix the upper to the bottom part. These, it will be seen, fit close up against the back, and when screwed in position secure both parts together (see Fig. 784).

Pedestal Cupboards, Figs. 786 to 791.—These two alternative designs for a pedestal cupboard match the other pieces of the suite, the first example being a legged specimen. The carcase top in this case would run through from back to front, instead of rails such as were introduced into the washstand, etc. The construction of the ends would be similar, namely, the ends dowelled between the legs. Inside the ends, grooves would be worked to receive the carcase bottom.

With pedestal cupboards, a pediment is usually introduced as a finishing feature; one such is shown in the example. This is screwed from the under-side, for which reason the top should overhang about 1 in. at the back. The overhang indicated also enables a cupboard top to fit close up against a wall above the skirting.

A panelled back is unnecessary in a small piece of this description.

A Bedroom Suite

Figs. 789 to 791 illustrate the front elevation and working details for a carcased pedestal cupboard. The spacing of the dovetails for both the carcase top and bottom is also shown. It will be seen that small dovetails are introduced at the back

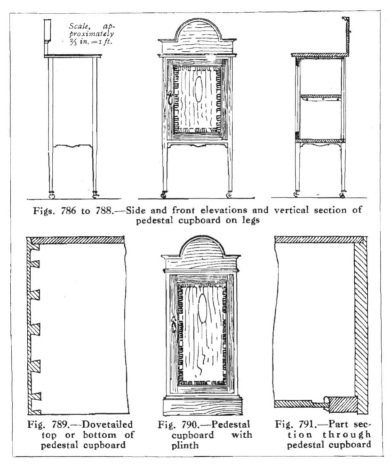

Figs. 786 to 788.—Side and front elevations and vertical section of pedestal cupboard on legs

Fig. 789.—Dovetailed top or bottom of pedestal cupboard

Fig. 790.—Pedestal cupboard with plinth

Fig. 791.—Part section through pedestal cupboard

and front similarly to the wardrobe. The other working detail shows the door stile rebated into the end.

With a cupboard of this description, one shelf would be necessary, supported by means of two fillets.

U

Chest of Drawers, Figs. 792 to 800.—In the chest of drawers shown, a panelled back is introduced, as this gives the maximum amount of stability. The pediment feature, though not altogether usual, adds to the general appearance, and prevents small objects from being pushed off the top.

The height of a chest of drawers ranges between 3 ft. to 3 ft. 3 in. The depth from back to front ranges from 18 in. upwards. In few other articles of furniture is systematic procedure so necessary as with the chest of drawers. A good plan is first to cut out all the carcase and plinth pieces, including drawer rails, divisions, runners, back stiles, panels, etc. Then all face sides should be planed up true and free from winding. The carcase ends, it must be noted, should have their round or heart sides on the outside, otherwise the round side, being placed inside the carcase, would bind on the drawer sides and prevent them running properly.

The carcase ends should be squared up together. Both face edges should be carefully lined up, and then the ends secured with the aid of hand-screws. Square the length lines across the face edges, and then return these lines across the ends with a striking knife. Saw the spare wood off about $\frac{1}{16}$ in. from the finished line, and then, with the ends still hand-screwed together, fix them in the bench vice, and plane down to the square lines. After this process has been effected the ends should be marked to width and planed down to the line. To complete this part of the work, well scour the inside of the ends across the grain with glasspaper, which enables the drawers to run easier. All carcase rails and bottom may now be shot to length.

Figs. 795 and 796 show the method of clamping the divisions between the top drawers. The long piece should, of course, be planed to width before the clamp is glued on. The top carcase rails and the carcase bottom are lap-dovetailed into the ends, whilst the drawer rails are slip-dovetailed into the ends, which necessitates their being shot $\frac{1}{2}$ in. longer than the shoulder size. An isometric view (Fig. 797) shows the drawer rail grooved to receive the dustboard, and after the rails are fitted, runners are fitted into grooves running

A Bedroom Suite

across the ends, a small stub tenon being formed at the front of each runner which fits into the groove of the drawer rail. The sectional plan (Fig. 799) shows the method of securing the double inside runners. These also are stub-

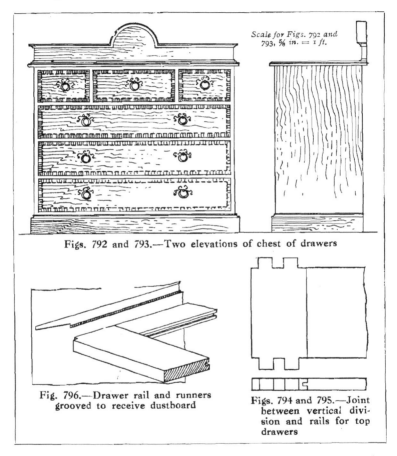

Figs. 792 and 793.—Two elevations of chest of drawers

Fig. 796.—Drawer rail and runners grooved to receive dustboard

Figs. 794 and 795.—Joint between vertical division and rails for top drawers

tenoned into the drawer rails, and for additional security they are screwed also to the edges of the divisions. The back should be made, fitted and screwed so as to keep the carcase square whilst the drawers are being fitted. The carcase should be made slightly larger at the back; $\frac{1}{32}$ in.

will ensure easy running of the drawers, which will be made as previously described.

Wooden Bedstead, Figs. 801 to 805.—Figs. 801 and 802 show the general design and proportion of the head and foot of the bedstead. The construction of the foot part is not

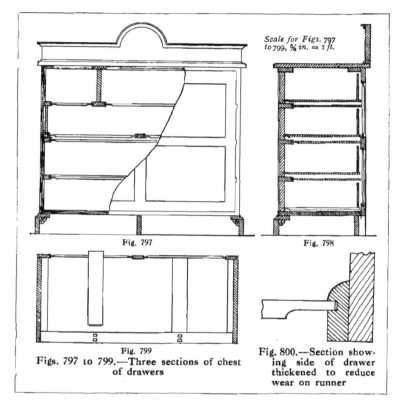

Fig. 797

Fig. 798

Fig. 799

Figs. 797 to 799.—Three sections of chest of drawers

Fig. 800.—Section showing side of drawer thickened to reduce wear on runner

dealt with separately, as the features described in connection with the head are almost exactly similar.

To construct the head, all the material should first be planed to width and thickness, then the tenons marked on the narrow and the centre splat with corresponding mortices on the rails. All of these should then be cut, after which the top and bottom rails should be tenoned into the

A Bedroom Suite

legs. Next inlaying is proceeded with, each splat and rail having grooves worked for the stringings, a scratch stock being utilised for this purpose, and then the stringings are glued down into the grooves. It will perhaps be hardly

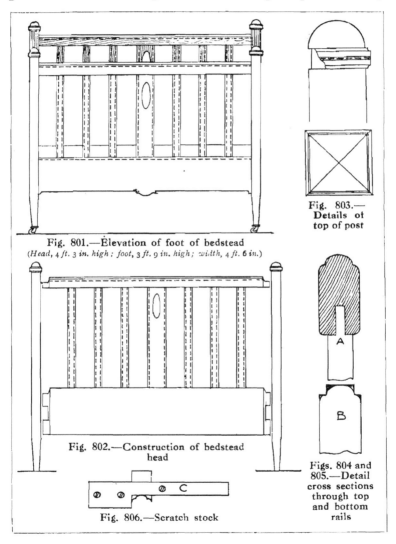

Fig. 801.—Elevation of foot of bedstead
(*Head, 4 ft. 3 in. high; foot, 3 ft. 9 in. high; width, 4 ft. 6 in.*)

Fig. 802.—Construction of bedstead head

Fig. 806.—Scratch stock

Fig. 803.—Details of top of post

Figs. 804 and 805.—Detail cross sections through top and bottom rails necessary to note that both the head and the foot parts should be mortised together before proceeding with the inlaying.

The next step is to work the mouldings on the top rails. Fig. 805 illustrates how this should be effected. Rebates are first worked on the top edges as indicated, and then a cutter is made from $\frac{1}{12}$-in. plate steel, filed to fit the moulding; this is fixed in the scratch-stock as shown by Fig. 806. The cutter just mentioned, and, indeed, all cutters of this type, must be filed in a certain way to obtain the best results. The edge, corresponding to the reverse of the moulding required, should be made perfectly square with the face of the cutter, and a burr is automatically produced on the edge by the action of filing, which really effects the cut. If the edge is not made perfectly flat and square, a part will, of course, bear on the material, and thus prevent the burr from cutting it. The bottom edges of all the rails and also the upright splats should be slightly rounded off.

The posts at the top are decorated as shown in Fig. 803. The posts are grooved round about $\frac{3}{16}$ in. deep in order to receive a moulding inlaid in the face side. This is prepared in lengths, rectangular in section and gauged to width and thickness. Inlaying should be proceeded with prior to moulding the edges, and both processes may be facilitated by improvising a piece of simple apparatus as follows: After the slips have been planed to size, cut a length of mahogany or other hard wood about 3 ft. long, and shoot one edge perfectly straight and true. Then drive in 1-in. stiff brads at distances of about 6 in. apart, allow the heads to project about $\frac{1}{4}$ in. from the edge, and then file the heads off and joint up the projecting ends with a file. Fix the board in the bench stop, and the slips of wood can then be temporarily secured by pressing the slip down into the points. The pressure exerted during the processes of inlaying and moulding is largely downwards but chiefly forwards; but it will be found that the slips can be held quite firmly enough by this means. An alternate method of securing the wood is to put $\frac{3}{4}$-in. screws through each end of the slips into the edge of the board, when the inlaying and moulding can be pro-

A Bedroom Suite

ceeded with without fear of the pieces buckling or breaking. A wooden mitre cut is, of course, necessary when fixing the moulding.

The " Vono " bedstead fitting is an admirable arrangement, economical, and easy to adjust. It has the advantage of keeping the bedstead thoroughly firm and rigid when the whole is fixed in position. Two angle-iron end pieces are screwed inside the head and foot frames, these being notched in order to receive the two side rails. The latter are secured to the end pieces by means of bolts and a key. Similar results are obtained by the ordinary fittings as described for the second bedstead design (*see* page 325).

CHAPTER XXVIII

Another Bedroom Suite

Wardrobe, Figs. 807 to 824.—The suite described in this chapter embodies a series of reasonable proposals capable of being carried out successfully by the average craftsman. With this end in view every part has been made as simple as possible.

A restrained type of design has been adopted throughout, and combined with good material will give pleasure far longer than the various transient "styles." Figured oak finished a light grey or green is suggested, or unpolished teak or mahogany would serve; a polished surface, however, would hardly be in keeping with the design.

Fig. 807.—Wardrobe

The wardrobe (Fig. 807) is the largest item in the suite, and has been designed to take to pieces, this being usually the more convenient system. Accordingly, as the base is comparatively small, it is made solid, and on it are placed

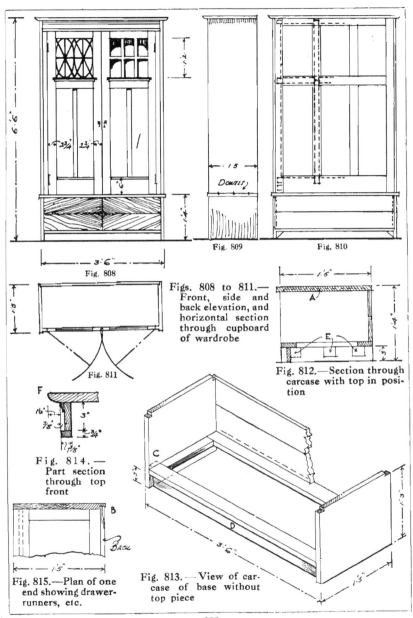

Fig. 808

Fig. 809

Fig. 810

Figs. 808 to 811.—Front, side and back elevation, and horizontal section through cupboard of wardrobe

Fig. 811

Fig. 812.—Section through carcase with top in position

Fig. 814.—Part section through top front

Fig. 815.—Plan of one end showing drawer-runners, etc.

Fig. 813.—View of carcase of base without top piece

the sides, fitting over a series of small oak dowels, and held together mainly by the flat top piece; but subsequently stiffened by the insertion of a back all in one piece of framing. The problem of fixing can be solved by a few fairly long screws judiciously used at the back and top, and if necessary a pair of small wrought-iron angles fixed inside near the top to ensure rigidity. Alternative arrangements for the glazing of the door panels are given, that on the left being intended for execution in leaded work with wide cames, and the other with simple wood glazing-bars. A pleasing surface treatment can be obtained by veneering the drawer front with quartered oak as shown in Fig. 808.

It is not proposed to give particulars of the drawer, which would require to be dovetailed and grooved together in the usual way, and is meant to finish when closed $\frac{1}{4}$ in. back from the front edges of the sides.

The carcase should be prepared as in Fig. 813, with $\frac{1}{2}$-in. by 1-in. notches cut out of the ends in order to house them into 15-in. by 1-in. by $\frac{1}{2}$-in. grooves in the under-side of the top (see A, Fig. 812), a $\frac{3}{4}$-in. by $\frac{1}{2}$-in. rebate down their inner back edges to take the back boarding (see B, Fig. 815), front division housed 2 in. by 1 in. by $\frac{1}{2}$ in. into the ends C (Fig. 813), plain skirting fixed $1\frac{1}{2}$ in. back D, runner fixed perfectly level with the front division by means of the angle blocks, three on each side as at E in Fig. 812, the whole of the work being strongly screwed.

For a quick job the back of the carcase could be composed of a panel of matchboarding, etc., 41 in. by 62 in., fixed on three horizontal ledges across its inner face, cut back $\frac{1}{2}$ in. from the ends in order to clear the sides of the wardrobe, although framing would be far better.

To begin the upper part, the top can be rounded off on its front and end edges as at F in Fig. 814, and grooved 15 in. by 1 in. by $\frac{1}{2}$ in. exactly like the top of the base (Fig. 820). The sides also should be as described, including a rebate down the back edges. In addition, they should be bored to fit over three projecting oak dowels firmly fixed as at G in Fig. 823, no actual fixing being employed, but an element

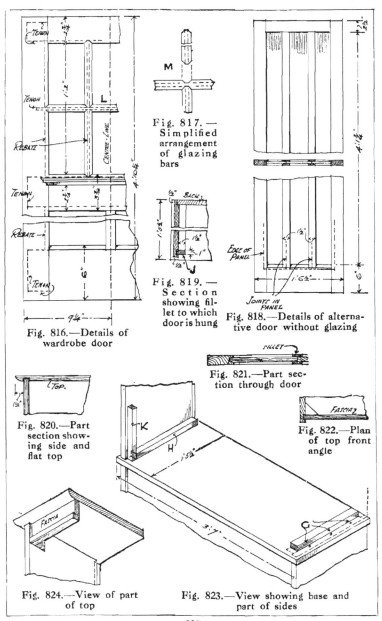

Fig. 816.—Details of wardrobe door

Fig. 817.—Simplified arrangement of glazing bars

Fig. 819.—Section showing fillet to which door is hung

Fig. 818.—Details of alternative door without glazing

Fig. 820.—Part section showing side and flat top

Fig. 821.—Part section through door

Fig. 822.—Plan of top front angle

Fig. 824.—View of part of top

Fig. 823.—View showing base and part of sides

of support afforded by means of two pieces as at H screwed in position close against the removable sides.

The top front is finished with fascia, fillet, and hollow moulding, all as in Fig. 814, the first being housed $\frac{1}{4}$ in. into the sides as in Fig. 822, which also shows an angle block which might be added; but it should be remembered that the whole is to take to pieces when required. The $1\frac{3}{4}$-in. by 1-in. fillets to which the doors are hung (J, Fig. 819) should be housed $\frac{1}{4}$ in. into the sides $\frac{3}{8}$ in. back from the front edge, and fixed permanently, being so small. One of them is shown at K in Fig. 823.

With regard to the panelled back, supposing this to be adopted, the whole must be tenoned together and grooved to take panelling in the usual manner, the panels being left free to expand or shrink. The middle rail lines with that of the doors, and the edges can be chamfered or rounded off slightly. In each case, whether the panelled or boarded back is adopted, it is well to remember that on this part the whole wardrobe depends for rigidity.

The doors need tenoning together in the customary manner, as shown by dotted lines in Fig. 816, first being grooved to take the panels as in Fig. 821, which also shows a fillet flush with the framing planted over the central butt joint. Note the increased width of the middle rail, also the small moulding planted on it and mitred and returned at the ends, also the splayed top edge to the bottom rail. The glazing bars are proposed to be kept square on the face, with angles slightly rounded off, and in order to minimise work can be fitted as follows: The horizontal bar L (Fig. 816) has a small tenon into the frame at each end; but the uprights are halved with it at the intersections, or else merely fitted against it as at M in Fig. 817, and fitted in the same way without tenoning against the frame.

The simpler alternative door in Fig. 818 is made on similar lines, and the figure will be found self-explanatory.

The fittings, which might be of the oxidised type, comprise two good strong pull handles, two smaller ones, a bullet catch, and sundry hooks, etc., for the interior. In some cases locks may be desired for the drawer and doors.

Another Bedroom Suite

Washstand, Figs. 825 to 835.—This part of the suite consists of quite a number of small parts, all requiring nice working and fitting. Its arrangement of central drawer and flanking cupboards is obvious, as will also be the towel-rail at each or either end, and the simple metal upright standards and curtain rod at the rear. This treatment of the back with a curtain constitutes a perfectly suitable finish,

Fig. 825.—Washstand

and one less hackneyed than those in which tiles, etc., are employed. It is intended to finish the table-top in oak (or whichever other wood is adopted), matching the general surface, and then to cover it with a sheet of clear plate glass of the same size, with rounded edges, and merely laid on it, the back angles being cut to miss the curtain standards.

Probably the best idea of the work can be obtained from Fig. 835, where the main framing of the back and front portions is shown quite distinct and separate. The former consists of 1¼-in. square legs at the ends, two 2-in. by 1-in. rails tenoned well into them, one at the top and the other 1 ft. 3½ in. from the floor, and both flush with the legs at the back. There are also two short upright rails, about 1¼ in. by 1 in., slightly tenoned in position to take the inner sides of the cupboards. Both these uprights and the legs should be grooved for the sides as at A and B in Fig. 835, and they can also be grooved for the three-ply back panels; or, if preferred, these can be merely fixed against the face of the framing or in rebates worked on the back edges of it.

For the front framing the four 1¼-in. legs shown are tapered to ⅞ in. in the bottom 1 ft. 3½ in. of their length. The end legs are connected by a top rail C 1¼ in. by 1 in., dovetailed into their tops as at D in Fig. 831, the dovetail being 1 in. long, and kept near the front in order to clear the mortice which will be required later for the joint with the top side rail. The intermediate legs can be stub-tenoned ½ in. into the under-side of the top rail, and the three shorter 1-in. by 1¼-in. lower rails might have tenons ⅜ in. thick projecting ¾ in. into the legs, which should be grooved at the backs as before.

The front and back framings are connected partially by means of six 1¼-in. by 1-in. rails, indicated by dotted lines in Fig. 835, tenoned as far as possible without spoiling the previous joints grooved for the panels or sides of the cupboards as at E in Fig. 829. In order to efficiently tie in the front and back, they are also connected by three 2½-in. by 1-in. pieces as F and G in Fig. 831, dovetailed well into the top rails. These pieces require ½-in. rebates as at H in Fig. 829, and must finish quite flush with the top of the framing, so that the wood top can be prepared in one slab and attached to these three dovetailed and rebated pieces only, by means of wood " buttons " as J and K screwed to it and properly fitting the rebate, thus allowing shrinking or expansion without the risk of splitting, which is seen directly a wide piece is fixed at more than one point. Fig. 828 shows these buttons in position.

When the sides of the cupboard are fitted it will be found that the inner ones have no rail at their tops (*see* L,

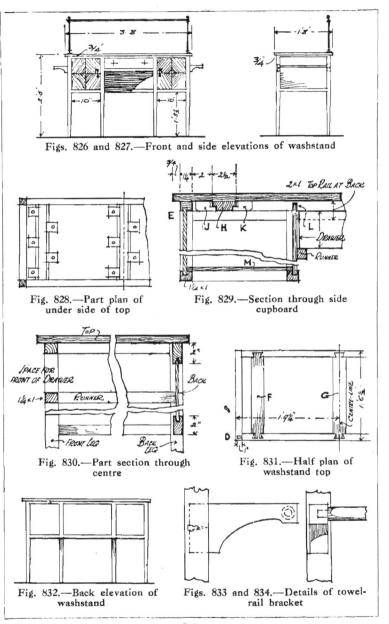

Figs. 826 and 827.—Front and side elevations of washstand

Fig. 828.—Part plan of under side of top

Fig. 829.—Section through side cupboard

Fig. 830.—Part section through centre

Fig. 831.—Half plan of washstand top

Fig. 832.—Back elevation of washstand

Figs. 833 and 834.—Details of towel-rail bracket

Fig. 829); but as they are comparatively small and are secured along all the three other sides, this is immaterial. As shown, they have runners fixed against them for the central drawer, level with the front central rail. The cupboard bottom also can be fixed as in this figure at M without any joints, and being thus above the flat rail, its edge will serve as a stop to the door concerned. This latter is intended

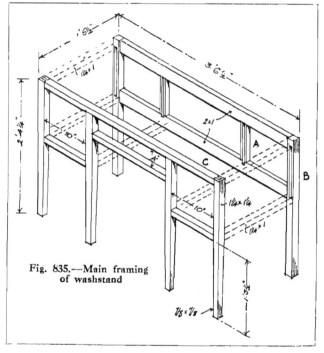

Fig. 835.—Main framing of washstand

to be a quite plain single piece; but its face should be veneered in quarters, and the inside also, to prevent twisting.

The drawer can be made in the ordinary manner, and a detail of the towel-rail is given in Figs. 833 and 834. The former gives the contour of the brackets, and the way in which it is proposed to secure them by means of a thin wedge inserted in a groove in the centre of the tenon of each. This widens out as the joint is closed, thus making a very secure

Another Bedroom Suite

job. Fig. 834 shows an end view, and indicates by a dotted line a tenon or dowel at the end of the circular rail.

The curtain rail and standards for the back can be in metal or wood.

Dressing-table, Figs. 836 to 846.—The dressing-table is very similar in design and construction to the washstand previously described. Its long mirror has been adopted as being preferable to the upright form, and can be curved at the head or merely rectangular.

The key to the construction of this dressing-table will be found in Fig. 843, and precisely the same system has been adopted as in the case of the washstand. The front framing should be tenoned together as before, but with the slightly different spacing of the legs and divisions. The back framing, also, should be prepared complete, including grooves for the side panels and grooves or rebates for the three-ply backs as in Fig. 844. The back legs (which, it will be remembered, are not tapered) are taken up to a total height of 4 ft., and shaped at the top as shown.

The back and front framings are connected first of all by means of six $1\frac{1}{4}$-in. by 1-in. bearers as at A, B, and C (Fig. 843), grooved or ploughed for the sides, and secondly by two pieces as at F (Figs. 840 and 843); these are kept as thick as the front legs, not so much for strength, but in order to keep the drawer on each side running quite smoothly; they should be tenoned in position, and grooved along the bottom edges for the thin filling below. The third connection between back and front should take the form of three $2\frac{1}{2}$-in. by 1-in. dovetailed and twice rebated bearers, to which the top is secured with " buttons " (L, Fig. 840), as before. To these last pieces the top should ultimately be fixed, forming a $\frac{3}{4}$-in. projection on the front and side edges, and cut to fit against the back legs as in Fig. 842.

Before the top is fixed the lower part should be fitted up with drawers. Ten oak runners (*see* Fig. 840) will be required, as will also six similar strips to H, J, and K, also shown, these being merely to serve as guides to the drawers, and fixed on the side parts as shown in section.

Each of the little compartments for the top side drawers

is fixed down on the finished surface of the main top piece. Each consists primarily of a ½-in. base measuring 1 ft. 5½ in. by 10 in. (*see* Fig. 842) between the uprights, the three short ones of which are set out over the legs of the under-framing, while the fourth at the outside back corner consists of the upper

Fig. 836.—Dressing-table

part of the back leg. These uprights are joined up by means of 1-in. by 4-in. sides, as at M and N, tongued into the uprights. They are also rebated to take a thin back piece as shown, so that when the whole has been correctly fitted together it should be a simple matter to fix it in position round the ½-in. base, which would have been previously

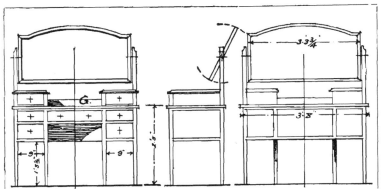

Figs. 837 to 839.—Front, side and back elevations of dressing-table

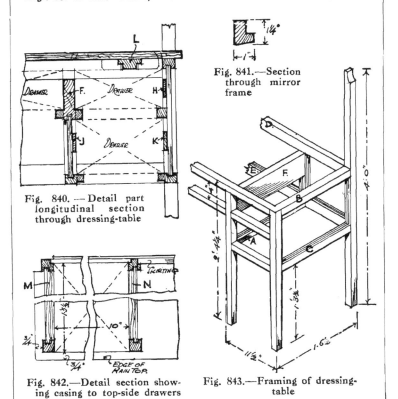

Fig. 841.—Section through mirror frame

Fig. 840.—Detail part longitudinal section through dressing-table

Fig. 842.—Detail section showing casing to top-side drawers

Fig. 843.—Framing of dressing-table

screwed in position, and to finish the compartment with a 1-ft. 7¼-in. by 12½-in. by ¾-in. top o (Fig. 845) with moulded edges, and one corner cut to fit round the back leg. The drawer would be of the usual type, except that as the depth available is more than is likely to be useful, it is suggested that the back be set forward several inches as at P on the lower drawer in Fig. 845, and the sides and bottom con-

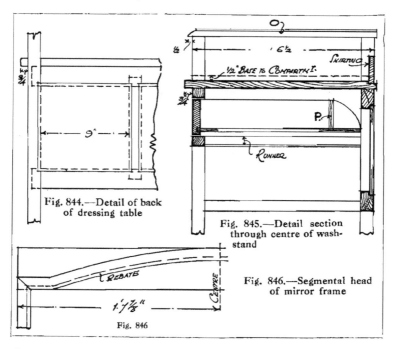

Fig. 844.—Detail of back of dressing table

Fig. 845.—Detail section through centre of washstand

Fig. 846.—Segmental head of mirror frame

tinued to the extreme depth, in order to keep the drawer in a straight position even when fully open. The same figure also shows a 2½-in. by ¼-in. skirting filled in at the back centre, the short uprights and back edge of the main top being slightly rebated for this.

With regard to the mirror frame, this is intended to be worked to the section in Fig. 841, it being advisable to employ quite a small width. The segmental top will require to be cut out of a 4½-in. width as in Fig. 846, to a curve of

Another Bedroom Suite

about 3-ft. 4-in. radius, and mitred with the side pieces, all four mitred joints being strengthened by means of small right-angled brass or wrought-iron straps screwed on at the back. The mirror should be cut by the merchant to fit exactly, and it will need ample protection at the back. A good pair of brass centres should be fitted a little more than half-way up the frame, to enable it to swing in the customary manner.

Wooden Bedstead, Figs. 847 to 860.—Joiners' work in connection with a bedstead is usually confined to the construction of a piece of framing, as in Fig. 850 for the foot, and another similar piece, 1 ft. 6 in. higher (*see* Fig. 855), for the head. Of course, these can be connected by means of horizontal wood bearers to carry the mattress, etc.; but the task is by no means simple if the work is to hold properly when in use; and in addition to this, an efficient all-wood structure would be difficult to take to pieces for removal purposes. The best course is to obtain a pair of the light iron bearers and connections usually employed, which will admit of a strong, light bed, easily dismantled. Most of these bearers have ends as at A in Figs. 859 and 860, fitting into sockets with strong lugs countersunk for 2-in. screws, which serve to attach them to the posts. This metalwork should be obtained before the posts are worked in order that they may be of sufficient thickness, and it should be so that the top horizontal surfaces are about 1 ft. 3 in. from the floor. On these surfaces it is intended to place, without any fixing, the wooden frame of a wire-spring mattress, which may usually be reckoned as occupying about 7 in. in thickness over all.

It should perhaps be mentioned that the length of legs quoted assumes " domes of silence " or similar fittings to be employed. Should, however, castors be adopted, the legs should be correspondingly shorter.

The foot is shown in detail in Figs. 851 to 854 and Figs. 857 and 858 inclusive. Fig. 852 illustrates a square leg tapered to $1\frac{1}{4}$ in. in its bottom 9 in. of length, and stub-tenoned about $\frac{3}{8}$ in. into the top capping at B. The two horizontal rails have tenons $1\frac{1}{4}$ in. long and $\frac{1}{2}$ in. thick, housed into the leg as at C and D, and are both worked in the manner shown in Figs. 853 and 854, from which it will be seen that in the centre they are 4¾ in. wide, grooved for a panel, and simply moulded ½ in. on the face (all as at E in Fig. 854); but that at the point required this moulding is mitred off at 45°, and the rails, both top and bottom, reduced to 4¼ in. in width as at F (Fig. 853). The upright rail G (Fig. 852) is tenoned to suit, and moulded and grooved as in Figs. 857 and 858, in order to meet the mitred moulding and continue it up-

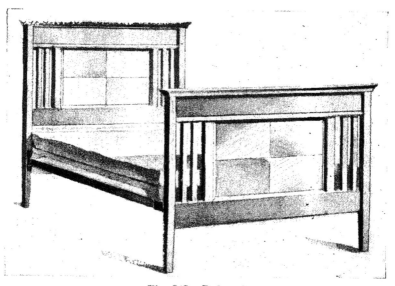

Fig. 847.—Bedstead

wards along the side of the panel to meet the mould on the under side of the top rail as in Fig. 852. The back edge round the panel might suitably be slightly rounded, and the panel itself is veneered in quarters on its outer face. The 1¼-in. by ¾-in. flat balusters flanking it should be slightly tenoned as shown in Fig. 853, and a small bead, as H in Fig. 854, should be planted on along the top rail only. These last two figures also serve to show the simple capping, worked to a cavetto on the solid and finished flat on the top, grooved to fit tightly over the top rail ¼ in., and

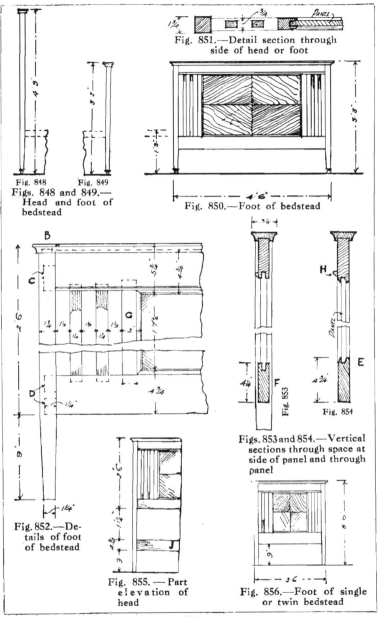

Fig. 851.—Detail section through side of head or foot

Fig. 848 Fig. 849
Figs. 848 and 849.—Head and foot of bedstead

Fig. 850.—Foot of bedstead

Fig. 852.—Details of foot of bedstead

Fig. 855.—Part elevation of head

Figs. 853 and 854.—Vertical sections through space at side of panel and through panel

Fig. 856.—Foot of single or twin bedstead

328 Furniture Making

mortised to fit the stub-tenoned top of the leg as at B in Fig. 852.

The head of the bed should be exactly as before described, but altered to suit Fig. 855, which shows an extra bottom rail, as at J, $4\frac{3}{4}$ in. by $1\frac{1}{4}$ in.

In the event of one or more single beds being required, the foot might be set out as in Fig. 856, all the details applying precisely as before, but the total width reduced to 2 ft. 6 in., and 3 in. taken off the height. The head framing might also be reduced at least 3 in. in height.

Cheval Glass, Figs. 860A to 867.—There is a strong

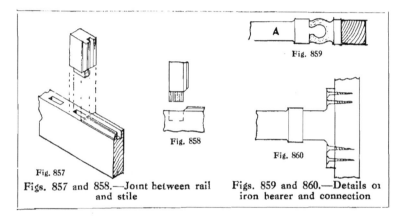

Figs. 857 and 858.—Joint between rail and stile

Figs. 859 and 860.—Details of iron bearer and connection

family likeness between the other parts of the suite and the cheval glass now illustrated, and it would be a distinct acquisition to any room already furnished. The details of the design might easily be modified slightly so as to harmonise sufficiently with any existing work. The supports consist of two square uprights tapering upwards from $1\frac{1}{4}$ in. by $2\frac{1}{4}$ in. to $1\frac{1}{4}$ in. by $1\frac{3}{4}$ in., shaped at the top, and tenoned into cut and shaped feet finishing $4\frac{1}{4}$ in. by $1\frac{3}{4}$ in. by 1 ft. 3 in. long (*see* Figs. 864 and 867): this joint should be particularly firm and can be tightened if found necessary by the insertion of thin hardwood wedges from below, or by letting in a strip of metal as at A in Fig. 864, drilled and countersunk for three long screws

Another Bedroom Suite

as shown, the centre one going well into the end of the tenon.

For their linking up, the uprights depend upon the mirror frame and centres at the top and the rail marked B in Fig. 862 at the bottom; this rail is 1 in. by $1\frac{3}{4}$ in. wide (C, Fig. 864) and is let into the uprights and screwed as at D in Fig. 865, where the dotted lines indicate the work subsequently to be added; this consists of a 1 in. by 1 in. rail (E, Fig. 864) slightly tenoned in position, an upright at either end (F, Fig. 867) let into the uprights about $\frac{1}{8}$ in., and a panel veneered in quarters on the face and secured with a small ovolo moulding and beads as in Figs. 864 and 866.

For the frame of the mirror, a moulding finishing not less than $1\frac{1}{8}$ in. on the face and $1\frac{1}{4}$ in. thick should be used, splayed slightly (as for the glass of the dressing table) and rebated $\frac{1}{4}$ in. deep as in Fig. 864 at G: the head can be worked out of a piece 2 ft. 3 in. by $4\frac{3}{4}$ in. by $1\frac{1}{4}$ in. Into this frame the glass should be accurately fitted and secured with small fillets as at H. The glass being necessarily comparatively heavy, it is essential to tie the frame well together at the back by means of a thin panelled back screwed fairly closely all round. A simple alternative is to use four cross-rails as in Fig. 861 notched and screwed into the sides of the frame, and rebated to suit the backing, which will be kept clear of the glass by the fillets as in Fig. 864.

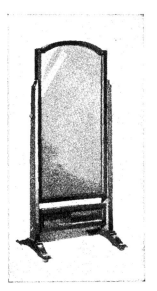

Fig. 860A.—Cheval glass

Brass pivots or centres, specially made for large dressing-glasses, should be procured before the frame is made, so that it may be adjusted to the precise width desired; it should work rather stiffly.

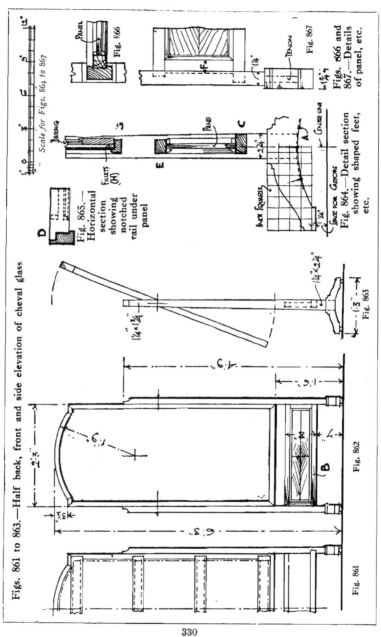

Figs. 861 to 863.—Half back, front and side elevation of cheval glass

Fig. 865.—Horizontal section showing notched rail under panel

Fig. 864.—Detail section showing shaped feet, etc.

Figs. 866 and 867.—Details of panel, etc.

CHAPTER XXIX

MISCELLANEOUS BEDROOM FURNITURE

Toilet Mirror or Dressing-glass, Figs. 867A to 872.— The toilet mirror illustrated by Fig. 867A has square-turned standards and a simple inlaid top, while the working drawings (Figs. 868 to 872) show circular turning and omit the inlay; other variations would be to alter or straighten the curved outline of the top of the frame, straighten the bowed front of the base, or omit the drawers in the latter. The 2 in. by $\frac{1}{2}$ in. rail at A (Figs. 868 and 869) also could be fretted on similar lines to the " gallery " of the urn stand on page 214.

The work consists first of two uprights or standards, round or square turned (if the former, note that portions are left square as in Fig. 868), finished not less than $1\frac{3}{8}$ in.; these are secured as in Fig. 870 to $\frac{7}{8}$ in. sides (B) rebated to receive a $\frac{1}{2}$ in. back C about $2\frac{1}{2}$ in. high, the whole being screwed from below through a stout base (D, Fig. 868) having moulded edges; this can be in one solid piece or framed to suit with an open centre, in which case small runners would subsequently be required for the drawers which otherwise slide on the base direct. It is subdivided by means of $\frac{3}{4}$-in. pieces as at E, worked to suit the front curve, and small drawers can afterwards be fitted, the side ones stopping against the standards, while the centre one goes a little farther. The front of the latter can be shaped out of a piece $1\frac{3}{4}$ in. thick, left square on the inside. A $\frac{3}{4}$-in. shaped top, also with moulded edges (F, Fig. 868), can then be fitted in position, being previously holed to pass over the standards; this need not be very accurately done as a small moulding is mitred round as at G.

The section of the mirror frame is shown in Fig. 871, and the shaped top should be worked from three pieces, secured with saw-kerfs and tongues across the angles. Before

332 Furniture Making

fixing the mirror, brush round the rebate with lamp-black mixed with a minimum of varnish to prevent the bright edge of the glass showing when fixed. Fix the glass with fillets H (Fig. 871) glued at intervals. Rebate the frame as at J all round to receive a thin backboard, and at the top and near the bottom fix pieces about 3 in. wide as at K in order to tie in the framework; these could project slightly without detriment, and should be rebated along their top and bottom edges for the thinner portions of the backfilling (see L, Fig. 871), as it is important that the mirror be properly enclosed.

Fig. 867A.—Toilet mirror or dressing-glass

There are several neat and simple fittings now sold for the pivoting of the glass to the standards, or the old-fashioned method shown in Fig. 872 can be adopted. In this, a long screw is inserted in a small brass or hardwood knob, and a metal plate with a corresponding thread is screwed to the inside of the mirror frame. A hole is bored through the standard and frame, large enough to allow the screw to pass easily until it reaches its plate.

Antique-style Toilet Mirror, Figs. 873 to 875.— This example is rather a pleasant change from the more orthodox types. It would be most suitable on the top of a dressing-chest or placed in some other moderately high position. It should be kept as slight in its proportions as possible, the standards being widened out only when

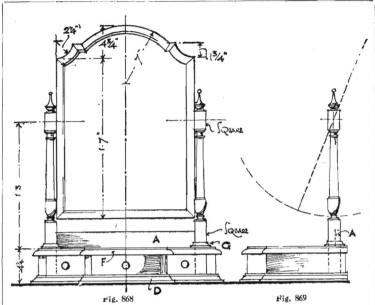

Figs. 868 to 870.—Two elevations and horizontal section of toilet mirror

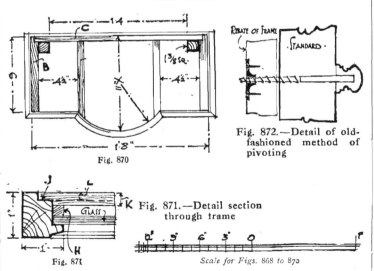

Fig. 870

Fig. 872.—Detail of old-fashioned method of pivoting

Fig. 871.—Detail section through frame

Fig. 871

Scale for Figs. 868 to 870

quite near the shaped feet, as in Fig. 875. The cornice can be worked out of the solid, and should consist of very small mouldings.

"**Wardrobe Top**," **Figs. 876 to 880.**—In bedrooms inadequately supplied with cupboards as well as in other instances, the expedient of concealing by means of a curtain

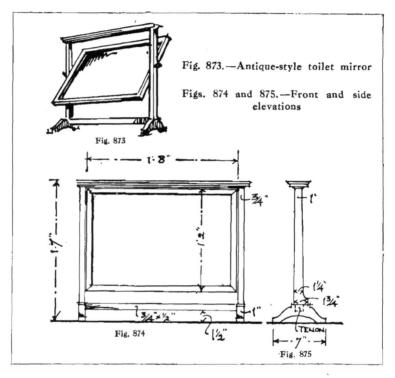

Fig. 873.—Antique-style toilet mirror

Figs. 874 and 875.—Front and side elevations

a number of garments hung in a row is a frequent solution of an embarrassing problem. Such an arrangement is convenient, but it has its objections, among which may be mentioned the unsightly appearance.

This is obviated by the " wardrobe top " the construction of which is very simple, consisting as shown of two end pieces or brackets A and B (Fig. 877) cut to the contour shown in Fig. 878, and dovetailed as indicated

Miscellaneous Bedroom Furniture

by the same figure to the ends of a backboard 3 ft. by 9 in. wide.

The backboard is shown in section by Fig. 880, from which it will be seen to project above the top edge of the

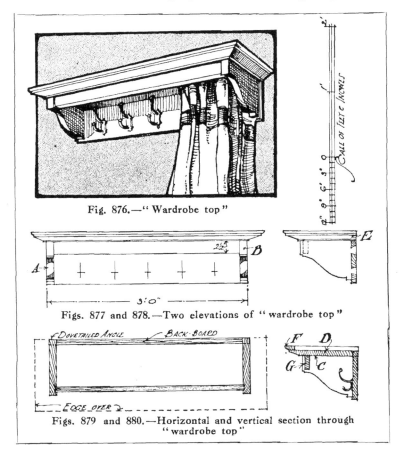

Fig. 876.—"Wardrobe top"

Figs. 877 and 878.—Two elevations of "wardrobe top"

Figs. 879 and 880.—Horizontal and vertical section through "wardrobe top"

end pieces or brackets (which finish at the line c) to a distance of about ¾ in., this being allowed for the thickness of a top piece D 3 ft. 5 in. long and 10½ in. wide, with three sides worked as shown. This is likely to prove of service as a shelf, and the reason that it is not continued over the backboard to the wall surface is that the easiest method of fixing the finished article will be by means of metal " wall plates " screwed on along the top back edge, and because these naturally should be attached to the part taking the most weight. Should, however, it be intended to fix by plugging the wall and nailing or screwing through the centre of the back, then the top piece D might be taken across to the wall face, thus reducing the width of the back by $\frac{3}{4}$ in., and obviating the need for a small piece of making out at E (Fig. 878).

The top is screwed to the ends and back, and made more important as a cornice by means of a moulded fillet as at F (Fig. 880) fixed along the edges and mitred at the corners. The final piece of wood required for the job will be a small fascia $2\frac{1}{2}$ in. deep fixed between the front edges of the ends G (Fig. 880), into which it is shown as being slightly housed in Fig. 879.

Five brass or iron hat and coat hooks, as indicated by crosses in Fig. 877, will be required, and also a neat rod suspended behind the fascia, on which a pair of curtains may slide. Their ends on the return to the wall are suspended from small hooks on the inside of the brackets near the top, as there will be no need for these portions of the curtains to move. Ample fullness of width should be allowed for these hangings.

Small Bedroom Chair, Figs. 881 to 884.—This chair has been designed with a view to a somewhat quaint effect (employing any of the cheaper woods), obtained with the minimum of material and work. It is suitable for use in either bedroom or hall. Its seat is rather low, while the back is elongated, and the only squared portions are the legs, seat rails and two horizontal backrails. The residue of the small bars are simply rounded pieces tapered off at the ends in quite the ordinary old-fashioned manner, and fitted into sockets formed with a brace and bit. The chair accordingly becomes quite light, and its maker could very appropriately have it finished with canework or, preferably, a rush bottom. If the latter is selected, the seat rails might be kept back about $\frac{3}{8}$ in., and strips of wood $\frac{3}{16}$ in. thick

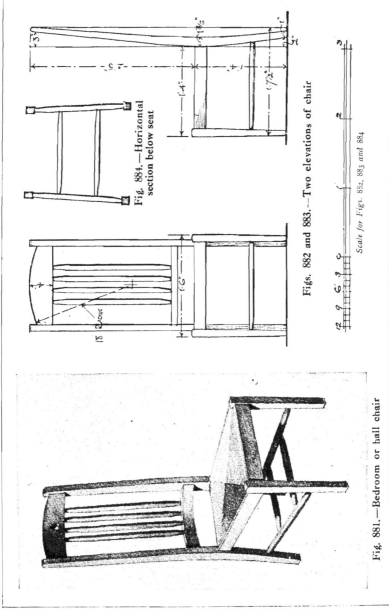

Fig. 884.—Horizontal section below seat

Figs. 882 and 883.—Two elevations of chair

Scale for Figs. 882, 883 and 884

Fig. 881.—Bedroom or hall chair

added to form a finish to the edges over which the rush or cord is turned. A small pierced heart to the top rail would not look amiss if desired.

Rush-seating or Cord-seating a Chair.—In chairs that are to have rush or cord seats, the sides of the seat frame are sunk below the front corners or tops of the front legs, so that the thickness of the rushes or cord will bring all flush. Fig. 885 shows how a typical seat is made, A B C D being the sides of the frame and E the back legs. The cording is simple, and proceeds from one corner regularly round to the others in succession, finishing at the centre. The cord is coiled on a stick and one end made fast to the right-hand back leg E. The coil is passed [up and out over A, then under A and up and out over B, under B, across the seat and over C, under C and up and out over A, next under A, across the seat and over D, then under D and up and out over C, and so on. The loose cord and the arrow in Fig. 885 show clearly the direction taken. The work when pulled up snugly will appear at each corner as shown in the illustration at F. Of course, in the case of rushes there will be a number of joins, and care must be taken to see that these come underneath. If desired, stuffing may be pushed in between the upper and lower layers of cord as the work proceeds. The seat is finished by securely knotting the end that was first tied to the back leg, then cutting off close to the knot, and generally by nailing a thin batten to each edge of the seat.

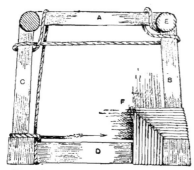

Fig. 885.—Method of forming chair seat in rush or cord

Shaving-stand, Figs. 886 to 896.—The mahogany shaving-stand here illustrated resembles in style the periods of Sheraton and Hepplewhite, when mouldings were used with restraint, and the value of finely figured veneers well

Miscellaneous Bedroom Furniture

appreciated. It is made in two parts, (a) the stand, with legs and cross-rails, and (b) the carcase, or cupboard part, surmounted by an elliptical mirror, the two parts meeting at A (Fig. 887), and secured together with screws. The legs are 2 ft. long, $1\frac{1}{8}$-in. square section at the top, and taper (on the inside faces only) to $\frac{5}{8}$ in. square at the bottom, with $1\frac{3}{4}$-in. by $\frac{3}{4}$-in. rails tenoned to them. Details of one of the corner joints are given by Figs. 889 and 890, and it will be observed that the construction is strengthened by an angle bracket. At a distance of 6 in. from the bottom of the legs two diagonal cross-rails are halved together and stump-tenoned to the legs. These cross-rails are $\frac{7}{8}$ in. by $\frac{1}{2}$ in. at the centre, and taper to $\frac{1}{2}$ in. by $\frac{3}{8}$ in. at the ends.

When the stand has been glued up and flushed off, a $\frac{3}{8}$-in. by $\frac{1}{4}$-in. rebate is worked on the front and sides, to receive the inlaid moulding as shown in Figs. 889 and 890.

Prepare the sides of the carcase 18 in. long by 12 in. wide by $\frac{1}{2}$ in. thick, and dovetail a $\frac{3}{8}$-in. bottom to them, slip-dovetailing a $\frac{1}{2}$-in. full division in position to form a 14-in. square door opening. Two 3-in. by $\frac{3}{8}$-in. top rails are jointed as shown in Fig. 892, the back one being set forward $\frac{5}{16}$ in. to allow for a mahogany back to fit into rebates in the sides.

Construct the drawer by the usual method, with a $\frac{5}{8}$-in. front and $\frac{1}{4}$-in. sides and bottom. Veneer the face of the drawer with two pieces of curl mahogany as shown.

The door is of $\frac{5}{8}$-in. mahogany, mitre-clamped at each end to prevent warping; or, as an alternative, the door may be made up of three pieces of $\frac{1}{4}$-in. stuff glued up in three-ply fashion, with the back veneered as well to prevent warping.

The finished size of the top is 16 in. by $12\frac{1}{2}$ in. by $\frac{1}{2}$ in., the edges being treated similarly to the inlaid stand moulding, and the veneer on the top is cut off clean at a distance of $2\frac{1}{2}$ in. from the back edge, to receive $2\frac{1}{2}$-in. by $\frac{1}{4}$-in. crossbanded strip glued down as shown in Fig. 888. The same figures indicate a 16-in. by 10-in. by $\frac{1}{4}$-in. piece of clear plate glass placed on top to protect the surface.

Fig. 886 shows clearly how the two standards which

Furniture Making

support the mirror are tenoned right through the top and back rail, and Fig. 895 is an enlarged detail of one standard top with an inlaid diamond of rosewood or of mother-of-pearl. The strongest construction for the mirror frame is to build it up in three layers of pieces glued together, brick-

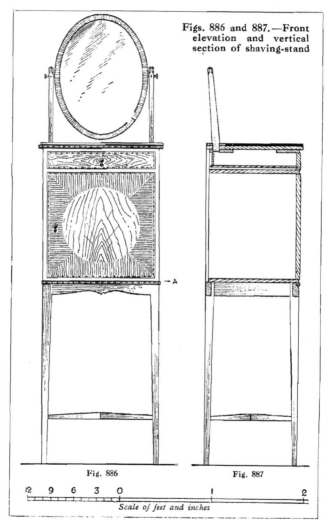

Figs. 886 and 887.—Front elevation and vertical section of shaving-stand

Fig. 886 Fig. 887

Scale of feet and inches

Miscellaneous Bedroom Furniture

work fashion, as follows : Draw an ellipse 16½ in. by 12¼ in. full size, and cut, fit, and glue eight pieces of ¼-in. mahogany as shown by Fig. 893. When dry, lightly tooth the surface, and glue down eight more pieces to form a second layer, with the butt joints halfway between those of the first layer. After laying the third layer, remove from the board, finish exact

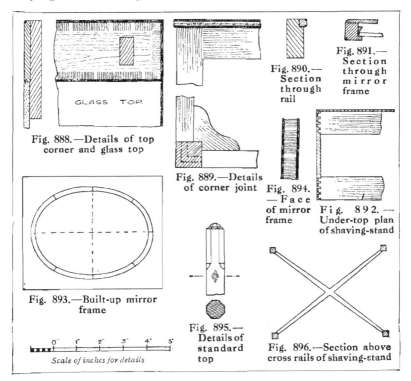

Fig. 888.—Details of top corner and glass top

Fig. 889.—Details of corner joint

Fig. 890.—Section through rail

Fig. 891.—Section through mirror frame

Fig. 892.—Under-top plan of shaving-stand

Fig. 893.—Built-up mirror frame

Fig. 894.—Face of mirror frame

Fig. 895.—Details of standard top

Fig. 896.—Section above cross rails of shaving-stand

Scale of inches for details

to shape, rebate the back for glass (see Fig. 891), and cross veneer the face (Fig. 894). The ebony corner line may be held in position after gluing by binding with damp string. Small wedge-shaped blocks glued and pinned to the rebate are sufficent to secure the mirror ; and before placing the latter in position it is advisable to darken the rebate and glass edge with a mixture of lampblack and size. A $\frac{3}{16}$-in. back completes this part of the work.

Furniture Making

The swing movement for mirrors of this type usually consist of screws which pass through the standard to the inside of the rebate, on which is fastened a small brass plate. No provision is shown for towels; but a light rod may, if desired, be attached by means of brackets to the side.

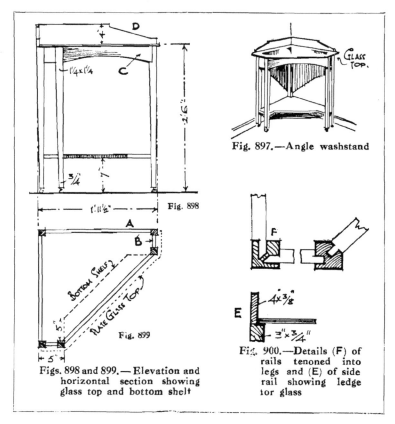

Fig. 897.—Angle washstand

Figs. 898 and 899.— Elevation and horizontal section showing glass top and bottom shelf

Fig. 900.—Details (F) of rails tenoned into legs and (E) of side rail showing ledge for glass

Angle Washstand, Figs. 897 to 900.—This consists of a clear ¼-in. plate glass top supported on white enamelled rails and legs, there being no marble or wood slab at the top as in most cases, although of course these could be fitted. The effect produced is novel and hygienic, making an excellent dressing-room or bath-room fitting.

Miscellaneous Bedroom Furniture 343

All sizes not quoted will be found on the drawings, which show four tapered legs in front and one in the corner not tapered. These are connected by 3-in. by $\frac{3}{4}$-in. rails as at A and B and a curved spandril of the same size at C, the joints being tenons as in detail F (Fig. 900), stopping $\frac{3}{4}$ in. short of the tops of the legs in order to make a presentable appearance when seen through the clear glass top. The legs are also connected near the floor by a bottom shelf as

Fig. 901.—Adjustable cot

in Fig. 899 notched into each. The side rails have a 4-in. by $\frac{3}{4}$-in. skirting shaped as at D (Fig. 898) and fitted as at E in Fig. 900, forming a ledge $\frac{3}{8}$ in. wide to receive the glass, which will be kept in place by its own weight, and should have polished rounded corners and edges projecting very little in front. The skirting can be dovetailed or merely mitred at the corner, and might be heightened in order to support a small angle-shelf if desired.

Adjustable Cot, Figs. 901 to 906.—The cot here illustrated was especially designed to permit of extension when required, to attain which object the foot rail

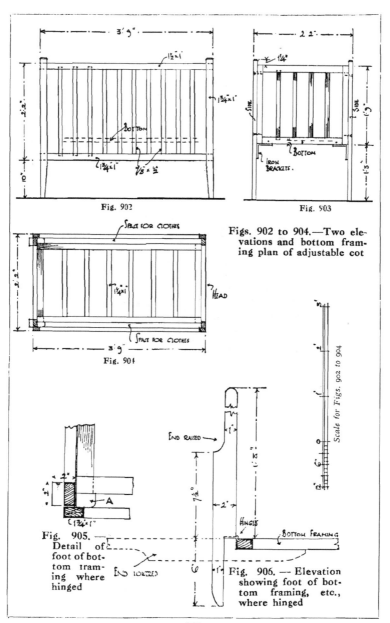

Figs. 902 to 904.—Two elevations and bottom framing plan of adjustable cot

Fig. 905.—Detail of foot of bottom framing where hinged

Fig. 906.—Elevation showing foot of bottom framing, etc., where hinged

Miscellaneous Bedroom Furniture 345

is made to fold down into a horizontal position level with the bottom of the cot. Another arrangement is made allowing the clothes to hang down on the inside of the rails; this enabling the little occupant to be well covered at the sides.

Fig. 902 shows how the two side frames are made; the horizontal rails are mortised and tenoned through into the corner posts or legs and wedged. The laths, of $\frac{7}{8}$-in. by $\frac{1}{2}$-in. material about 3 in. apart, are stump-tenoned. Fig. 903 is the head frame, which has four haunched mortise and tenon joints, and is fitted in between the sides and fixed with screws.

The swing foot frame is made in much the same way, but with stiles 2 in. by 2 in. shaped as in Fig. 906 the lengthened portion below the joint acting as a stop when altered to the horizontal position. The foot frame is fixed firmly with three hinges; the two positions are shown in Fig. 906. Both the end frames of the cot fit in between the side frames; this enables buttons or small barrel-bolts to fasten the foot frame when closed.

The bottom frame is shorter than the side frames by the amount of 1 in. each end. It is narrower than the end frames by $1\frac{1}{4}$ in. each side, to allow the clothes to overhang (*see* Fig. 904). The bottom frame is fixed at the head with screws from the outside, and from the sides at the bottom corners where small packing pieces $1\frac{1}{4}$ in. thick are necessary at these corners A (Fig. 905) to make a good fixing. Four angle irons are screwed underneath the bottom frame and to the legs as shown in Fig. 903. This is for additional strength, which is especially necessary at the foot end of the cot. Rounded top edges will be very suitable for the four top rails, and castors may can be fitted if desired.

CHAPTER XXX

Bedside Tables and Reading-stands

Three Bedside Tables, Figs. 907 to 916.—The three designs of tables given by the figures referred to have double tops, so that when one top is opened, it may be projected over the bed into a convenient position for the occupant. When open it is supported by a flat board in quadrant shape

Fig. 907.—Two styles of bedside tables

(*see* A, Fig. 913). The dotted lines in that figure show it when pushed in, while those in Fig. 908 show the top opened and supported by the quadrant.

Fig. 908 shows a small drawer and shaped diagonal braces below, which could be merely straight if preferred: Fig. 909 has a square cupboard with panelled door, the sides being plain or panelled as preferred; while Fig. 910 is simply finished with a lower shelf and shaped rails as shown.

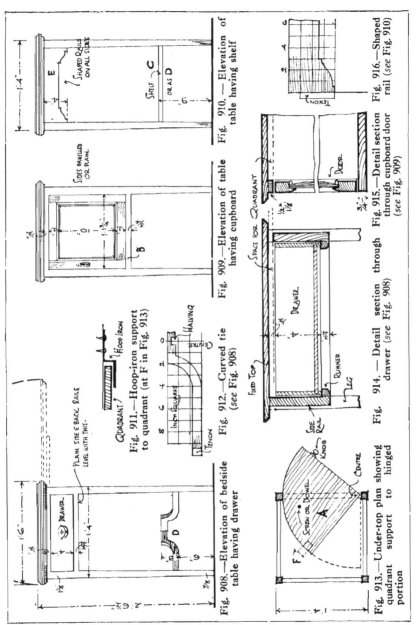

Fig. 908.—Elevation of bedside table having drawer
Fig. 909.—Elevation of table having cupboard
Fig. 910.—Elevation of table having shelf
Fig. 911.—Hoop-iron support to quadrant (at F in Fig. 913)
Fig. 912.—Curved tie (see Fig. 908)
Fig. 913.—Under-top plan showing quadrant support to hinged portion
Fig. 914.—Detail section through drawer (see Fig. 908)
Fig. 915.—Detail section through cupboard door (see Fig. 909)
Fig. 916.—Shaped rail (see Fig. 910)

Furniture Making

The main measurements of each table are the same; tops when closed 1 ft. 6 in. square, and height from floor 2 ft. 6½ in.

In setting out the full-size working drawings, the following thicknesses of stuff must be taken into consideration: Legs, tapering from 1⅛ in. full at the top to ⅞ in. square at the bottom; tops, shaped side rails, and stretchers of ¾-in. or ½-in. stuff. The bottom board B (Fig. 909) and shelf C (Fig. 910) are of ¾-in. stuff. The stretchers or braces D (Fig. 908) are ¾ in. by ⅝ in. The door framing of Fig. 909 is of 1-in. stuff; see enlarged section of framing and panel in Fig. 915. The panels of the doors and ends are of ½-in. stuff.

The shaped span-rails E (Fig. 910; see enlargement in Fig. 916) are tenoned into the legs, and it will be understood that one side must be less in width than the thickness of the quadrant A (Fig. 913) in each case, so that this may swing out freely as shown (*see* top of Fig. 914).

The quadrant must be made to draw out without friction, a small brass knob as in Fig. 913 being attached. A screw put in where shown in the same figure forms a centre for the working of the quadrant, and another screw or dowel prevents it being drawn out too far. To prevent all risk of the quadrants dropping when pushed in, a lath of ½-in. stuff extended from the outer rails should be fitted beneath it; or if the table has a drawer as in Fig. 908, a piece of hoop-iron as in Fig. 911 may be fixed to the under face of the top, as at F in Fig. 913, for the same purpose. By drawing the same number of squares on the full-size drawing as in Figs. 912 and 916, the outlines passing through each square may be copied readily.

The fixed top in each case is fixed by slanting screws driven from the inside faces of the shaped rails, and the two tops are hinged together with card-table hinges. The stretcher part D (Fig. 908) is interchangeable with the shelf C in Fig. 910, this form being useful for holding books, etc., or it might be adapted to support a small central shelf.

In Fig. 908 due consideration must be given to the drawer

Bedside Tables and Reading-stands

passing freely under the quadrant, and its back should be narrower than the sides, so that it will pass under the screw or dowel marked in Fig. 913.

It will be understood that the tenoning of the various horizontal rails to the legs and the notching of the lower shelves in Figs. 909 and 910, as well as the construction of the drawer, etc., have been taken for granted, there being no especial point in connection with them. Beds vary somewhat in height, and consideration should be given to the length of the table legs, which might in some cases be shortened a little to suit a lower bedstead.

Invalid's Bed-table and Reading-stand, Figs. 917 to 927.—The stand shown on page 350 forms an invalid's table which can be raised, lowered, revolved, and tilted, to extend over a bed or couch, and the height of table to be adjustable from 2 ft. 6 in. to 4 ft. high. To avoid the expensive metal fittings in such appliances wood is used almost exclusively.

Fig. 918 is a side elevation showing pillar, arm, top and base; Fig. 919 is an elevation looking on the end of the arm from the side away from the "top." The pillar may be compared to a tuning-fork of two prongs, with slots A (Fig. 918) cut through each prong, the slots allowing the bolt and winged nut seen in the first three figures to slide up or down as required. A wood pin B (*see also dotted lines at* C *in* Fig. 919), in conjunction with the bolt and winged nut, keeps the arm, with the bracket, at right angles to the pillar. The arm for the greater part of its length is circular, and extends through blocks D and E (Figs. 918 and 921). By tightening the screws shown in these the top is secured in a horizontal position as a table, or tilted as a reading-stand to any angle. According to the length of the arm, so can the table top be extended over the bed or brought near the pillar, if desired.

The portion of base under the arm is extended in order to prevent the table from tilting should heavy articles be placed on it. To stiffen and prevent the top from warping, a lower plate or board F (Figs. 918, 919, and 921) is secured with screws to the top. Before the latter is fixed the blocks D and E are fastened with screws driven through F. When adjusting the arm up or down the pillar it is not necessary to screw up the winged nut at each adjustment, as the friction of the bolts against the inner sides of the slots A prevents the arm with the top from falling. By slightly lifting the top and arm at the extreme end the end of the arm will move freely up or down the pillar.

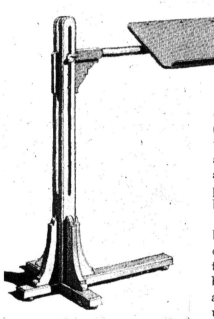

Fig. 917.—Invalid's bed-table and reading-stand

When using the stand for reading, a ledge as in Fig. 920 is added; holes are bored in the top near the two longer edges, and iron pins G (Fig. 920) are fitted in the ledge, which being adjusted at two edges allows the stand to be placed at either side of a bed or chair.

If desired, the top could be made to revolve laterally on a centre connected to the board F and the top; but there is no particular advantage in this, as when used as a table the ledge is better away, a cloth being then spread over the table. By making the pin B movable, or by providing a second bolt and winged nut, the arm could be raised to a vertical position for stowing away. Should the peg B be a fixture, the prongs must be sprung open at the top when inserting the arm between the prongs.

In constructing, the pillar may be got out of three thicknesses of 1-in. stuff, the centre piece H and the two sides J (Fig. 919), the three pieces being glued together, at the lower

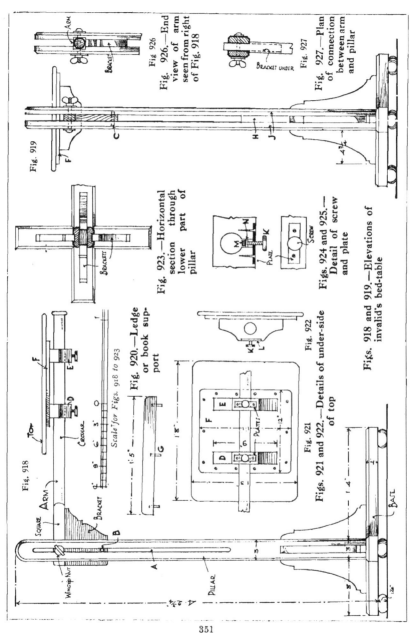

Fig. 926.—End view of arm seen from right of Fig. 918

Fig. 927.—Plan of connection between arm and pillar

Fig. 923.—Horizontal section through lower part of pillar

Figs. 924 and 925.—Detail of screw and plate

Fig. 920.—Ledge or book support

Figs. 921 and 922.—Details of under-side of top

Figs. 918 and 919.—Elevations of invalid's bed-table

end of course. The base is of 2-in. stuff and the arm of $1\frac{1}{2}$-in. stuff, worked or turned to $1\frac{3}{8}$ in. diameter and reduced where connected to the pillar as in Fig. 927, also the bracket (Fig. 918), so that it will slide freely between each prong of the pillar. The lower brackets connecting the base to the pillar (Figs. 918 and 919) are of 1-in. stuff, the blocks D and E (Fig. 918, etc.) of $1\frac{3}{4}$-in. stuff, and the top and board F of $\frac{3}{4}$-in. stuff planed to about $\frac{1}{2}$ in. thick.

The base should be halved together, and the pillar connected to it by means of dowels passing through the halved portions of the base, or alternatively by a stub-tenoned joint. The brackets here should also be fixed with dowels and glue and can be let into the built-up central pillar as in Fig. 923. The turned ball feet may be about $1\frac{1}{4}$ in. thick and dowelled in position, or if preferred castors might very suitably be fitted.

To allow the bolt to work freely the slots should be $\frac{1}{16}$ in. wider than its diameter. It will be seen that the lowest and highest point of the slot determines the limit of adjustment of the table. The outer edges of the pillar are bevelled as shown, and likewise the upper edges of the base.

Fig. 922 is a side view of blocks D and E. The screw K and plate L are shown in detail by Figs. 924 and 925. To prevent the screw from bruising the arm, a circular disc or wad of soft wood M is placed above a metal disc N and the end of the screw K or the plate L; an ordinary piece of thick strip brass or iron will do, with the screw holes for fixing and the centre hole tapped for the screw K. Most ironmongers will supply the latter and suitable bolts with winged nuts.

CHAPTER XXXI

STUFFOVER CHAIR AND SETTEE

Chesterfield Settee and Divan Chair, Figs. 928 to 935.—These drawings give all the necessary measurements for a seven-foot Chesterfield settee and a divan chair to correspond. The dotted outlines indicate the shape of the upholstery. The timber for making the frames may be "chairmakers' birch," which is very cheap, and may be reckoned at the rate of about 2d. per square foot of 1 in. thickness. All the joints may be dowelled or tenoned in the usual way. The feet may be of mahogany or birch stained, and round as in the sketches or square-tapered as in the details. If the seats have to be double sprung, it would be better to use a soft material for upholstering, but if Pegamoid is decided on, large springs should be used, single, and the frames made with longer legs and the lower rails 3 in. or 4 in. higher.

With the frames made to the illustrations, the materials for stuffing and upholstering should be about as follows: For the settee, two pieces of web; $2\frac{1}{2}$ doz. 12-in. springs for seat, and nine 9-in. springs for the front rail; $4\frac{1}{2}$ doz. 7-in. springs for the back and arms; $3\frac{1}{2}$ yd. of spring canvas; $4\frac{1}{2}$ yd. of scrim; 2 yd. of common canvas for the outside back and ends; 7 yd. of calico; 8 yd. of wadding; 9 yd. of Pegamoid; 18 lb. of fibre for first stuffing and stitched edges; 18 lb. of wool flock; 20 lb. of hair; 1 ball of stitching twine; 1 ball of spring twine for lashing the springs; 1 packet of webbing tacks; 1 packet of $\frac{1}{2}$-in. tacks; 6 yd. of banding; 1 gross of studs.

For two of the divan chairs: two pieces of web; $1\frac{1}{2}$ doz. 12-in. springs for the seats, and ten 8-in. springs for the front rails; $3\frac{1}{2}$ doz. of 5-in. springs for the backs and arms; $2\frac{1}{2}$ yd. of spring canvas; $3\frac{1}{2}$ yd. of scrim; 2 yd. of common

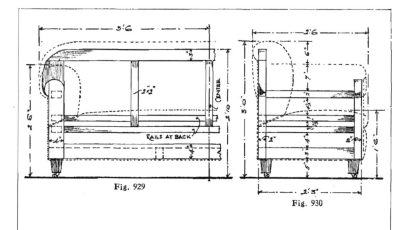

Fig. 929

Fig. 930

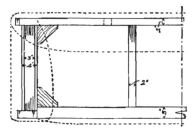

Fig. 928.—Stuffover settee

Figs. 929 to 931.—Framework of settee
(*Dotted lines indicate upholstering*)

Fig. 931

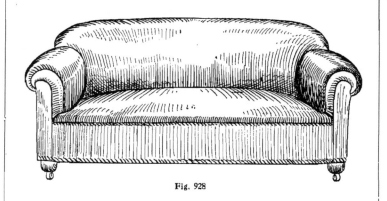

Fig. 928

Stuffover Chair and Settee

canvas; 8 yd. of calico; 8 yd. of wadding; 7 yd. of Pegamoid; 16 lb. of fibre; 16 lb. of wool; 20 lb. of hair; 1

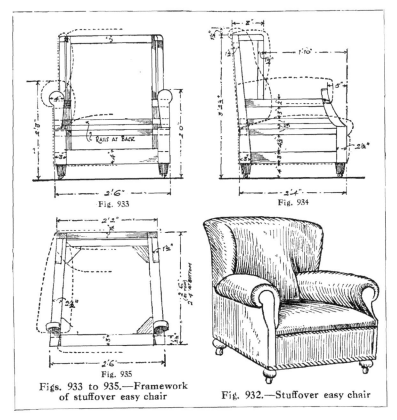

Figs. 933 to 935.—Framework of stuffover easy chair

Fig. 932.—Stuffover easy chair

packet of webbing tacks; 1 packet of $\frac{1}{2}$-in. tacks; 7 yd. of banding; and 1 gross of studs.

CHAPTER XXXII

A French Side Table

Carved Walnut Table, Figs. 936 to 948.—The small table described in this chapter was exhibited at the South Kensington Museum, where it is described as " a stand for a cabinet, carved walnut, French, second half of sixteenth century." It is most attractive in appearance, and while it is free from very complicated work, can be readily simplified if desired. It is proposed to mention various modifications, and then to describe the construction of a replica of the table.

There are eight turned legs, and of these the two middle back ones could be omitted, and the two others at the back might be made plain and square. The little ornament projecting in the middle of the drawer front might be left out, as might also the carved ornament between the legs immediately below it, which would seem to be by a different hand from, and is certainly much inferior to, the narrower pieces of carving at the sides. These latter should be retained if possible; but the table would still be of good style without them (as in the right-hand portion of Fig. 937). Other alterations or adaptations will probably occur to the worker

As it stands, the table consists first of a top 3 ft. 2 in. by 1 ft. 6¾ in. and ⅞ in. thick, finished sizes, and simply moulded on three edges. This is made up of a 2¾-in. margin framed together and grooved for a flush panel, which is the best method, although the top could be made up of plain boards side by side, with their edges tongued together. A hollow square framed up of 3¼-in. by ⅞-in. stuff, measuring about 3 ft. by 1 ft. 5½ in., outside sizes, is then prepared, moulded on three sides as before (*see* E, Fig. 944, *and* F, Fig. 946), to go below the drawer, and grooved along the sides and back to take upright pieces as at G, the ends of the back

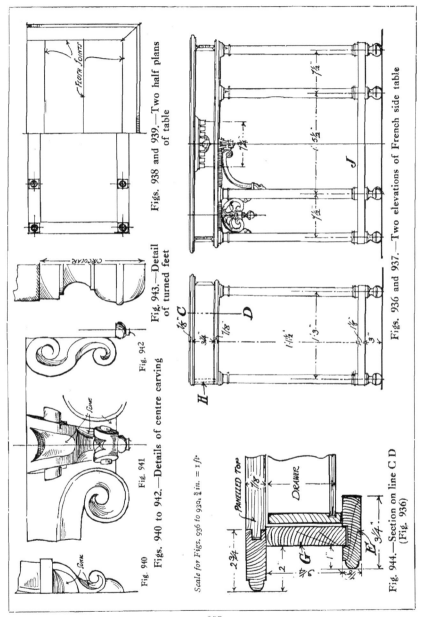

358 Furniture Making

piece H (Fig. 936) being housed into the sides. The top is fixed flush on these three pieces, and a drawer of the ordinary type then made to slide into the boxing so formed. The ornament to the centre would be applied afterwards if desired. The tiny winged cherub's head is a metal fastening on the original, and the dentils are cut away to suit it. Drawer handles if used should be fixed centrally over the spaces between the end pairs of legs, and the bevelled front ends to the side pieces, which are planted on (not worked on the solid), can be added or not, as desired.

The under-framing consists of another hollow square J

Fig. 945.—French side table, sixteenth century

A French Side Table

(Fig. 937), 2 ft. 10¾ in. by 1 ft. 5¼ in. outside measurement, and made of 1⅛-in. by 2-in. stuff, mitred and tenoned at the angles as in Fig. 947, a method of framing which applies also to the two upper parts already mentioned. This portion is connected to the top by eight turned legs as shown in Fig. 946, the square parts of the caps and bases to which are finished 2 in. by 2 in., while the upper diameter of the

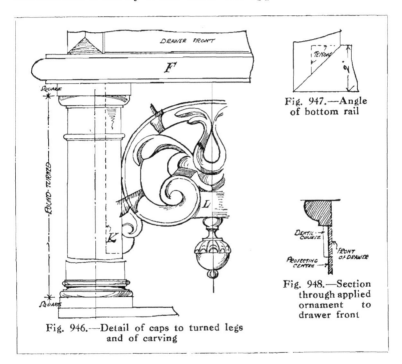

Fig. 947.—Angle of bottom rail

Fig. 948.—Section through applied ornament to drawer front

Fig. 946.—Detail of caps to turned legs and of carving

shaft (which tapers slightly upwards) is 1½ in. The length of the legs is 1 ft. 11½ in., with stub-tenons extra at the ends, fitting into mortises in the top and bottom framings. Turned feet 3 in. high, as in Fig. 943, are fixed in a similar manner under each of the legs, or oak dowels might be used instead of these tenons.

All that now remains is the carving, which is cut and pierced out of about ¾-in. stuff, housed into grooves in the legs as at K (Fig. 946). The illustrations will probably suffice to explain this work, which is clean and bold in execution. The portion marked L bays out slightly on plan, and the turned pendant below it (which has a little simple cut ornament) is not fixed until afterwards. The carving in the centre is as illustrated. The truss or key has very pronounced spiral curves or "fiddle ends," as they are sometimes called. The curve of the scroll which connects the parts in Figs. 940 and 941 is not above reproach, and might easily be made rather more graceful and flowing.

CHAPTER XXXIII

Recess Fitments

Recess Fitment with Cupboard and Drawers, Figs. 949 to 955.—Recesses occurring at the sides of fireplace projections form excellent positions for various forms of cupboard fittings, a convenient example of which is here shown. The recess is 2 ft. 10 in. wide and 1 ft. 2 in. deep, this being about the most usual size.

The dimensions given for the various parts will be a good guide for most cases, and it will be observed that the fitting projects $1\frac{1}{2}$ in. into the room. The illustrations show fully the principal parts of the construction, and the following is a description of the main features, which can all be carried out in 1-in. stuff. It should be noted that in all probability it will be necessary to avoid an existing skirting-board, as in Fig. 950, the work being adjusted accordingly.

The first part to be made is the framework for the drawers, comprising the lower portion. The two stiles A and B, and the bottom and two intermediate rails, are housed together as shown at C, whereas the top joint at A, between the top rail and side, should be dovetailed as at D. The runners E should tenon into the front rails F, and if it is desired to have panels to separate the spaces between the drawers, the runners and rails should be ploughed as shown.

Next, the rails and stiles should be fixed together and then fastened temporarily to the sides of the recess. Fillets G about $\frac{1}{2}$ in. thick and 3 in. wide should be prepared and cut so as to fit close against the back wall. The runners should next be cut off true to length, and to the back and edges of these the fillets should be nailed.

The front should now be taken out, the runners attached to it, and the whole pushed into the recess. The runners should be adjusted so that they are horizontal, and the

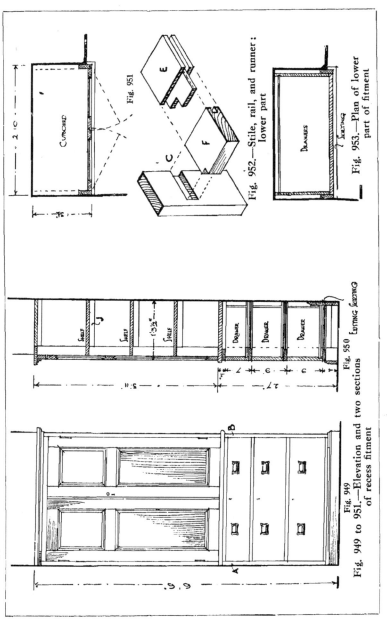

Fig. 949 to 951.—Elevation and two sections of recess fitment
Fig. 952.—Stile, rail, and runner: lower part
Fig. 953.—Plan of lower part of fitment

Recess Fitments

fillet may be nailed to the wall. After this the front should be fixed to the sides of the recess.

To make a good job, two brick joints on each side should be found and small plugs driven in. To find the joints without damaging the plastering, drive in a bradawl.

The top of the drawers has a rounded edge, and should next be prepared and fixed. The construction of the drawers is on customary lines and guide strips should be made to go between the runner and fillet as shown at II, and a piece of skirting or plinth fixed to the bottom, mitred and returned if the front projects, as in the instance shown. The upper frame to receive the doors should present little difficulty.

The joint between the head piece and stile is shown at the top of Fig. 954, the head piece serving as a top member to the cornice, which can be suitably built up in the simple manner shown in Fig. 955, or an ordinary moulding can be employed. This framing should be fixed in

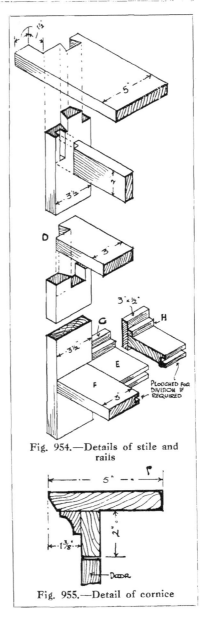

Fig. 954.—Details of stile and rails

Fig. 955.—Detail of cornice

364 Furniture Making

a similar manner to the lower part. Fillets as at J in Fig. 950 should be nailed to the sides to receive the shelves and top.

The door, stiles and rails require mortising and tenoning together, and next ploughing for the panels; then, when these are prepared, the joints should be glued, cramped, and wedged.

The appearance of the doors will be improved if a mould-

Fig. 956.—Bookshelf fitments in recesses

ing is mitred and bradded in, or a small moulding could be worked on the solid.

Bookshelf Fitment for Recess, Figs. 956 to 967.—Well arranged books always help to give a furnished appearance to a room, and the recess usually found on each side of a fireplace is a convenient position for setting up the bookshelf fitment here described.

The design is simple, for the entire construction can be made without mortise and tenon or dovetail joints, enabling the whole to be readily taken apart for removal. The timber suggested is American whitewood, " faced up " with walnut or some other hard wood such as oak or mahogany.

Recess Fitments

The fitment goes into a recess 3 ft. 9 in. wide and 1 ft. 2 in. deep, with a total height of 6 ft. 9 in. from the floor to the top of the cornice ; but these dimensions may be modified to suit a larger or smaller opening. If the room has a picture

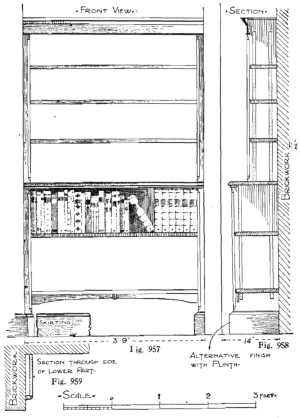

Figs. 957 to 959.—Front elevation and vertical and horizontal sections of bookcase fitment

moulding, a good plan is to make the top of the cornice to line with the under edge of the moulding. It will be clear from the sectional view that the fitment is arranged in two parts. The lower portion, which is 11½ in. deep and 3ft. 3 in. high, terminates at the moulded shelf, and provides accommodation for large bound volumes, atlases, etc. The upper portion is made $7\frac{1}{2}$ in. deep for the smaller books. For the lower sides prepare two pieces of whitewood, each 3 ft. 2 in. by $10\frac{7}{8}$ in. by $\frac{3}{4}$ in., and proceed to tongue and groove to the front edge of each a strip of walnut $1\frac{3}{4}$ in. wide and $\frac{7}{8}$ in. thick, as indicated in Fig. 965. This pilaster, besides improving the appearance, facilitates the fitting of the sides to any irregularities in the walls. The pilasters cause a space of 1 in. between the sides and the walls, which is easily filled by screwing two battens each $10\frac{1}{2}$ in. by $1\frac{1}{2}$ in. by 1 in. to the back of each side.

For the moulded shelf, which forms the division between the upper and lower portions, plane a piece of walnut 1 ft. $0\frac{1}{2}$ in. wide and $\frac{7}{8}$ in. thick, and, after moulding the front edge, glue and screw to the under-side a 2-in. by $\frac{1}{2}$-in. strip of walnut to form an under-moulding. Carefully cut this shelf to fit between the walls, and notch a piece from each of the upright sides to make room for the under-moulding; a detail is shown by Fig. 961.

The sides of the upper portion are made in a similar manner to the lower sides, the whitewood being cut to 3 ft. $5\frac{5}{8}$ in. long and $6\frac{7}{8}$ in. wide before being tongued to the pilasters. As shown in Fig. 960, the whitewood sides project $3\frac{5}{8}$ in. above the tops of the pilasters, in order that the tongues may receive the cornice front. This cornice consists of a length of whitewood $3\frac{3}{8}$ in. deep by $\frac{5}{8}$ in. thick, "faced up" by gluing on lengths of walnut moulded to the section given in Fig. 962. Notice that the top moulding projects $\frac{3}{8}$ in. above the whitewood, thus forming a rebate, into which a $\frac{3}{8}$-in. dust-board is afterwards screwed. Fig. 963 shows the position of the groove that is cut at each end of the cornice back, to fit the tongues on each side as indicated in Fig. 960.

Make all the shelves of whitewood to finish a full $\frac{7}{8}$in. thick, facing the front edges with $\frac{3}{8}$-in. walnut. The finished width for the upper shelves is $6\frac{7}{8}$ in., and for the lower ones $10\frac{7}{8}$ in. Fig. 966 is a detail of the $2\frac{3}{4}$-in. by $\frac{1}{2}$-in. curved piece, which is tongued to the under-side of the bottom shelf, and strengthened with blocks glued at the back. The

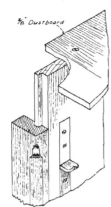

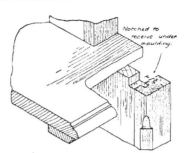

Fig. 961.—Detail of notch for under-moulding

Fig. 960.—Detail at top corner.

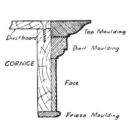

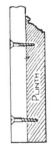

Fig. 962.—Section through cornice and dust-board

Fig. 963.—Back of cornice

Fig. 964.—Section through plinth

Fig. 965.—Section through pilaster

Fig. 966.—Section through bottom shelf

Fig. 967.—Shelf moulding

moulded shelf which forms the division between the upper and lower portions is, of course, a fixture; but all other shelves (including the bottom one) are adjustable. A good arrangement for supporting the shelves is to have grooves shaped as shown in Fig. 965 ploughed in the sides, and shelving-strips screwed into them as in Fig. 960; or the other method mentioned in Chapter III. might be adopted.

If the room has a skirting-board, the pilasters should be scribed over it, and a finish obtained by working, moulding, and mitreing a length of skirting along the sides. Should there be no skirting-board, a neater finish can be made by mitreing and screwing (from the back) a 6-in. plinth of walnut, details of which are shown by Fig. 964. The appearance of the pilasters is improved by working a $\frac{1}{2}$-in. stop-chamfer on the edges prior to finally setting up the parts in position. After staining the whitewood to match the walnut, finish the whole with either french or wax polish, according to choice.

Proceed to set up in position as follows: First place the lower sides against the walls, and screw down the wide moulded shelf to them. The screw-heads will be covered by placing the upper sides into position, after which fit the cornice on to the tongues, and screw the $7\frac{1}{4}$-in. by $\frac{3}{8}$-in. dust-board into the cornice rebate and also into the top of the upper sides. Finally insert the metal supports into the ladders, and place the shelves as required. If the work has been carried out as described there should be no need to screw the sides to the walls. The position and number of shelves is a matter of choice, for any shelf not in use can be placed on the top of the dust-board.

The fitment can be quickly taken to pieces for removal in the following order: (1) Remove all shelves and metal supports; (2) unscrew and remove the dust-board and the cornice; (3) remove the upper sides; (4) unscrew and remove the moulded shelf, and, lastly, the lower sides.

This fitment may be regarded as a tenant's fitting.

CHAPTER XXXIV

Kitchen and Scullery Furniture

Small Kitchen Table, Figs. 968 to 978.—An excellent though somewhat uncommon wood for the framing of such a table as this is larch, which is probably stronger and more durable than any other coniferous timber; but red or white pine may be used. The dimensions are: length of top, 3 ft. 4 in.; breadth, 1 ft. 11 in.; height (over-all), 2 ft. 4 in. The table legs are dressed $2\frac{1}{4}$ in. square, and bevelled from the edge of the rails to $1\frac{1}{2}$ in. at the foot. The back and end rails are finished 5 in. by 1 in. The top front rail and bearer-rail for the drawers are $2\frac{1}{4}$ in. by 1 in., as is also the upright between the drawers, and the longitudinal and bottom rails 2 in. by 1 in. The table top is a solid 23-in. wide yellow pine board 1 in. thick by 3 ft. 4 in. long, and projects 2 in. over the framing at the ends and $1\frac{1}{4}$ in. at the front and back. Should a solid board of sufficient width for the top be unobtainable, the breadth may be made up by shooting the edges of two or more pieces, and dowel-jointing and gluing them together.

The stuff for the drawers is $\frac{3}{8}$-in. birch, with $\frac{5}{8}$-in. thick fronts, the latter being made of home-grown walnut, which when polished or varnished contrasts well with the lighter-coloured framing. The drawer knobs may be bought, or turned from the same stuff (walnut) as the drawer fronts, and, instead of the usual screwing, glued in tight with plain turned pins.

The back and end rails are bridge mortised into the legs, and the end bottom rails are also mortised, while the front top rail is dovetailed into the top of the front legs and the drawer bearer. The upright between the drawers is double-mortised into the rails; but the tenons may be mortised right through and glue-wedged, which tends to

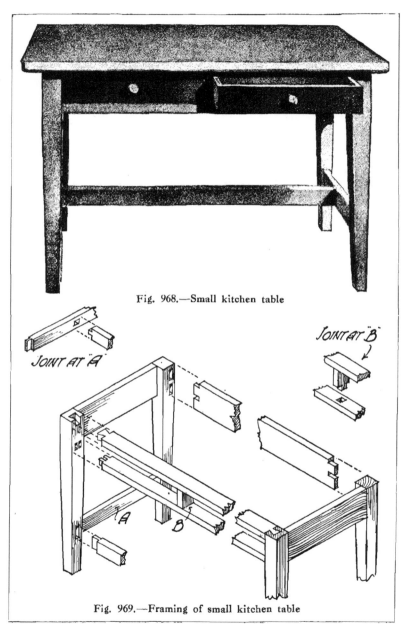

Fig. 968.—Small kitchen table

Fig. 969.—Framing of small kitchen table

Kitchen and Scullery Furniture 371

prevent the weight and use of the drawer working the joints open at the shoulders. The drawer runner is fixed between the bearer and back rail of the table with small blocks glued on underneath. The drawer guide is on top of the runner. The end runners are similarly fixed at both ends of the table.

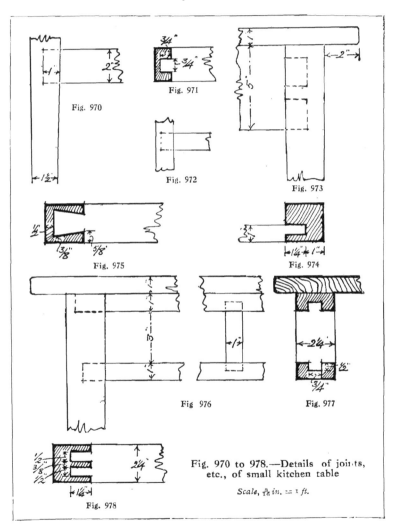

Fig. 970 to 978.—Details of joints, etc., of small kitchen table

Scale, ⅛ in. = 1 ft.

Furniture Making

Fig. 979.—First dresser design—cottage type

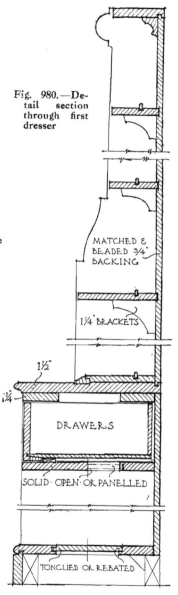

Fig. 980.—Detail section through first dresser

The longitudinal bottom rail is mortised midway into the bottom end rails with stump-tenon joints.

In putting the framing together, the end, top, and bottom rails are glued and cramped together, and then placed aside until the joints set. The short upright is at the same time glued into the front rails, and, in the latter case especially, care must be observed that the rails are not distorted from parallelism in cramping. Next, everything being prepared, the various joints are manipulated into their respective positions with mallet or hammer, taking care not to bruise the wood, and

Kitchen and Scullery Furniture 373

finally cramped tightly together and tested for squareness. Any defect of this sort (provided the rails are correct for length and shoulders) should be remedied by slacking, and slightly altering the position of the cramp.

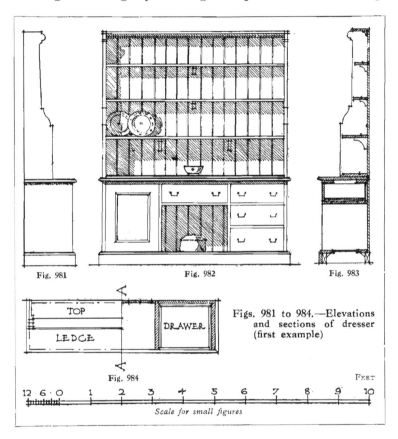

Figs. 981 to 984.—Elevations and sections of dresser (first example)

It should also be noted that the bottom end-rail shoulders are bevelled to suit the legs.

The drawers are 1 ft. $3\frac{1}{2}$ in. wide and 3 in. deep at the front, and may be made 1 ft. 6 in. from front to back, dovetailed and glued together. The drawer back is flush at the top and bottom with the dovetail pins, so that the grooving

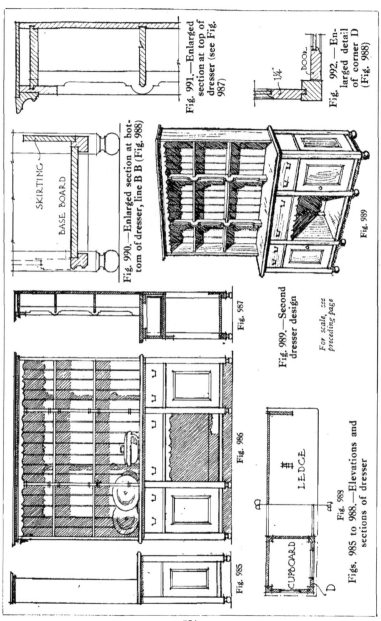
Figs. 985 to 988.—Elevations and sections of dresser

Kitchen and Scullery Furniture

for the bottom is flush with the under-side of the back, and permits the bottom being slid in from the back after the

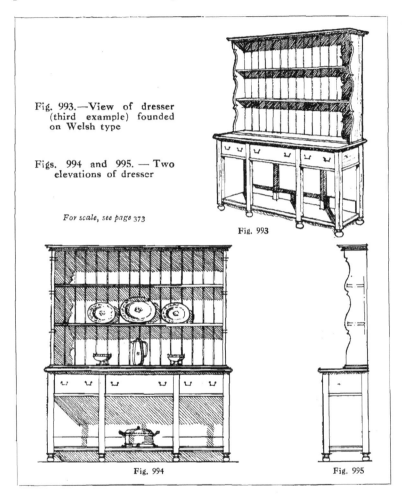

Fig. 993.—View of dresser (third example) founded on Welsh type

Figs. 994 and 995. — Two elevations of dresser

For scale, see page 373

Fig. 993

Fig. 994

Fig. 995

front, sides, and back are framed together. Fillets are finally fixed to give breadth for wear, and prevent the thin drawer sides wearing tracks in the bearer and runners. As provision against shrinkage, which often occurs in drawer bottoms, the bottom may be advantageously left projecting a little beyond the back and held in place with a fine screw-nail through it into the drawer back. Thus, if it shrinks from

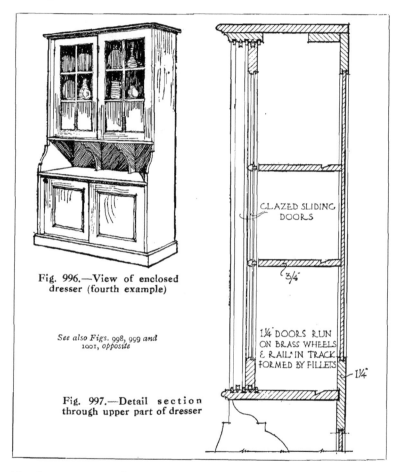

Fig. 996.—View of enclosed dresser (fourth example)

See also Figs. 998, 999 and 1001, opposite

Fig. 997.—Detail section through upper part of dresser

the front groove the screw can be withdrawn and reinserted after pushing in the bottom.

Two methods of fixing the table top may be employed, either by glued angle blocks, or angled countersunk screw-nails, or a combination of both.

Kitchen and Scullery Furniture 377

Dressers and Pantry Cupboards, Figs. 979 to 1014.
—These dressers are suitable for the kitchen or living-room. Some of them illustrate simple types based on the lines of the old cottage dresser, while those with legs are examples of a modern treatment characteristic of the old Welsh type

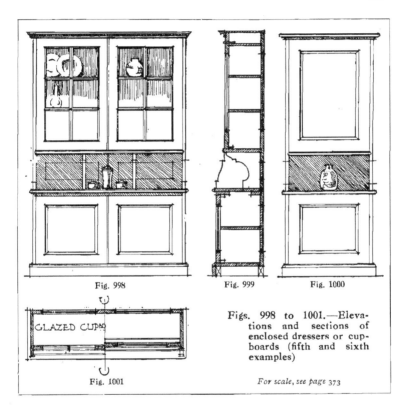

Figs. 998 to 1001.—Elevations and sections of enclosed dressers or cupboards (fifth and sixth examples)

For scale, see page 373

of fitting. Their simple character is determined by consideration for good proportion and straightforwardness of design and the absence of all elaborate and unnecessary ornation. Those shown by Figs. 979 to 984 and 1007 to 1010 lend themselves to oak or deal construction, while those shown by Figs. 998 to 1006, to be in keeping with their style, should preferably be of oak.

Fig. 1002   Fig. 1003   Fig. 1004

Fig. 1005

Figs. 1002 to 1005.—Elevations and sections of enclosed dresser or cupboard (seventh example)

For scale, see page 373

Fig. 1006.—General view of enclosed dreser (seventh example)

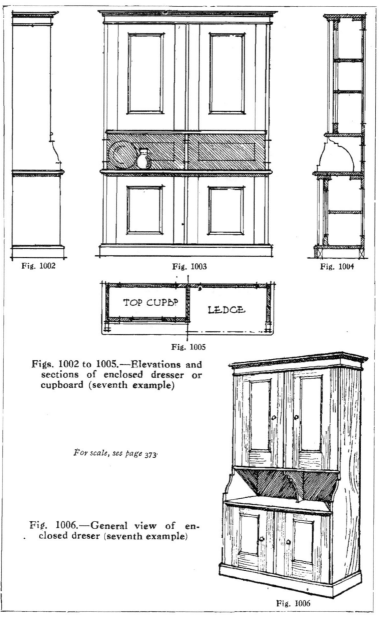

Fig. 1006

Kitchen and Scullery Furniture

The lower portions are filled in with cupboards and drawers, and the upper parts with plain shelving housed into

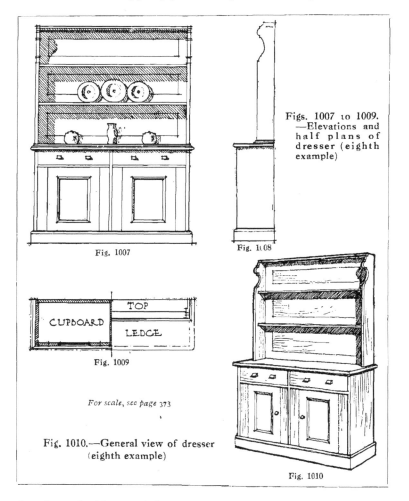

Figs. 1007 to 1009.—Elevations and half plans of dresser (eighth example)

Fig. 1007

Fig. 1008

Fig. 1009

For scale, see page 373

Fig. 1010.—General view of dresser (eighth example)

Fig. 1010

the shaped sides and into the wood backing. The shelves would be fitted with cup hooks as necessary, and the drawer fronts with metal drop handles.

The enlarged section (Fig. 980), whilst constructionally

Furniture Making

explaining Fig. 979, is a typical section of a dresser of this type. The base or pot board may be in one solid piece or filled in with a rebated or tongued panel, and the same applies to the division below drawers. The $\frac{3}{4}$-in. matchboarding to the upper part may be tongued to the ledge and top pieces as illustrated, or cut square and screwed at these places, the former construction making a firmer and neater job. The plates, etc., can be kept in slanting positions

Fig. 1011.—Elevation of dresser with cupboard (ninth example)

on the shelving by means of grooves or fillets (alternate sections are illustrated in the various designs).

The enlarged sections (Figs. 990 and 991) are taken through the top and bottom of Fig. 986; and the enlarged section (Fig. 992) through the angle leg shows the detail of the door and side panels and the grooved jointing of the latter to the leg.

Alternate designs for serviceable pantry cupboards, providing ample storage accommodation for china or silver, etc., with hinged and panelled, and sliding glazed and panelled doors are also given; and a smaller cupboard is illustrated in addition. These would be constructed of deal, painted white.

Kitchen and Scullery Furniture

Dish and Plate Rack, Figs. 1015 to 1022.—The fronts and backs of the rack here shown would be made complete with the bars fixed and then tenoned into position to the two sides. The sides comprise back, angle posts, and top rail. The back and angle posts of the sides would be mortised

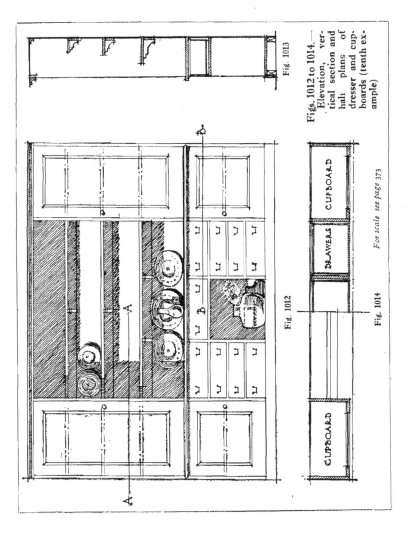

Figs. 1012 to 1014.—Elevation, vertical section and half plans of dresser and cupboards (tenth example)

to receive the tenons of the top and bottom front and back rails, and, on one side only, mortised to receive the horizontal intermediate rails, also tenoned at bases to fit into the top bracket pieces, as fully shown in the illustrations. The $\frac{1}{2}$-in. top would now be nailed to the fixed framing, leaving the carcass complete and ready for jointing into the bracket pieces after the brackets are fixed to the wall. To make a good strong job of the brackets, the following method of

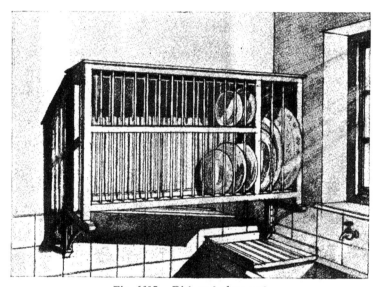

Fig. 1015.—Dish and plate rack

fixing is recommended :—Having well secured the back pieces to the wall, screw the iron brackets to the top pieces and complete the fixing by well screwing the brackets to the back pieces already fixed. The enlarged isometric detail shows the application of the tenon joints to the rails, etc. The $\frac{1}{2}$-in. circular bars are housed into the top and bottom rails, $2\frac{1}{2}$ in. apart (centre to centre) for the plate divisions, and $3\frac{1}{2}$ in. apart (centre to centre) for the dish divisions. These bars are carried right through the front and back intermediate rails, as shown in the isometric detail.

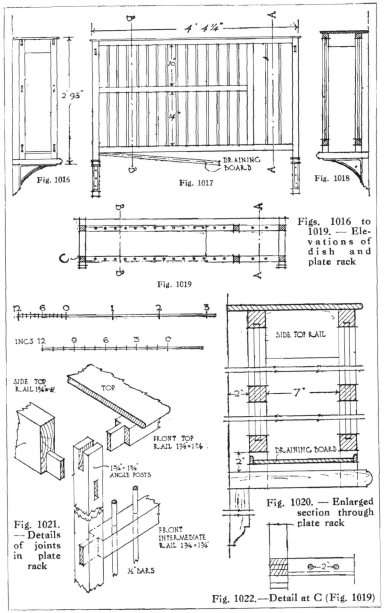

Fig. 1016. Fig. 1017. Fig. 1018.

Figs. 1016 to 1019. — Elevations of dish and plate rack

Fig. 1019.

Fig. 1021. — Details of joints in plate rack

Fig. 1020. — Enlarged section through plate rack

Fig. 1022.—Detail at C (Fig. 1019)

Furniture Making

The draining-board, as here shown, is arranged to suit this particular example, where it is necessary to drain the water towards the front of the sink, and is open to adjustment according to the relative positions of the sink and rack.

This form of rack lends itself to any particular length, according to the accommodation required.

Trough Plate Rack, Figs. 1023 to 1031.—The plate rack here illustrated should prove of considerable assistance in "washing up," and is intended to be suspended as nearly over the sink as may be found practicable. The way in which it accommodates plates will be seen, and it should also be of service for various small articles which would otherwise

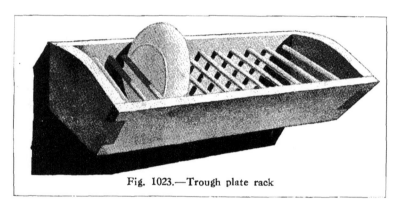

Fig. 1023.—Trough plate rack

occupy valuable space on the draining-board. The rack can be varied indefinitely in length, and it is intended to be made out of $\frac{3}{4}$-in. or 1-in. wood, which should be of as impervious a character as possible, oak and teak being the ideal materials.

The most explanatory of the illustrations is the transverse section (Fig. 1028), in which there is an upright back piece A 2 ft. by 8 in., seen at B in Fig. 1030 (which incidentally shows two holes by which the completed rack can be hung). Then at C (Fig. 1028) is a sloping front piece 2 ft. long and $5\frac{1}{4}$ in. wide, splayed off along the bottom as shown, so that when fitted together this splayed edge will be at right angles to the face of the back piece A. The front and back are con-

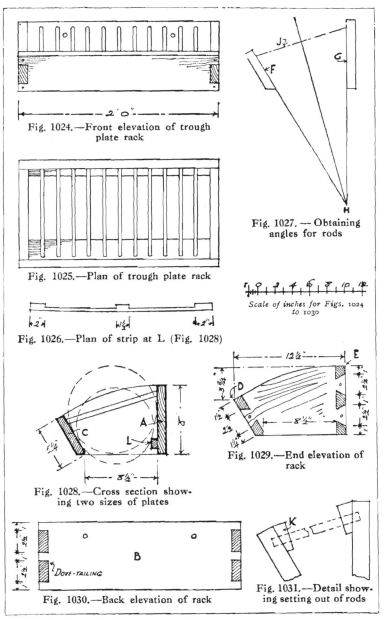

Fig. 1024.—Front elevation of trough plate rack

Fig. 1025.—Plan of trough plate rack

Fig. 1026.—Plan of strip at L (Fig. 1028)

Fig. 1027.—Obtaining angles for rods

Scale of inches for Figs. 1024 to 1030

Fig. 1028.—Cross section showing two sizes of plates

Fig. 1029.—End elevation of rack

Fig. 1030.—Back elevation of rack

Fig. 1031.—Detail showing setting out of rods

Z 385

nected by a pair of end pieces, each cut out of 12½-in. by 8-in. stuff to the contour shown in Fig. 1029, the slope of the front being easily set out by means of a 60° set-square, and the slight curve introduced in order to join up lines at right angles from the points D and E.

The four pieces should be dovetailed as in Fig. 1029.

Before fixing together, arrange for the insertion of the small rods forming the 1½-in. wide divisions. These rods had better be of oak, even if the bulk of the work is not, and they should be fixed by housing into suitable sockets formed with a brace and bit. These rods can be purchased in ready-made lengths of about 10 ft., or garden canes would form very durable substitutes. In any case, the difficulty lies in readily making a close joint at each of the twenty-two or so ends. The way in which to arrange this is to set out full size on paper a section of the work similar to that in Fig. 1028, continue the lines F and G (Fig. 1027) until they meet at H, then measure 1 in. down from the top ends of F and G, and join across the angle by means of a line J, this being the centre line for the circular rods. Halve this and join to H, and then, taking a strip of wood 1 ft. 10 in. long and about 1½ in. wide, plane it off to the same angle as that made by the centre line with either of the side lines F and G. Next, at a distance of 1 in. from the wider edge of the strip, set out a line of eleven equidistant points as centres. The strip can then be lightly glued or bradded to the back of the front piece as at K in Fig. 1031, and the sockets bored through. The fact that the brace and bit are worked at right angles to the splayed faces of the fillet will cause them to form a hole entering the wood below at the correct angle (*see* dotted lines in Fig. 1031). For the back line of holes, the same fillet can be used reversed. Now adjust the rods to the lengths required, and fix the work together.

The larger dotted circle in Fig. 1028 indicates how far an average dinner-plate would go into the rack. To prevent smaller plates slipping too far, fix a strip L along the back, and, so that this may collect as little moisture as possible, cut it neatly away at the back as shown in Fig. 1026, leaving three small parts for fixing.

CHAPTER XXXV

MISCELLANEOUS FURNITURE

Small Stand or Occasional Table, Figs. 1032 to 1039.—This stand or table consists of a square top having a small ledge or "gallery" round it, and is carried on a four-way support, cruciform on plan, and composed of one piece from A to B, with two others, C and D, fixed at right angles to it, as will be described. The wood employed is all quite light in thickness, and can be of oak or any other description, while the work involved is of the simplest nature.

First of all the $\frac{1}{2}$-in. top, 1 ft. 4 in. square, should be prepared, with a $\frac{1}{4}$-in. by $\frac{3}{16}$-in. groove worked all round its upper surface $\frac{1}{2}$ in. from the edges, which are rounded off as in Fig. 1034. Here it should be noted that the rounding is not semicircular in section, the upper portion being flattened and the lower made correspondingly sharper; this will be found to give a more refined appearance. A $1\frac{11}{16}$-in. by $\frac{1}{4}$-in. length should then be prepared for fitting into the grooves, very carefully mitred at the corners, rounded off on its upper edge, and neatly secured with fine brads at the angles, and also with small screws inserted from the under-side of the top, through small holes bored from above through the centre of the groove, before it is filled by the ledges.

The lower portion is prepared as follows: The continuous piece A B (Fig. 1033) is shaped as shown in Fig. 1038, 2 ft. $3\frac{1}{2}$ in. long, 11 in. wide at the bottom, reducing to $8\frac{1}{2}$ in. at the top, curved each side to the contour shown in detail by Fig. 1039. This illustration can be very easily enlarged to full size by setting out a sheet of paper with lines at right angles 2 in. apart, measuring along its height, and with 1-in. spaces horizontally across its width, to correspond with the rectangles on the figure, by means of which the curves can be set out with precision. Note that the string of dimensions along two sides of the figure all read from the point E. Each of the pieces C and D will be cut to the same outline as in Fig. 1039, except that along the line E F they will be reduced by one-half the thickness of the wood employed, so that assuming this to be $\frac{1}{2}$ in. (as would be very suitable), the line E F would require to be moved up $\frac{1}{4}$ in. for these two pieces, thus making them, when in position as in Fig. 1033, of precisely the same overall dimension as A B. The simplest way in which to secure them will be by means of a metal strap about 3 in. long as in Fig. 1037, countersunk for screws and let slightly into the under edges at G (Fig. 1038). At the top a connection will be effected by screwing down from above as indicated on plan in Fig. 1036, the holes being very carefully set out and bored previously, as accuracy in this part of the work is imperative. These screws should be sunk a little below the surface and concealed with stopping ; and if a couple of long oak dowels can be inserted through the three parts of the support as indicated at H and J, a sound job will be made of the table, which, however, is obviously not suited for heavy wear unless stouter thicknesses are substituted for those specified.

The table might be varied if desired by using a circular or hexagonal top, or by setting the square top on the supports in such a way that the latter comes under its diagonal lines (this would incidentally tend to afford greater security from overturning, supposing the stand to be employed as a coffee table, for instance).

Square Palm Stand, Figs. 1040 to 1047.—For this palm stand, four legs are required, 1 in. square and 3 ft. $5\frac{5}{8}$ in. long ; these will be linked up by diagonal rails measuring $\frac{1}{2}$ in. by $1\frac{1}{4}$ in. high, fixed at the two levels marked A and B ; these rails are tenoned into the legs as shown on plan at C, an elevation of the joint being given in Fig. 1043. This joint is made by first of all taking off the inner angle of the leg to a width of $\frac{1}{2}$ in. as at C, for a height of $1\frac{1}{4}$ in. at the correct level (as dimensioned in Fig. 1040), and then working a mortise $\frac{3}{16}$ in. wide and about $\frac{3}{4}$ in. long in the middle of the angle as indicated. Where the rails cross in the centre they must be halved together, one being cut

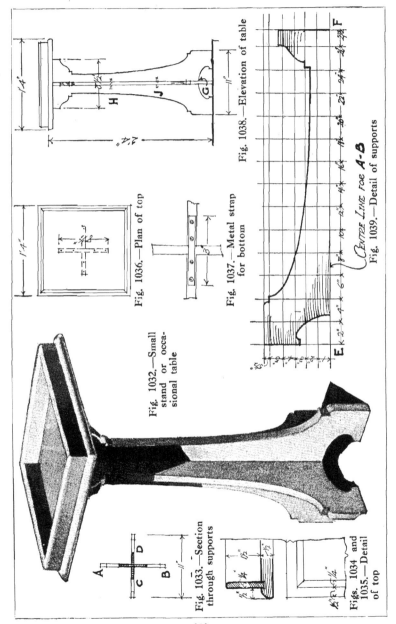

Fig. 1038.—Elevation of table

Fig. 1036.—Plan of top

Fig. 1037.—Metal strap for bottom

Fig. 1039.—Detail of supports

Fig. 1032.—Small stand or occasional table

Fig. 1033.—Section through supports

Figs. 1034 and 1035.—Detail of top

out at the bottom as shown at D, and the other with the same sized piece ($\frac{1}{2}$ in. by $\frac{5}{8}$ in.) cut out at the top, the two thus fitting into one another. Supported on the upper pair of diagonals there is intended to be a flat shelf $\frac{1}{2}$ in. thick and $9\frac{7}{8}$ in. square, slightly rounded off on all four sides, and notched out at each corner as in Fig. 1046 in order to fit round the legs ; this part will obviously require very careful fitting.

Before any parts of the work are fixed together, the legs should be double-rebated as in Fig. 1044, for a height of about $11\frac{3}{4}$ in. above the top of the shelf; this will leave room for four fretwork sides $\frac{1}{4}$ in. thick, of a simple geometric pattern which by reason of its series of vertical bars will be found quite effective in appearance. These fret sides should be set out with square and compasses as shown in Fig. 1041, $9\frac{1}{2}$ in. wide and $11\frac{3}{4}$ in. high, with top curved concavely to a radius of about $7\frac{1}{4}$ in., and the five straight slots cut on each face with great accuracy, as any irregularity is far more noticeable with a simple rectilinear figure than in the more usual flamboyant types of design.

The sides, of course, fit into the $\frac{1}{4}$-in. rebates in the legs, and it will be sufficient to butt them against the top of the flat shelf, after which they can be glued in position and further secured by means of small fillets splayed as necessary to fit in position as at E ; these should be made to continue the inner angle of the legs as nearly as possible. Work will be completed by fixing small caps $1\frac{5}{8}$ in. square by $\frac{3}{8}$ in. thick with rounded edges (Fig. 1041) on top of each leg, when the whole stand will be ready for staining, etc., as desired.

Hall or Bedroom Seat, Figs. 1048 to 1054.—The box-seat here shown would be equally suitable for a hall or in a bedroom, where it might perhaps find a suitable position in front of a window. It has a hinged top, giving access to a trough or box for which many uses might be found, while below there is a space of the height and length required to accommodate several pairs of boots. The length of the whole could very easily be varied to conform to any particular position, and the top could be upholstered if desired, or a loose flat cushion prepared to cover it and be removed when the lid is raised. The slightly inclined front

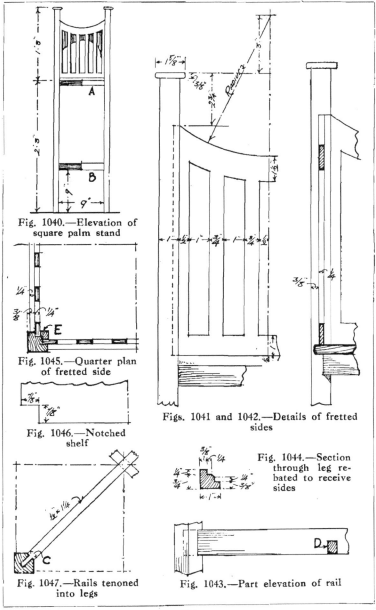

Fig. 1040.—Elevation of square palm stand

Fig. 1045.—Quarter plan of fretted side

Fig. 1046.—Notched shelf

Figs. 1041 and 1042.—Details of fretted sides

Fig. 1044.—Section through leg rebated to receive sides

Fig. 1047.—Rails tenoned into legs

Fig. 1043.—Part elevation of rail

of the box might be composed of, say, 1-in. framing, with either one or three panels, and moulded if desired. Alternatively, the work might be kept solid as shown, but enriched with a sunk carved ornament; a 4-in. circle or a diamond about 6 in. long would be very suitable in the centre of the front or at the ends, always provided that the device is kept simple.

The construction of the seat is as follows: First the two end-pieces, 22 in. by 12 in. and out of 1-in. stuff, are

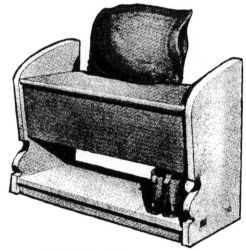

Fig. 1048.—Hall or bedroom seat

prepared, their back and bottom edges square, but shaped on front and top as indicated by the contour of Fig. 1050; this outline can be rapidly and accurately set out by dividing the front 4 in. in the width of one side into 1 in. spaces horizontally and vertically, this giving a corresponding number of squares to those in Fig. 1053; it will be advisable to number them as in the figure, and it will be found a very simple matter to draw the curves correctly by noting where they cut across any particular line or corner and joining up the points thus obtained. In order to save space the finish of the simple top curve at A is curtailed, but there can be

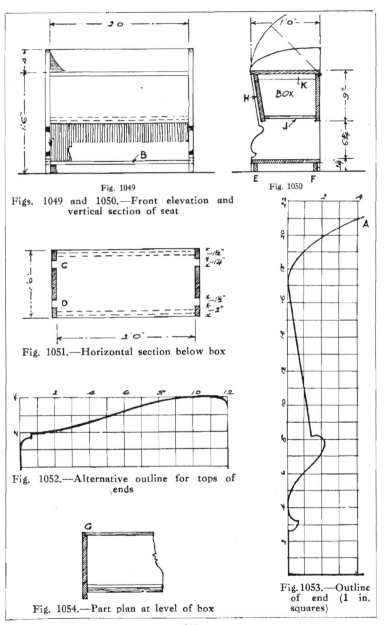

Fig. 1049

Figs. 1049 and 1050.—Front elevation and vertical section of seat

Fig. 1050

Fig. 1051.—Horizontal section below box

Fig. 1052.—Alternative outline for tops of ends

Fig. 1053.—Outline of end (1 in. squares)

Fig. 1054.—Part plan at level of box

no difficulty in completing this on the actual work. There is perhaps a possibility that this curve will be considered too simple by some, and accordingly an alternative suggestion for it will be found in Fig. 1052 ; this can be enlarged square by square, as before described.

The boot shelf B, 26 in. by 12 in., and finishing about $\frac{5}{8}$ in. thick, should have its ends cut back 1 in. in order to leave projections as at c and D of the widths there shown, the front ones being kept back a little in order to keep them away from the parts where the front is cut into for the curved portions ; these projections are intended to be driven into slots cut in the sides to suit them, with the tops $2\frac{1}{4}$ in. up from the floor level ; the projecting ends can easily be cleaned off at the finish, and the bottom should ultimately be completed with two small filling-in pieces as at E and F, fixed about $\frac{1}{4}$ in. back from the edges of shelf and ends. A back piece 25 in. by $8\frac{3}{8}$ in. and $\frac{5}{8}$ in. or so thick, fixed 9 in. above the floor by letting into rebates prepared for it in the ends as at G, will help to secure the upper part of the ends, as will also a similar front piece H fixed on the slope parallel to the inclined portion of the end and $\frac{3}{16}$ in. back from the front ; on account of this inclination its top edge will require splaying off a little in order to be made horizontal. This front could be fixed by merely strongly screwing through the ends into it, or much better methods would be to dowel it in position, or to house it bodily into the uprights.

The bottom of the box J can be quite light, and should present no difficulties in fixing ; its ends might be supported on very small fillets fixed against the uprights. The lid also is quite simple, merely a 24-in. by 12-in. board $\frac{3}{4}$ in. thick resting on the front and back of the box, and hinged to the latter ; its front edge should be rounded and it will be as well to put small strips under it at the ends (as at K) fixed to the uprights, in order to support it and obviate any danger of its splitting along the grain under any extra weight.

Pedestal for Vase or Bust, Figs. 1055 to 1058.— This has points of resemblance with the pedestals described on pages 218 to 222. The half-section (Fig. 1056) explains the construction, o representing a 2-in. by 2-in. central

Miscellaneous Furniture

post to which are secured three series of fir blocks (crossed as described for the earlier examples). These take a 2-in. by

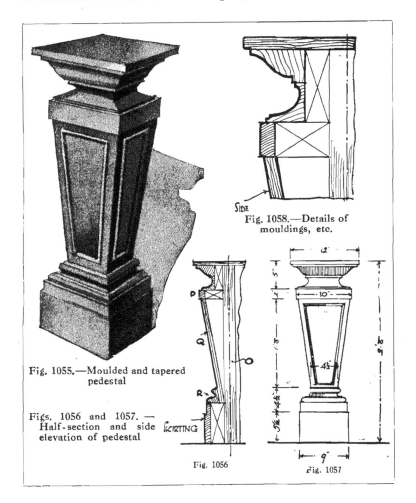

Fig. 1055.—Moulded and tapered pedestal

Figs. 1056 and 1057. — Half-section and side elevation of pedestal

Fig. 1058.—Details of mouldings, etc.

1-in. piece P, a heavily moulded portion as in Fig. 1058, surmounted by a plain top as shown, and a simple skirting in one or two pieces. A few fitted fixing-pieces will also be required to take the four sloping sides Q, which should leave just enough room for a bold base moulding as at R. Very careful making and fixing are essential to a good result.

Hall Fitting with Mirror and Pegs, Figs. 1059 to 1070.—This model is rather a departure from the usual types of such fittings, and its shape will be found to permit of its being placed in positions too narrow for the majority of patterns. It will serve for hats and coats in the ordinary way, or could be reserved as a rack for sticks, etc. ; and, of course, if preferred, metal hooks could be substituted for the wooden pegs shown.

Oak is the best material for use throughout, and the main framework can best be understood from the back view shown by Fig. 1069. Here are shown two side pieces and top and intermediate rails, all $2\frac{1}{2}$ in. wide and about $\frac{7}{8}$ in. thick, together with a bottom rail 4 in. wide and fixed $\frac{1}{2}$ in. up from the bottom edges of the upright sides. A detailed setting out of the joint is given in Fig. 1061, and Fig. 1062 gives a section of the joint in order to prevent misunderstanding. The dotted lines at A indicate the rebate about $\frac{1}{2}$ in. wide and $\frac{1}{2}$ in. deep, which should be worked round both the openings in the framing before the various parts are fixed together. The top rail should be secured in exactly the same manner, but with a smaller dovetail as in Fig. 1069, while for the middle rail an ordinary simple halved-joint will be sufficient, as the work is securely held together by the joints at the top and bottom. If desired, the joints may be fixed with pegs driven through them, and these might project a little or be smoothed off flush, as preferred.

The bottom opening is filled in with a $\frac{1}{2}$-in. oak panel, having its margins planed off to a slight slope about $1\frac{1}{4}$ in. wide, in order to show about $\frac{5}{8}$ in. on the face, as in Fig. 1060, where the panel is seen in section, and is held in position by means of a small bead as at B. The top panel could be merely filled in with a mirror, either bevelled or plain ; but in order to produce the diamond shape shown, a piece of fretwood, say $\frac{3}{16}$ in. thick, is prepared with the opening carefully set out and cut as shown, and the exposed edges chamfered off, the whole being put into the rebate before

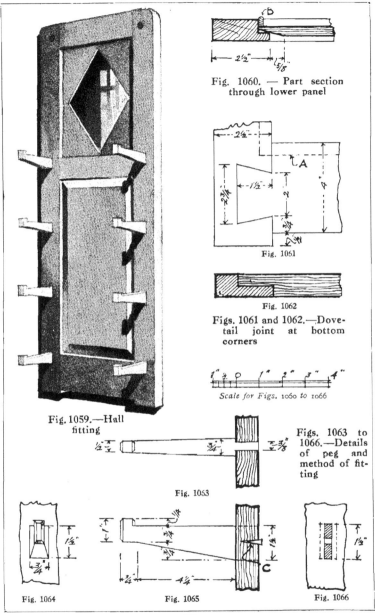

Fig. 1060. — Part section through lower panel

Fig. 1061

Fig. 1062

Figs. 1061 and 1062.—Dovetail joint at bottom corners

Scale for Figs. 1060 to 1066

Fig. 1059.—Hall fitting

Figs. 1063 to 1066.—Details of peg and method of fitting

Fig. 1063

Fig. 1064

Fig. 1065

Fig. 1066

Furniture Making

the mirror, which, when suitably protected at the rear, will not leave any space in the rebates.

If simple oak pegs are desired rather than metal ones, they can be made as shown by Figs. 1063 to 1066, from pieces 1¾ in. by ¾ in. and 6 in. long, cut to the outline and dimensions shown. They are tapered on plan, and tenoned

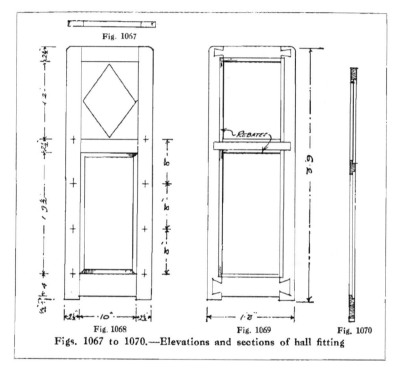

Figs. 1067 to 1070.—Elevations and sections of hall fitting

at the wider end of each, and chamfered at the ends. For fixing the pegs, slots ⅜ in. by 1½ in. should be cut where indicated by crosses in Fig. 1068, tightly to fit the tenoned ends; these should have small V-shaped pieces taken out of them as at c in Fig. 1065. When the pegs have been driven home, small wedges should be inserted from the back as shown, in order to fix the work as tightly as possible.

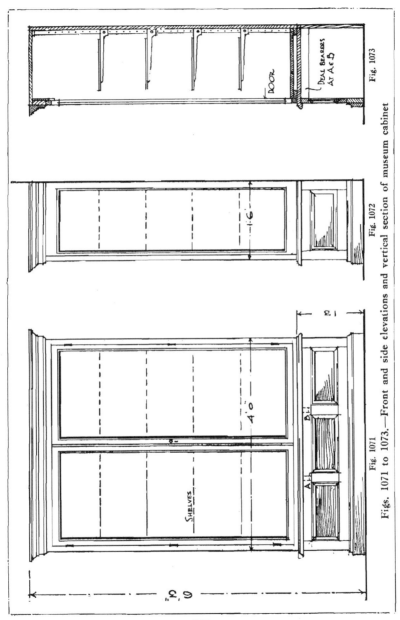

Figs. 1071 to 1073.—Front and side elevations and vertical section of museum cabinet

Museum Cabinet, Figs. 1071 to 1077.—This museum cabinet is suitable for storing curiosities and antiquities. The outside dimensions are 4 ft. wide by 1 ft. 6 in. deep by 6 ft. 3 in. high. Wainscot oak can be used for all outside parts, while the parts that are hidden are of best yellow pine. All the materials must be perfectly seasoned. The lower part of the cabinet, or base, is panelled and moulded and could easily be adapted for a cupboard if desired; it is made independent of the upper part or cabinet proper, the latter being constructed on the air-tight principle, the opening sashes or doors having hook-joints on the meeting stile and air-tight beads to the hanging stile as in Fig. 1075. The frame has air-tight fillets at the top and bottom as in Fig. 1076, the ends being framed to match the front, and glazed with polished plate glass. The inside of the cabinet can be lined with velvet plush on the back, the latter being composed of $\frac{3}{4}$-in. matchboarding, and should be papered before being covered. The bottom is also lined with plush.

The cabinet is fitted with plate-glass shelves, shaped as shown (Fig. 1074) and supported on bronzed iron or brass shelf brackets, screwed with set-screws to vertical standard bars, which are holed at intervals of $1\frac{1}{2}$ in. to 2 in. for convenience in raising or lowering the position of the shelves. The doors are hung on brass arrow butts, three to each door. The left-hand door is fitted with a brass bolt at the top and bottom the right-hand door has an eccentric handle and catch, and a small sash lock.

Plain Bookcase, Open or Glazed, Figs. 1078 to 1082.—The bookcase here illustrated can equally well be made as a fixture or as a movable piece of furniture, and, if desired, could be fitted with glazed doors. The main supports are the two side uprights A, which should extend from the level of the floor to that marked B. If in deal, these should be from $\frac{7}{8}$ in. to $1\frac{1}{4}$ in. thick, according to the size of the bookcase, and about $9\frac{1}{2}$ in. wide will suffice, unless large books are to be accommodated. If it is proposed to leave the shelving open at the back, the width could be reduced about $\frac{3}{8}$ in. by omitting the rebate and $\frac{1}{2}$-in. back boarding at c. This is not advisable, however, as the solid back makes a much better finish,

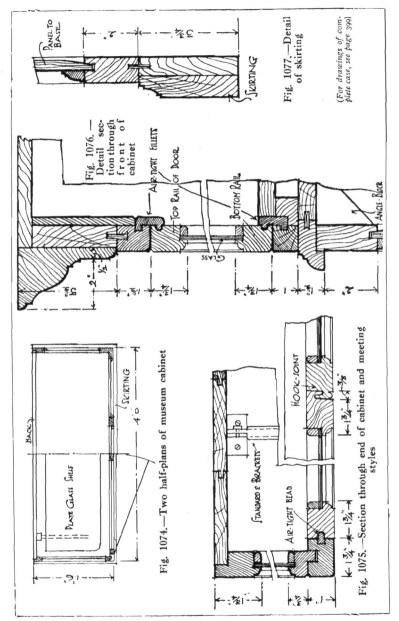

Fig. 1077.—Detail of skirting

(For drawings of complete case, see page 399)

Fig. 1076.—Detail section through front of cabinet

Fig. 1074.—Two half-plans of museum cabinet

Fig. 1075.—Section through end of cabinet and meeting styles

and also serves to tie the whole together thoroughly if fixed with the grain horizontal.

With its top about 4½ in. above the floor, a bottom shelf D, of the desired length and the same width as the sides,

Fig. 1078.—Plain bookcase

should be fixed so as to keep the ends in their proper relationship, and this is further secured by fixing down on top of their ends a thin top shelf or cover as at B. Under the front edge of this, and flush with the edges of the sides, should then be fitted a 4½-in. by 1-in. fascia E, butting against the

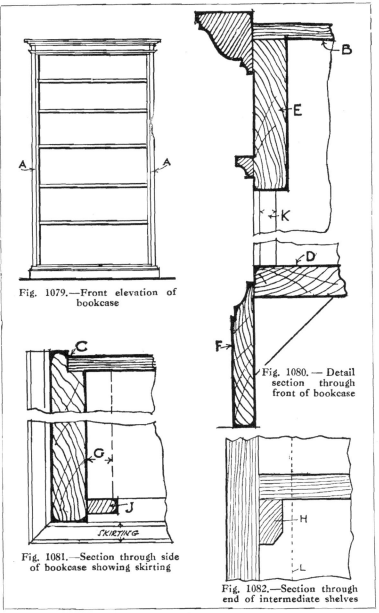

Fig. 1079.—Front elevation of bookcase

Fig. 1080.—Detail section through front of bookcase

Fig. 1081.—Section through side of bookcase showing skirting

Fig. 1082.—Section through end of intermediate shelves

sides at each end, where it can be secured with angle-blocks on the inside, if required. On this fascia, as shown, are fixed a cornice moulding about $1\frac{1}{4}$ in. by $1\frac{1}{2}$ in., and $2\frac{1}{2}$ in. below it a moulded fillet or necking about $\frac{5}{8}$ in. high. These are, of course, both mitred and returned along the sides to the back, and then cut off flush. The bottom may be finished in a similar manner with a 4-in. by $\frac{5}{8}$-in. moulded skirting F, fixed along the front with angle-blocks under the shelf D as indicated.

The levels of the various shelves having been decided, these should be prepared about 8 in. wide and of just sufficient thickness to avoid the slightest sagging when filled. They are intended to be supported on fillets about $1\frac{1}{4}$ in. by $\frac{1}{2}$ in., as at G and H. These supports should be screwed to facilitate any subsequent alterations of their positions, and as they would appear comparatively unsightly when seen from the front, they are concealed by means of small fillets $\frac{7}{8}$ in. by $\frac{1}{2}$ in. square, fixed a little back from the edges of the sides, as at J, K, and L.

INDEX

ANGLE chair, etc. (see Corner)
Armchair with adjustable back, 200
——, dining-room, 201
——, stuffover, 353
"Armoire" hall fitment, 92

BANDINGS, 84
Bathroom fitment, 60
Bedroom chair, 336
—— seat, 390
—— suites, 289-330
Bedside tables, 346-352
Bedstead fitting, Vono, 311
——, wooden, 308, 325
Bookcase, built-up or sectional, 28
——, bureau, 43
—— or cabinet, 19
——, dwarf, with glazed doors, 25
——, plain, open or glazed, 400
—— table, double-shelf, 1
—— ——, single-shelf, 1
—— with underneath cupboard, 22
Book-racks, 6-11
Bookshelf, dwarf, 12
—— fitment for recess, 364
—— and smoker's cupboard combined, 167
Bookstands, 1-11
——, double-tier, 8
——, double trough, 7
——, single trough, 6
"Bottle-end" glazing, 16
Box, rug, 126
Bracket clocks, 65, 72
Bust pedestals, 218-222, 395
Bureau bookcase, 43
Bureaux, 35-47

CABINETS, 19-34, 135-147, 157-167
—— with bookshelves, 13
——, china, 19-34, 170
——, curio, 19-34, 398
——, hanging, 157-167
——, medicine, 157, 166
——, museum, 398
——, music, with leadlight doors, 141
——, ——, modern, 144
——, ——, with trays and drawers, 135
——, smoker's, 157, 163
——, writing, 35-47
—— and writing-table combined, 40
Card table, folding, 236
Cauls, veneerer's, 89
Chair (see also Seat)
——, angle, 195
——, arm, with adjustable back, 200
——, ——, dining-room, 201
——, bedroom, 336
——, Chippendale, 188
——, corner, 195
——, dining, 182, 184

Chair, divan, 353
——, drawing-room, 186
——, modern, 189
——, rush- or cord-seating 338
Chest, dressing, 294, 321
——, Flemish, 122
—— or rug box, 126
Chesterfield settee, 353
Chest-of-drawers, 306
Cheval glass, 328
Child's cot, 343-345
China cabinets, 19-34, 170
Chippendale chair, 188
Clock, eighteenth-century English, 72
——, grandfather, 74
——, hanging wall, 66
——, mantel with side shelves, 65
Coffee table, 232
Cord-seating chair, 338
Corner chair, 195
—— cupboard, 168-174
—— ——, antique, 168
—— —— to hang or stand, 170
—— fitting with shelves, 205
—— seat, upholstered, 208
—— stand, 106
Cot, adjustable, 343
Cottage sideboard, 281
Couch, stuffover, 353
Credence, Flemish, 122
Cupboards, 157-167, 168-174, 376
——, antique corner, 168
——, bookcase with, 22
——, Flemish, 122
——, hanging corner, 170
——, medicine, 157, 166
——, music, 141
——, overmantel with, 48
——, pantry, 376
——, pedestal, 304
——, recess fitment with, 361
—— with shelves, 13
——, smoker's, and bookshelf combined, 167
Curio cabinets, 19-34, 398
—— tables, 239-244

DAMP walls: precautions, 21
Desk, 245-254
——, pedestal kneehole, 248
——, table, 245
Dining chairs, 182, 184, 201
—— table, extension, 264
—— ——, modern style, 260
—— ——, Pembroke, 255
Dish racks, 380
Doors with geometric glazing-bars, 26
Drawer construction, 34
—— fronts, inlaid, 86
Drawers, chest of, 306
——, recess fitment with, 361
Drawing-room chair, 186

405

Index

Dresser, kitchen, 376
——, sideboard, 286
Dressing chest, 294, 321
—— glass, 331
—— ——, antique style, 332
—— table, 294, 321
Duet music stool, 132

EASEL, drawing-room, 152, 154

FARAGO, EDMUND, chair by, 189
Fire-screen, lead-glazed, 150
Fitment, "Armoire" hall, 92
——, bathroom, 60
——, bookshelf, for recess, 364
——, corner, with shelves, 205
——, recess, with cupboard and drawers, 361
Flemish credence, 122
—— cupboard, 122
Folding card table, 236
French stools, 175-181
—— table, carved, 356
—— ——, modern, 223

GATELEG table, 258
Gatelegsystem dining-table, 255
Glass (see also Mirror)
——, cheval, 328
——, dressing, 331
——, ——, antique style, 332
Glazing, lead, explained, 16, 286
Glazing-bars, geometric, doors with, 26
Gothic side table, 232
Grandfather clock-case, 74

HALL fitment, 396
—— ——, "Armoire," 92
—— —— with cupboard, 104
—— furniture, 92-113
—— mirrors and racks, 56, 58
—— seat, high-back, 110
—— ——, semicircular, 111
—— stand, modern style, 98
—— ——, narrow, 96
—— stool, 175
—— table, 232
Hammer, veneerer's, 89
Hanging cabinets or cupboards, 157-167
—— corner cupboard, 170
Hat racks and mirrors, 56-60
Hepplewhite urn-stand, 214
Hungarian chair, 189

INLAYER'S stock and cutter, 298
Inlaying, 84-91
—— bandings, 84
——, coloured woods for, 84
——: designs, 85, 87
—— drawer fronts, 86
——: marquetry effects, 86
——: mosaics, 84
——: scratch-stock, 88
—— stringings, 84
——, veneer, 90
Invalid's bed table and reading stand, 349

JEWEL boxes, 299

KITCHEN dressers, 376
—— table, 369
Kneehole pedestal desk, 248

LADY'S work table, 234
Lavatory fitment with mirror, 60
Lead glazing, 16, 286
Leather work, decorative, 193
Long or grandfather clock, 74-83
Looking-glasses (see Glass and Mirror)
Louis XIV. stool, 175

MANTEL enclosures, 61-64
—— clock, eighteenth-century English, 72
—— clock-case with side shelves, 65
Marquetry, inlaying, 86
Medicine cabinets and cupboards, 157, 166
Mirror (see also Glass), 48
——, bathroom, 60
——, cheval, 328
——, dressing, 331
——, hall, 396
——, hanging, 54
—— and rack, 56, 58
——, shaving, 336-342
——, toilet, 331
——, ——, antique style, 332
Mosaics, inlaid, 84
Museum cabinet, 398
Music cabinets, 135-147
—— —— with drawers and trays, 135
—— ——, modern, 144
—— —— with shelves, 13
—— stools, 129-134
—— —— with box seat, 129
—— ——, double, 132

NEST of three tables, 228

OCCASIONAL tables, 223-236, 387
Office table, small, 244
Overmantels, 48-60
——, architectural, 48
—— with cupboard, 48
——, modern style, 53

PALM stand, 388
Pantry cupboards, 376
Pedestal cupboards, 304
—— kneehole desk, 248
——, octagonal, 218
—— sideboard, 276
——, square, 218, 395
——, tapered, 222
Pegs, hall mirror and, 396
Pembroke dining table, 255
Piano stools (see Music Stools)
Picture easels, 152-156
Pierced tracery, 123
Pigeonholes, 43
Pipe racks, 166, 167
Plant stands, 213-222
—— ——, mahogany, 213
—— ——, modern style, 217
—— ——, square, 388
Plate rack, 380
—— ——, trough, 382
Pyke, George, clock by, 72

Index

RACKS, book, 6-11
—— and hall mirrors, 56, 58
——, hat, 56-60
——, pipe, 166, 167
——, plate and dish, 380
Reading stands, 346-352
Recess, bookshelf fitment for, 364
—— fitment with cupboard and drawers, 361
Rug box or chest, 126
Rush-seating chair, 338

SAW, veneerer's, 89
Scratch-stock, 88
Screens, 148-156
——, fire, 150
——, four-leaf, 148
——, three-leaf, 148
Scullery furniture, 369-386
Seats, etc., 114-128, 182-212 (*see also* Chair)
——, bedroom, 336, 390
——, hall, 110, 114, 175, 390
——, upholstered corner, 208
——, —— window, 202
Sectional bookcases, 28
Settee, Chesterfield, 353
—— with loose spring-seat, 196
Shaving stand, 338
Sheraton pedestal sideboard, 276
Showcase tables, 239-244
Side table, Gothic, 232
Sideboard, cottage, 281
—— dresser, 286
——, pedestal, 276
——, Sheraton, 276
——, veneer decorated, 269
Smokers' cabinets, 157, 163
—— cupboard and bookshelf, 167
Stand, book, 1-11
——, corner, 106
——, Hepplewhite, 214
—— or occasional table, 387
——, palm, 388
——, plant, 213, 217, 388
——, reading, 349
Stationery case, 38
Stool or hall seat, 175
——, Louis XIV., 175
——, music, 129-134 (*see also* Music)
Stringings, 84
Stuffover armchair, 353
—— couch, 353

TABLE, bed, and reading-stand, 349
——, bedside, 346-352
—— bookcase, double-shelf, 1
—— ——, single-shelf, 1
——, card, 236
——, carved French, 356
——, coffee, 232
——, converting, into writing-table, 247

Table, curio, 239-244
——, dining, 255, 260-268
——, dressing, 294, 321
——, extension, 264
——, gateleg, 258
——, Gothic, 232
——, hall, 232
——, kitchen, 369
——, modern French, 223
——: nest of three tables, 228
——, occasional, or stand, 213-217, 387
——, office, 244
——, Pembroke dining, 255
——, showcase, 239-244
—— tops, securing, 4, 5
——, work, 234
——, writing, 245
——, ——, and cabinet combined, 40
——, ——, converted from plain table, 247
Terminals, vase-shaped, 80
Toilet glass (*see* Glass, Mirror, etc.)
Towel rail and mirror, 60
Tracery, pierced, 123
Trough bookstands, 6, 7
—— rack, 382

UMBRELLA pans, 98, 104, 108, 110
—— stand, corner, 106
——, ——, straight, 109
Upholstered corner seat, 208
—— window seat, 202
Urn stand, Hepplewhite, 214

VASE pedestal, octagonal, 218
—— ——, square, 218, 395
—— ——, tapered, 222, 395
—— terminal, 80
Veneering, 84-91, 296
——: blisters, 90
——: curved work, 90
——: laying veneer, 89
——: tools, 89
——: veneer inlaying, 90
Veneers, 89
Vono bedstead fitting, 311

WALL clock, hanging, 66
——, damp: precautions, 21
Wardrobe, 289, 312
"Wardrobe top," 334
Washstand, 300, 317
——, angle, 342
Window seat, upholstered, 202
Work table, 234
Writing cabinet and table, 40
—— desk, kneehole, 248
—— table, 244
—— —— converted from plain table, 247

Lightning Source UK Ltd.
Milton Keynes UK
UKHW040734161122
412291UK00004B/219